Ali Vakili-Ardebili
Halim Boussabaine

Ecological Building Design; Fuzzy Approach

Ali Vakili-Ardebili
Halim Boussabaine

Ecological Building Design; Fuzzy Approach

An Eco-Design Model

VDM Verlag Dr. Müller

Impressum/Imprint (nur für Deutschland/ only for Germany)
Bibliografische Information der Deutschen Nationalbibliothek: Die Deutsche Nationalbibliothek verzeichnet diese Publikation in der Deutschen Nationalbibliografie; detaillierte bibliografische Daten sind im Internet über http://dnb.d-nb.de abrufbar.

Alle in diesem Buch genannten Marken und Produktnamen unterliegen warenzeichen-, markenoder patentrechtlichem Schutz bzw. sind Warenzeichen oder eingetragene Warenzeichen der jeweiligen Inhaber. Die Wiedergabe von Marken, Produktnamen, Gebrauchsnamen, Handelsnamen, Warenbezeichnungen u.s.w. in diesem Werk berechtigt auch ohne besondere Kennzeichnung nicht zu der Annahme, dass solche Namen im Sinne der Warenzeichen- und Markenschutzgesetzgebung als frei zu betrachten wären und daher von jedermann benutzt werden dürften.

Coverbild: www.ingimage.com

Verlag: VDM Verlag Dr. Müller GmbH & Co. KG
Dudweiler Landstr. 99, 66123 Saarbrücken, Deutschland
Telefon +49 681 9100-698, Telefax +49 681 9100-988
Email: info@vdm-verlag.de
Zugl.: Liverpool, The University of Liverpool, PhD, 2005

Herstellung in Deutschland:
Schaltungsdienst Lange o.H.G., Berlin
Books on Demand GmbH, Norderstedt
Reha GmbH, Saarbrücken
Amazon Distribution GmbH, Leipzig
ISBN: 978-3-639-04681-6

Imprint (only for USA, GB)
Bibliographic information published by the Deutsche Nationalbibliothek: The Deutsche Nationalbibliothek lists this publication in the Deutsche Nationalbibliografie; detailed bibliographic data are available in the Internet at http://dnb.d-nb.de.

Any brand names and product names mentioned in this book are subject to trademark, brand or patent protection and are trademarks or registered trademarks of their respective holders. The use of brand names, product names, common names, trade names, product descriptions etc. even without a particular marking in this works is in no way to be construed to mean that such names may be regarded as unrestricted in respect of trademark and brand protection legislation and could thus be used by anyone.

Cover image: www.ingimage.com

Publisher: VDM Verlag Dr. Müller GmbH & Co. KG
Dudweiler Landstr. 99, 66123 Saarbrücken, Germany
Phone +49 681 9100-698, Fax +49 681 9100-988
Email: info@vdm-publishing.com

Printed in the U.S.A.
Printed in the U.K. by (see last page)
ISBN: 978-3-639-04681-6

Copyright © 2010 by the author and VDM Verlag Dr. Müller GmbH & Co. KG
and licensors
All rights reserved. Saarbrücken 2010

Acknowledgement

At the beginning we would like to thank our God for his blessing and favour that we could complete this work successfully. We believe that without his help we could not finish it. We are grateful for everything.

Also we would like to express our gratitude to our families for helping us to manage our time to write this book.

Table of Contents

Acknowledgement
Table of Contents   i
List of Abbreviations   vii
List of Tables   ix
List of Figures   xi

CHAPTER 1: Sustainable Building Design (SBD)   1
1.1 Introduction   1
1.2 Ambiguity in SBD   2
1.3 Complexity in SBD   2
1.4 Subjectivity in SBD   3
1.5 Flow of Design Value through Life Cycle of Assets   3
1.6 Development of a New SDB Paradigm   8
1.7 Implications   9
1.8 Conclusions   10

CHAPTER 2: Sustainability and Sustainable Development   11
2.1 Introduction   11
2.2 Environmental Considerations   11
2.3 Towards the Definition of Sustainability and Sustainable Development (SD)   12
2.4 Sustainable Development Review   13
2.5 Concept Focused Definitions   15
    2.5.1 Intergenerational Equity Focus   15
    2.5.2 Human (Intergenerational equity), Activities and Environmental Focus   15
    2.5.3 Human Activities and the Environment (Limitations) Focus   15
    2.5.4 Economy, Environment, Human Activities Focus   16
    2.5.5 The Virtue of Economic Growth Focus   16
    2.5.6 Ecological Justice Focus   16
    2.5.7 Sustainable Development and Business and Society Focus   16
    2.5.8 Sustainability and Mechanism of Education and Knowledge Focus   16
    2.5.9 Sustainability and Science Focus   17
2.6 Sustainable Development Dimensions   17
    2.6.1 Environmental Aspect of SD   18

2.6.2 Economical Aspects of SD	18
2.6.3 Social Aspects of SD	19
2.7 Emergence of Sustainable Development	21
2.8 Determinant of SD	22
2.9 The Environment as the Main Determinant of the Equilibrium in SD	24
2.10 Design for the Environment (DfE)	25
2.10.1 Clean Production	25
2.10.2 Eco-efficiency	26
2.11 Sustainability and Quality Concept (Overall Review)	28
2.11.1 Design for Maintainability (DfM)	29
2.11.2 Design for Serviceability (DfS)	30
2.11.3 Design for Performance (DfP)	30
2.11.4 Design for Durability (DfD)	30
2.11.5 Design for Flexibility (DfF)	31
2.11.6 Design for Deconstruction (DfD)	32
2.12 Conclusions	32
CHAPTER 3: Sustainable Building; Concepts, Overviews and Scopes	**34**
3.1 Introduction	34
3.2 Building as a Product	34
3.3 Building Impacts on the Environment	35
3.4 Sustainable Building (SB)	35
3.4.1 Sustainable Building Design (SBD)	36
3.4.2 Sustainable Building Principles	37
3.5 Performance Concept and SBD	38
3.6 SBD Overviews	39
3.7 Concept of Flexibility in SBD	40
3.8 Different Philosophies in SD and SBD	41
3.9 Eco-design, Eco-building design (EBD) Scope	41
3.9.1 Key Indicators in EBD	42
3.10 Innovation in EBD	43
3.11 Role of Designer in EBD	44
3.12 SBD Assessment Method and Science	44
3.13 SBD Assessment Methods	45
3.13.1 BRE's Environmental Assessment Method (BREEAM)	46

3.13.2 BEPAC	47
3.13.3 Leadership in Energy and Environmental Design (LEED)	47
3.13.4 LCA and LCA id	47
3.13.5 GBA (Green Building Assessment) and (GB Tools)	48
3.13.6 Checklists (Checklist 2002) & Checklist for Sustainable Development	48
3.13.7 Standards	48
3.13.8 Other Building Assessment Methods	50
3.14 Assessment Methods in Industry	51
3.15 Eco-building Design Assessment Method	53
3.16 Development of Eco-indicators in the Research	54
3.16.1 Building Design Factors	54
3.16.2 Environmental Profile Attributes	55
3.16.3 Energy and Resources Profile Attributes	55
3.16.4 Socio-economics Attributes	55
3.17 Conclusions	56
CHAPTER 4: Eco-Building Design Conceptual Model	**58**
4.1 Introduction	58
4.2 Emergence of Sustainable Development (SD)	58
4.3 Design Overview	60
4.4 Building Design and Customer Satisfaction (Kano Model Analysis)	61
4.5 Kano Model Adaptation with Design	63
4.6 Conceptual Paradigm of SBD	64
4.7 An Eco-Building Design (EBD) Conceptual Paradigm	66
4.8 EBD Conceptual Model	68
4.9 EBD Implications	70
4.9.1. Design Eco-efficiency Enhancement	70
4.9.2 Design for Whole Life Cycle (WLC)	71
4.10 Conclusions	72
CHAPTER 5: Eco-Indicators Knowledge Elicitation through Fuzzy Theory	**73**
5.1 Introduction	73
5.2 Modelling Technique for SBD	74
5.3 Measurements and Values	75
5.4 Scoring Methods	75

5.5 Fuzzy Theory Application and Scoring	76
5.6 Fuzzy Theory and Logic Application in Various Fields of Science	77
5.6.1 Fuzzy Techniques and Manufacturing	77
5.6.2 Fuzzy Techniques and Engineering Modelling	77
5.6.3 Fuzzy Techniques and Electronics	78
5.6.4 Fuzzy Techniques and Science	78
5.6.5 Fuzzy Techniques and Managements	78
5.6.6 Fuzzy Techniques and its Overall Applications	78
5.7 Fuzzy Theory Method (Methodology)	79
5.7.1 Fuzzy Membership Functions (MBF)	79
5.7.2 Fuzzy Linguistic Variables	80
5.7.3 Defuzzification (Method of Computation)	80
5.8 Advantages of Fuzzy Theory Techniques	81
5.9 Fuzzy Theory and Eco-Building Design (EBD)	81
5.10 Conclusions	89
CHAPTER 6: Eco-Design Indicators Extracted Knowledge	**90**
6.1 Introduction	90
6.2 Knowledge Extraction Findings	91
6.2.1 Respondent's General Information Finding (Questionnaire first page)	91
6.2.2 Eco-design Indicators Findings	98
6.2.2.1 Building Design-Function Characteristic Eco-indicators	102
6.2.2.2 Building Design-Space Characteristic Eco-Indicators	109
6.2.2.3 Building Design-Form Characteristic Eco-indicators	111
6.2.2.4 Building Design-Technology Characteristic Eco-indicators	114
6.2.3 Environmental Profile and Eco-efficiency	122
6.2.4 Energy and Resources Consumption	130
6.2.5 Socio-Economics	138
6.3 Conclusions	141
CHAPTER 7: Eco-Design Indicators Knowledge Organisation	**142**
7.1 Introduction	142
7.2 Methodology of Study	142
7.3 Analysis and Ranking of Eco-indicators	146
7.4 Measuring Architects Concordance	147

7.5 Ranking Based on Statistical Data	148
7.5.1 Building Design	148
7.5.1.1 Function	148
7.5.1.2 Space	149
7.5.1.3 Form	150
7.5.1.4 Technology	151
7.5.2 Environmental Profile and Eco-Efficiency	152
7.5.3 Energy and Resources	153
7.5.4 Socio-Economic Aspects	154
7.6 Summary of the Findings from the Overall Ranking	155
7.7 Kendall's Concordance Analysis Employing SPSS	156
7.8 Average Severity Indices of Eco-Building Design Category	157
7.9 Average Severity Indices of Building Design Characteristics	158
7.10 Conclusions	159
CHAPTER 8: Eco-Design Indicators Combination	**160**
8.1 Introduction	160
8.2 Research Methodology	160
8.3 Factor Analysis	161
8.4 Analysis of the Findings	162
8.4.1 Scree Plot	164
8.5 Interpretation of the Clusters	172
8.5.1 Cluster 1: Environmental Impacts	173
8.5.2 Cluster 2: Environmental Design Passive and Active Strategies	173
8.5.3 Cluster 3: Site Analysis	173
8.5.4 Cluster 4: Social Aspects	174
8.5.5 Cluster 5: Economy	174
8.5.6 Cluster 6: Design Aspects and Strategies	175
8.6 Conclusions	175
CHAPTER 9: Fuzzy Eco-Building Design Model Development	**177**
9.1 Introduction	177
9.2 Background	178
9.3 Applied Methodology	178
9.4 Fuzziness of Eco-Building Design Indicators	181

9.5 Construction of the membership Functions	181
9.6 Statistical Data Used to Develop Membership of Functions (MBFs)	183
9.6.1 Membership of Functions (MBF) of Eco-Indicators	186
9.7 Defuzzification	190
9.8 Linguistic Variables and Linguistic Terms (Possible Scenarios)	190
9.9 Combinations of Scenarios and Fuzzy Computation	192
9.9.1 Notes in Computation	194
9.10 Fuzzy Eco-Building Design Model (FEBDM)	200
9.11 Conclusions	201

CHAPTER 10: Overview of Ecological Building Design Indicators Application — 202

10.1 Introduction	202
10.2 Indicators Affecting Eco-Building Design (EBD)/Eco-Indicators	202
10.2.1. Design Strategy Indicators	203
10.2.2 Environmental Design Strategy Indicators	204
10.2.3 Site Analysis Indicators	204
10.2.4 Environmental Impact Indicators	205
10.2.5 Social Indicators	205
10.2.6 Economical Indicators	205
10.3 Modelling Technique	206
10.3.1 Differences	206
10.3.1.1 Conceptual Differences in Indicators Selection	206
10.3.1.2 Methods of Analysis of Data	206
10.3.1.3 Assessment Categories	206
10.3.1.4 Model Development	207
10.3.2 Model Testing	207
10.3.3 Advantages	215
10.3.4 Comparison with Other Methods	215
10.4 Scope	218
10.5 Impacts	218
10.6 Conclusions	218

References   **220**

List of Abbreviations

a	Weighted Average Mean
b	Standard Deviation
a	Alpha Cut
CoV	Coefficient of Variation
DF	Degree of Freedom
DFD	Design for Durability
DfE	Design for Environment
DfF	Design for Flexibility
DfM	Design for Maintainability
DfS	Design for Serviceability
DfP	Design for Performance
EBD	Eco-Building Design
FEBDM	Fuzzy Eco-Building Design Model
$F_{ij}(x)$	Membership Function at a Certain Alpha Cut (a)
FL	Fuzzy Logic
IOU	Intensity of Use
M	Weighted Mean Value
MBF	Membership Function
N	Number of Observed Samples
NGO	Non-Governmental Organizations
PSS	Product Service System
S	Standard Deviation
SB	Sustainable Building
SBD	Sustainable Building Design
SD	Sustainable Development
S.I.	Severity Index
W_j	Weighting coefficient for Criterion (a)
BREEAM	BRE's Environmental Assessment Method
BEPAC	Building Environmental Performance Assessment Criteria
LEED	Leadership in Energy and Environmental Design
LCA	Life Cycle Assessment
GBA	Green Building Assessment

LIST OF ABBREVIATIONS

RE	Rebound Effect
RIBA	Royal Institute of British Architects
W	Kendall's Coefficient of Concordance
WLC	Whole Life Cycle
WLCC	Whole Life Cycle Costing

List of Tables

Chapter 2:
Table 2.1 Capital Stock and Flows of Benefits: a Modernised Economic Model for SD. (Parkin, 2000)   21

Chapter 3:
Table 3.1 Existing SBD Methods in Building   49
Table 3.2 Comparison of the Four Famous Assessment Methods   50
Table 3.3 Existing SD and Eco-design Methods in Industry   51-52

Chapter 5:
Table 5.1 Categories of Eco-Building Design   85-88

Chapter 6:
Table 6.1 Descriptive Information Obtained from Questionnaire Survey   99-102

Chapter 7:
Table 7.1 Building Design Category-Function Attributes   149
Table 7.2 Building Design Category-Space Attributes   150
Table 7.3 Building Design Category-Form Attributes   151
Table 7.4 Building Design Category-Technology Attributes   152
Table 7.5 Environmental Profile and Eco-Efficiency Category   153
Table 7.6 Energy and Resources Category   154
Table 7.7 Socio-Economic Category   155
Table 7.8 The 30 Most Important Ranked Indicators Extracted for Eco-Building Design   156
Table 7.9 Kendall's Concordance Analysis Employing SPSS   157

Chapter 8:
Table 8.1 Total Variance Explained   163
Table 8.2 Rotated Component Matrix (a)   166-169
Table 8.3 Data Analysis: Elementary Factor Reduction   170
Table 8.4 Factor Reduction: Six New Categories (Final Data Reduction and Factor Analysis)   172

Chapter 9:

Table 9.1 Design Aspects and Strategies Cluster Data	184
Table 9.2 Environmental Impacts Cluster Data	185
Table 9.3 Design Environmental Strategies Cluster Data	185
Table 9.4 Social Aspects Cluster Data	185
Table 9.5 Site Analysis Cluster Data	185
Table 9.6 Economy Cluster Data	186
Table 9.7 Possible Combinations (Alternatives) of Eco-Indicator	196
Table 9.8 Possible Alternatives Fuzzy Computation of Eco-Indicators	197-198
Table 9.9 Calculation of Lower, Middle, and Upper Bands of Eco-Building Design Clusters	199

Chapter 10:

Table 10.1 Application of Environmental Assessment Methods (Crawley and Aho, 1999)	203
Table 10.2 Project 1 (New Primary School)	209
Table 10.3 Project 2 (Royal Mill Apartments)	211
Table 10.4 Project 3 (Kaskenmaw School for Disabled)	213
Table 10.5 Scopes of Assessment Methods	217

List of Figures

Chapter 1:
Fig 1.1 the Whole Life Cycle (WLC) of a Building Asset   5
Fig 1.2 Flow of Design Value in the Building Process   6
Fig 1.3 Design and the Context   9

Chapter 2:
Fig 2.1 Different Perspectives of SD (Chaharbaghi and Willis, 1999)   14
Fig 2.2 Three Fundamental Principles Connected to Sustainable Development (Ryding, 1998).   17
Fig 2.3 Step Model of Eco-Design Innovation (Charter and Chick, 1997)   22
Fig 2.4 Material Flows: Cradle to Grave (today condition) (Dickson, 1997)   26
Fig 2.5 Process of Design in SD and SBD   33

Chapter 3:
Fig 3.1 The Framework for Development of Eco-Indicators   56

Chapter 4:
Fig. 4.1 Restriction, Sustainability, Extravagancy   60
Fig 4.2 Need-Goal-Function Model, (Crawley and de Weck, 2001)   61
Fig 4.3 Kano Model (Ullman, 1997)   62
Fig 4.4 Kano Model and Design Evolution   64
Fig 4.5 Conceptual Paradigm of SBD   65
Fig 4.6 EBD Conceptual Paradigm   67
Fig 4.7 Eco-Building Design Model as a Sub-set of SBD and SD   68
Fig 4.8 Eco-Building Design for Adding Value, and Risk Mitigation   70
Fig 4.9 Transition or Evolution of Eco-Building Design   72

Chapter 5:
Fig 5.1 Scaling Based on Eco-Indicator Degree of Significance   76

Chapter 6:
Fig 6.1 Number of Architectural Companies in the UK, Involved in SBD   91

LIST OF FIGURES

Fig 6.2 Respondents Job Descriptions	92
Fig 6.3 Organisation Type	92
Fig 6.4 Respondents Years of Experience	93
Fig 6.5 Rate of Interest in Eco-building Design among Affiliated Professions	94
Fig 6.6 Number of Architects in the Company	94
Fig 6.7 Expertise in Sustainable Building (Eco-Building Design)	95
Fig 6.8 Sustainable Projects Handled by Companies	96
Fig 6.9 Training Regarding Sustainable Building Design	96
Fig 6.10 Application of Assessment Programmes by Companies	97
Fig 6.11 Rate of Interest in Receiving a Copy of Survey Report	98
Fig 6.12 Histogram and Normal Curve for Adaptability to New Changes (Q4)	103
Fig 6.13 Histogram and Normal Curve for Adaptability to Surroundings (Q5)	104
Fig 6.14 Histogram and Normal Curve for Adaptability to the Environment (Q6)	105
Fig 6.15 Histogram and Normal Curve for Upgradeability and Extension (Q7)	106
Fig 6.16 Histogram and Normal Curve for Flexibility in Use Stage (Q8)	106
Fig 6.17 Histogram and Normal Curve for Performance regarding Longevity (Q11)	107
Fig 6.18 Histogram and Normal Curve for Control of Emission (Q26)	108
Fig 6.19 Histogram and Normal Curve for Energy and Eco-Efficiency (Q27)	108
Fig 6.20 Histogram and Normal Curve for Natural physical Conditions (Q36)	109
Fig 6.21 Histogram and Normal Curve for Building Orientation (Q37)	110
Fig 6.22 Histogram and Normal Curve for Climate (Q38)	110
Fig 6.23 Histogram and Normal Curve for Maintainability (Q43)	111
Fig 6.24 Histogram and Normal Curve for Durability Regarding Flexibility (Q46)	112
Fig 6.25 Histogram and Normal Curve for Component Detailing and Design (Q47)	113
Fig 6.26 Histogram and Normal Curve for Reliability and Usability (Q49)	113
Fig 6.27 Histogram and Normal Curve for Reusability and Recycle-ability (Q51)	114
Fig 6.28 Histogram and Normal Curve for Longevity Regarding WLC (Q59)	115
Fig 6.29 Histogram and Normal Curve for Maintainability Regarding WLC (Q60)	115
Fig 6.30 Histogram and Normal Curve for Energy Efficiency Regarding WLC (Q61)	116
Fig 6.31 Histogram and Normal Curve for Embodied Energy Regarding WLC (Q62)	117
Fig 6.32 Histogram and Normal Curve for Eco-efficiency and Recycle-ability (Q63	118
Fig 6.33 Histogram and Normal Curve for Reliability Regarding WLC (Q64)	118
Fig 6.34 Histogram and Normal Curve for Function Fit to Purpose (Equipments wise) (Q65)	119
Fig 6.35 Histogram and Normal Curve for Access to Equipment for Repairing (Q67)	120

LIST OF FIGURES

Fig 6.36 Histogram and Normal Curve for Pollution Generation (Q68)   120
Fig 6.37 Histogram and Normal Curve for Environmental Adapted Technology (Q69)   121
Fig 6.38 Histogram and Normal Curve for Noise Generation by Equipments in Building   122
Fig 6.39 Histogram and Normal Curve for Green House Effect (Q76)   123
Fig 6.40 Histogram and Normal Curve for Ozone Layer (Q77)   124
Fig 6.41 Histogram and Normal Curve for More Efficient Use of Water (Q78)   124
Fig 6.42 Histogram and Normal Curve for Energy Consumption (Q79)   125
Fig 6.43 Histogram and Normal Curve for Air Pollution (Q80)   126
Fig 6.44 Histogram and Normal Curve for Water Pollution (Q81)   126
Fig 6.45 Histogram and Normal Curve for Earth Pollution (Q82)   127
Fig 6.46 Histogram and Normal Curve for Ecological Deterioration (Q83)   128
Fig 6.47 Histogram and Normal Curve for Landfills (Q84)   129
Fig 6.48 Histogram and Normal Curve for Solid Residues (Q85)   129
Fig 6.49 Histogram and Normal Curve for Natural Light (Q86)   130
Fig 6.50 Histogram and Normal Curve for Passive Heating (Q87).   131
Fig 6.51 Histogram and Normal Curve for Natural Ventilation (Q88)   131
Fig 6.52 Histogram and Normal Curve for Passive Cooling (Q89)   132
Fig 6.53 Histogram and Normal Curve for Insulation and Airtight ness (Q90)   133
Fig 6.54 Histogram and Normal Curve for Water Saving Devices (Q91)   133
Fig 6.55 Histogram and Normal Curve for Biomass (Q94)   134
Fig 6.56 Histogram and Normal Curve for Low Embodied Energy (Q95)   135
Fig 6.57 Histogram and Normal Curve for Energy and Eco-efficient Design (Q96)   135
Fig 6.58 Histogram and Normal Curve for More Energy Efficient Equipments and Appliances (Q97)   136
Fig 6.59 Histogram and Normal Curve for Environmentally Adapted Technology (Q58)   137
Fig 6.60 Histogram and Normal Curve for Healthier and Safer Energy and Resources (Q99)   137
Fig 6.61 Histogram and Normal Curve for Maintenance Costs Regarding WLC (Q109)   138
Fig 6.62 Histogram and Normal Curve for Pollution Rehabilitation Costs (Q111)   139
Fig 6.63 Histogram and Normal Curve for Pollution Preventing Costs (Q112)   140
Fig 6.64 Histogram and Normal Curve for Saving Running Costs (Q115)   140

Chapter 7:

Fig 7.1 Hierarchy in the Questionnaire   143
Fig 7.2 Eco-Indicators Questionnaire Structure   145

Chapter 8:

Fig 8.1 The Process of Data Reduction and Factor Analysis 161
Fig 8.2 Scree Plot of 115 Eco-indicators of the Study 164

Chapter 9:

Fig 9.1 The Process of Calculation and Developing the *Fuzzy Eco-Building Design Model* (FEBDM) 180
Fig 9.2 Membership Function of Eco-Building Indicators 183
Fig 9.3 Probabilities Associated with a Normal Distribution, Adopted from Montgomery and Runger (1999). 184
Fig 9.4 Membership of Functions of *Environmental Impacts* Cluster 186
Fig 9.5 Membership of Functions of *Economy* Cluster 186
Fig 9.6 Membership of Functions of *Social Aspects* Cluster 187
Fig 9.7 Membership of Functions of *Site Analysis* Cluster 187
Fig 9.8 Membership of Functions of *Design Environmental Strategies* Cluster 188
Fig 9.9 Membership of Functions of *Design Aspects and Strategies* Cluster 189
Fig 9.10 Membership Function of Eco-Indicator Significance 191
Fig 9.11 Number of Alternatives (Possible Scenarios) for Each Eco-Indicator 192
Fig 9.12 The Process of Combination of Alternatives 193
Fig 9.13 Example of Fuzzy Computation A×B 194
Fig 9.14 Calculation in Triangle with an Angle of 90 Degree 195
Fig 9.15 Illustration of Lower, Middle, and Upper Bands for Eco-building Design 200
Fig 9.16 Illustration of Lower, Middle, and Upper Bands for Eco-building Design, with New Scale 201

Chapter 10:

Fig 10.1 Project 1 Assessment 210
Fig 10.2 Project 2 Assessment 212
Fig 10.3 Project 3 Assessment 214

CHAPTER 1[*]

Sustainable Building Design (SBD)

1.1 Introduction

SBD embraces various aspects and it is considered as an inclusive response to sets of variables. SBD is providing "construction ... that weaves together the ethical, human, scientific, aesthetic and other aspects of three contexts of [nature, culture and technology]" (Wiliamson et al., 2003). "while acknowledging how a technical performative approach to understanding environmental design has brought undoubted benefits in terms of highlighting the issues of energy efficiency in buildings, one must fundamentally revise the focus and scope of debate about sustainable architecture and reconnect issues of technological change with the social and cultural context within which change occurs" (Guy, 2005, p. 471). Hence, it is induced from the current debates that "it is necessary to understand the developmental priorities as well as cultural context" (Du Plessis, 2001). Such definitions are contextual approaches explaining how alliance of several contexts is needed in building design. Also Papanek in *The Green Imperative* looks at design process as a three steps model including *inform, reform* and *give form* stages by stating: "when our designs are succinct statements of purpose, easy to understand, use, maintain and repair, long-lasting, recyclable and benign to the environment, we **inform.** If we design with harmony and balance in mind, working for the good of weaker members of society we **reform**. Being willing to face the consequences of our design interventions, and accepting our social and moral responsibilities, we **give form**" (Papanek, 1995, p. 53). This conceptual framework implies that there are three main contexts influencing design process. The first step addresses challenges which should be responded in design, while the second stage highlights the customers of design whereas the last step identifies designer responsibilities and their commitments to existing society, and environment. According to Papanek description design process is addressing many contexts, while interacting with different levels of society in a harmonised ethical, moral and responsible manner. This paradigm is followed in this fact is considered as a background in this paper to provide innovative theoretical thinking on SBD and its characteristics. In spite of existence of a wide-ranging description in Papanek's point of view, there is a level of ambiguity and vagueness in this statement. The questions arising are:

---

[*]**Note**: *The main part of this chapter was published in the journal of Green Building by College Publishing (Vakili-Ardebili, 2007).*

- What are the contextual objectives mentioned in *inform* step and how are they achieved in design process?
- Who is the weaker member of the society in *reform* step in other words what are the distinctive criteria?
- What are the extents of responsibilities in *give form* step?

The answers to these questions might vary based on individual perception of reality. Hence, design process encounters with the ambiguity founded on essence of systematic complexity and subjectivity of opinions intrinsic in SBD. Clarification of the ambiguities will help to define horizons of SBD as well as facilitating the proceedings trends in design process. To tackle these theoretical assumptions following objectives should be considered:

- To identify design contexts over building WLC stages
- To acknowledge the trends of value management in building WLC process
- To suggest SBD as a contextual based building process
- To present a new conceptual paradigm in rethinking design process

1.2 Ambiguity in SBD

SBD consists of diverse aspects and it is the responsibility of design stakeholder to find balance among these components through a new design process paradigm. . Complexity and subjectivity are two problems encountered in SBD. The main reason for such problems is related to variety of components and their types and levels of interaction. The complexity arises because of existence of various components and the existing relations or interactions among them; and subjectivity relates to interpretation of these events by individuals. Subjectivity takes place because individuals perceive the components interactions according to their knowledge, understanding and type of experience. Overcoming ambiguity needs clarification of design complexity and better perception of subjectivity issue and its associated terms in design stage.

1.3 Complexity in SBD

SBD process is a complex dynamic system, inherently constantly changing and evolving. The purpose of SBD is to create an innovative and sustainable building in order to fulfil economical, social, environmental, and organisational objectives efficiently.
This study considers SBD as a complex system based on the fact that:

1. That both organisation and business are considered to be complex adaptive systems (Stacy, 1996); and
2. That is when these systems find themselves on the so called "edge of chaos" that innovation and creativity arise, which are concepts that are very much linked to design complexity.

Complexity theory perceives building design as a complex adaptive system. It is believed that SBD process can be portrayed as complex when one or some of the following criteria are present (Backlund, 2002).
1. SBD consists of many attributes and sub-attributes (Components);
2. There are many interactions between design attributes and sun-attributes;
3. Interactions in (2) are neither symmetric nor predictable; and
4. Arrangement of design attributes or sub-attributes are not symmetric.

1.4 Subjectivity in SBD

Various definitions of SBD are advocated by individuals based on their understanding and experience in a profession oriented framework. The term *"sustainable building"* has diversity of meanings depending on the context and background of those using term (Larsson, 1998). Also "for certain designers, the latest advances in engineering and environmental technology are central to their objectives; while for others, it is important to return to the lesson of history and the use of indigenous methods and materials. For another group, the resource of topography, vegetation, solar energy and earth itself are means to achieve an expanded vision of organic buildings" (Wines, 2000). Such definitions not only verify the existence of subjectivity but also imply to variety of contexts and components dealt in SBD. The authors believe despite the broadness of components types and their interactions a stable balance (edge of chaos) situation have to be developed through the design process so that the asset design service is maximised. This must be addressed through the life cycle of building assets. The following section presents a new paradigm on to deal with this important aspect. Here, building process stages and existing contexts overview is suggested; consequently it might help to clarify some of ambiguities addressed in SBD.

1.5 Flow of Design Value through Life Cycle of Assets

In this work the life cycle of building assets into four stages illustrated in Fig 1.1. In each stage design value(s) is created and exchanged based on the nature of activities that carried out within a particular phase.

The categorisation of activities in the life cycle of building assets is presented as follows:
a) The process of acquiring construction materials beginning with extraction of raw materials from the natural environment and then processing them in factories. In this stage issues such as technology, product management, environment impacts, economics and efficiency are addressed by stakeholders concerned.
b) Pre-Use stage which includes all activities such as design, procurement and construction needed to develop a building asset. This stage is assumed as a part of building process adding value to the materials through application of technology, design strategies and concepts. In this stage technical, managerial and economical aspects are addressed. Basically developmental priorities and objectives followed in this stage are limited to time, cost, quality, safety and health.
c) Use stage which starts after accomplishment of construction process. The essence of building process is based on existence of use stage. Hence, a process is more valuable when it is providing more values in use at operation stage for users for a longer period of time. Here one of the goals in building process would be creating more durable building which conserves design values for longer time. Durability in it own is inefficient to prolong the life span of assets. Other issues related to the fulfilment of customer satisfaction during use stage should be addressed as well. Serviceability, maintainability, flexibility to probable change in societal values, eco-efficiency are issues that are also essential in providing quality, performance and ease of use for customer in occupied asset. In the use stage all objectives should be followed according to social and cultural values in order to fulfil end users expectations otherwise functionality of a building involves risk of obsolescence and it is obvious that adding value in such circumstances seems to be redundant. Hence, the success of a building asset emerges from the use stage and this area should be pivotal in SBD.
d) Obsolescence stage relates to an asset not used because no value is found in the building to convince the user to carry on the use of property. Because of this building is abounded and probably dismantled. The appraising of this critical phase is based on costing the salvage value. The asset might be carrying a negative value and all efforts are must be directed to bring the value to the level of zero. The main objectives in this stage are:
- To minimise the cost of dismantling;
- To minimise the time of dismantling;
- To provide health and safety during the process is carried out;
- To control and minimise the rate of pollution during activity is carried out: and
- Or to eliminate this stage through renovation and reusing the asset (Optimum condition)

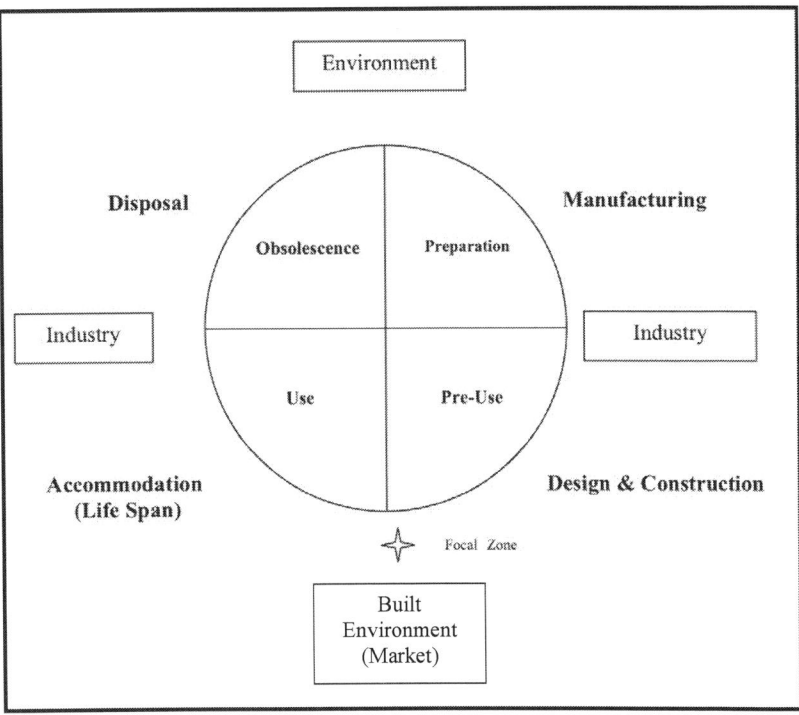

Fig 1.1 the Whole Life Cycle (WLC) of a Building Asset

In Fig. 1.1, although building process operationally seems to be consisting of independent stages but in reality there is a high correlation between these stages. For example, a durable building and functional longevity in use stage attributes can not be achieved unless a prudent selection of materials, a proper design and an accurate construction are applied in the construction process of asset.

Fig. 1.2 shows the flow of design value in building process over time. As it is illustrated there is an increase of value for material from the time they are extracted from natural environment and then processed and manufactured. Afterward they are used in construction process and combined in build the asset. By materialisation of building asset, design value is on the highest point of value curve. As shown in the figure this peak point is the maximum price or value is presented by the market. From this point on, the property starts to lose its design value. The main objective of this study (SBD) is to create conditions enabling assets to conserve design values close to maximum value and not let the value drop down over WLC.

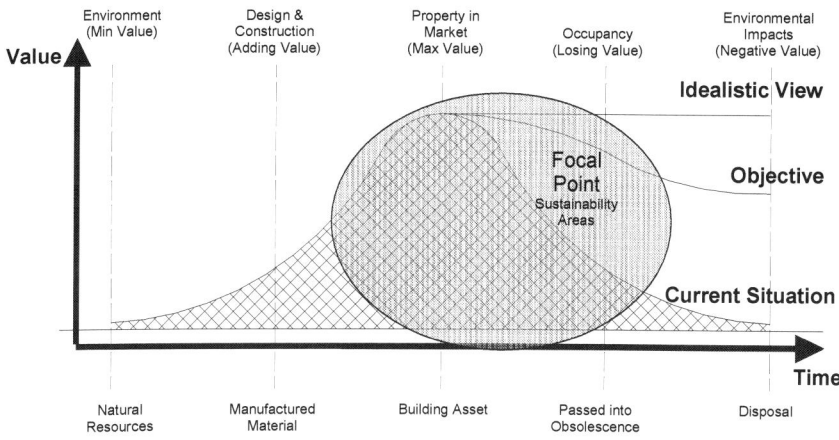

Fig 1.2 Flow of Design Value in the Building Process

The endeavours of designer are to extend the peak value of the design to form flat curve rather bell shaped curve. In this fashion we extended the service life of building assets. This is the area that should be addressed by SBD communities. In this area SBD attempts to provide design with concept enhancing services in use and minimising obsolescence as illustrated in Fig 1.1. To fulfil this objective, durability of building assets and its related issues could be used as a driver to increase the life span of building in use. Hence, the following are some aspects of durability that should be considered in increasing design value.

Building durability is one of the foremost concerns in SBD process while it employs concepts and strategies enabling building to conserve design values over WLC. It is considered as a foundation in building design processes in order to create new values on it. Longevity issue also involves in higher level of property management over life span period. The main goal is to find out how the life span of a building could probably expand and what services should be provided to maintain the values created at optimum levels.

The following strategies might be used:

- Longevity of functional operations regarding aging population;
- Maximisation of efficient use; and
- Mitigation of environmental impacts due to less call for construction.

Durability in a building does not exist unless objectives such as longevity of functionality, performance and efficiency are achieved in the operation stage. In other words there is a mutual relation between durability of building as a goal and its objectives as the required contexts.

To achieve durability, fulfilment of certain requisites is necessary. The requisites comprise activities such as:

- To fulfil aging population expectations over use stage of building. Flexibility in use based on customer satisfaction should be addressed in early stages of design.
- To consider efficiency as a general issue over WLC and particularly in use stage.
- The design should embrace obsolescence and disposal stage of building process in order to mitigate environmental impacts through revision of waste management.

Norman Foster and Partners describe sustainable building as: "creating buildings which are energy efficient, healthy, comfortable, and flexible in use and designed for long life" (ARBE 121) [Online source]. From this description it is perceived that durability would be one of characteristics of sustainability. The induction is based on this fact that the conservation of a value for a longer time is more logical and beneficial. Functional longevity is not feasible unless physical conditions are achieved. This means that spiritual durability and customer intension to use the building could be emerged when the physical existence and secure conditions are assured. Durability in a building can not be defined without deliberation of issues such as performance (Brochner *et al.*, 1999; Gibson, 1982), serviceability, maintainability (Blanchard *et al*, 1995) and flexibility of use (Keymer, 2000; Slaughter, 2001). In other words the materialisation of durability is depending on position of the abovementioned attributes in building service provided for the use stage. As performance concept focuses "on 'output' of technical description" therefore "performance should give sharper focus on quality instead of price only" (Brochner *et al.*, 1999, pp. 369-370). The overall objective of building performance is tied with the meaning of effectiveness regarding design.

Hence, this study takes durability and efficiency term in two aspects; one could be related to longevity of function based on building physical performance and the latter focuses on longevity of use based on customer satisfaction and intension to exploit asset. The following two aspects of durability are of paramount importance in creating value in design.

Physical Durability

This aspect of durability is based on building physical performances. Therefore it is fulfilled through activities pertained to design and construction and conditions established in these stages. It depends on materials adjacency, technical terms and balance created in design process. In this scope dematerialisation concept (Kibert *et al*, 2000) attempts to accomplish high quality design trough reflection of performance and efficiency while addressing functionality.

Spiritual Durability

This aspect of durability is addressing customer satisfaction fulfilment regarding use stage of asset. It focuses on design strategies and concepts put forward in early stages of design for providing service in use and obsolescence stages. It implicates SBD and its associated issues encouraging customer to use the asset for longer period. Based on this theory "Sustainable development is a process of continual evolutionary change toward lifestyles that lie within the ecological carrying capacity of our planet" (Shipworth, 2002). Accordingly, this paper places the emphasis primarily on this arena of durability and introduces SBD as a method of design which attempts to create value enabling building assets to offer better quality of performance over WLC responding functionality and efficiency.

1.6 Development of a New SDB Paradigm

Authors of this study believe that SBD should be a human oriented design addressing all existing contexts. Since customer satisfaction is the pivotal objective in SBD, therefore this approach works as a filter for extraction of indicators based on customer's expectations fulfilments (Vakili-Ardebili, 2005). According to this conceptual framework, durability of building is overviewed due to longevity of functions while customer satisfaction over use stage is provided. Durability as an attribute of SBD is an example of design concepts and strategies which is tied with all stages in building process. It embraces design functional and technical aspects as well as interacting with design contexts such as environmental impacts, socio-economics, energy and resources profile. Durability is innately an attribute that its essence depends on other attributes fulfilment in design. Flexibility, serviceability, maintainability and supportability are those design attributes endorsing durability of building assets. As a general rule durability emerges through amalgamation of various parameters in design with the existing contexts reflecting existing conditions and facilities over the time factor.

The new paradigm in SBD is illustrated in Fig 1.3 modelling design characteristics as the core of activity; environmental and socio-economical, energy and resources aspects as the existing contexts in design.

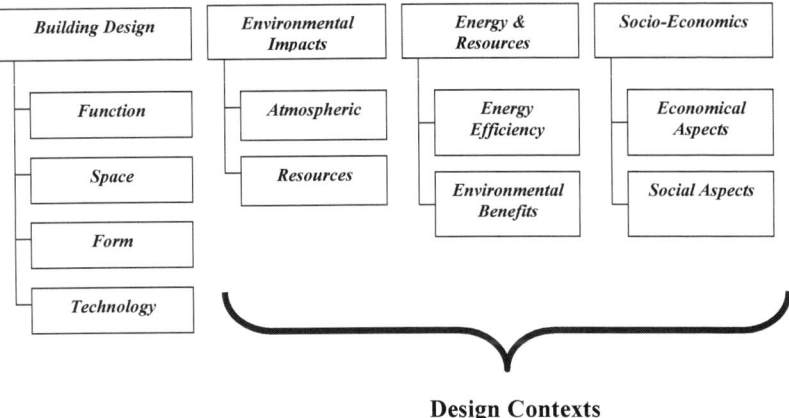

Design Contexts

Fig 1.3 Design and the Context

Objectives in SBD are sought based on design characteristics and relevant contexts which are filtered through customer satisfaction component. In this scope the priority is with proper response to functionality then values through concepts, thoughts and strategies based on design contexts are added. The procedure is directed in accordance with customer satisfaction

1.7 Implications

The direction of SBD strategies applied in design towards providing building assets with a high value after construction phase over their use and obsolescence periods. Design objective is to create value throughout the life cycle of the asset. The proposed SBD paradigm might have the following implications:
- Generation and extending the value building of assets;
- Property management enhancement over WLC;
- Control and mitigation of environmental impact focusing on waste management;
- Efficiency enhancement; and
- Customer satisfaction fulfilment as a guaranteed factor of design success.

The SBD theory presented here is a value based system geared towards customer benefits and satisfaction. The new philosophies could be used in creating value through the building design process by focusing on:

- Design for durability focusing on life span;
- Design for flexibility (Slaughter, 2001) focusing on life span and functionality;
- Design for serviceability focusing on life span and functionality;
- Design for maintainability (Blanchard and Lowery, 1969) focusing on life span and functionality;
- Dematerialisation in energy, resources, labour and time (Kibert *et al*, 2000) focusing on efficiency, embodied energy and environmental impacts;
- Rematerialisation including; waste management; reuse, recycle and reduce (Pearce, 2001) focusing on efficiency, embodied energy and environmental impacts; and
- Design for disassembling (Macozoma, 2002) focused on simplified disassembly (ease of dismantling and disassembly; the concept behind design that considers recycling and time and costs reduction) focusing on efficiency, environmental impacts, embodied energy and functionality.

1.8 Conclusions

In this work, SBD is presented as a complementary dynamic mechanism of contemporary design focusing on contextual aspects of design rather than the pure functionality and design technical profiles in order to re-think and revise the current conditions. Here, SBD is a dynamic process of creating value throughout the life cycle of building assets. In this scope SBD is not just a design process but it is assumed as a value creating mechanism in the built environment. SBD must be geared toward the conservation of value over longer time.

CHAPTER 2

Sustainability and Sustainable Development

2.1 Introduction

The European industrial revolution began in the 1700s and not only impacted upon the urban makeup and life style but also the production methods and material application. Attentions were drawn towards two main terms, speed and mass production, leading to rapid and dramatic changes to the social and economic structure of society impacting on the life style as well as environmental and social conditions being created.

Large quantities of raw materials and energy were demanded by the industrialised process and investment. The growth and development of technological advancement had become the major priority of industrial countries. As a consequence pollution generation was accepted as an environmental outcome of industrialising. There was increased use of land as well as water, air and soil that have become polluted.

However industrialisation brought the economical growth for society and economic stability provide communities with comfort. Pollution and limited resources to sustain a reasonable quality of life developed a conscience regarding sustainability. This is the pivotal reason why in the last few decades a strong awareness about sustainable development has been globally advocated and formed. Today sustainability is only a political topic which is recently encountered not only by local communities but also by the global community. Increased awareness towards impacts upon environment and the limited resources have evolved a new political conscience on all aspects of design. The concept and vision are based on individuals' points of view and varies in general; the implications will lead to the long term benefits of preservation of the planet for both present and future generations through consideration of social, environmental and economical requirements. The crux of the problem is laid in the heart of industries and their impacts on the natural environment.

This chapter reviews definition, concepts and relevant terms, regarding sustainability and achieving sustainable development.

2.2 Environmental Considerations

The movement for environmentalism started in the early seventies concern over environmental issues was caused by public awareness. As a pioneer in 1962, Rachel Carson through her book

'Silent Spring' highlighted the environmental disasters to the public (Carson, 1962). It was in 1980s that Sustainable Development became a political agenda and involved politicians all around the world. The environment became a pivotal part of the political agenda worldwide and the study embraces not only the local view in affected areas but also the global and predictive issues. The UN Conference on Environment and Development (UNCED) in Rio de Janiro led to 'Agenda21' and was followed by many other international and national meetings and conferences as implications of the aforementioned movements (Parkin, 2000). Human activities based on needs are like a coin with two sides providing two dissimilar features. The first side includes features needed for economic development whereas the other side generates impacts on the environment. The main objective of humans towards environmental effects focuses on controlling rates of impacts concerning desired developments.

2.3 Towards the Definition of Sustainability and Sustainable Development (SD)

There are diverse views on understanding SD and this leads to a variety of definitions. The meaning of development in different professions for individuals varies and this fact affects on SD as well. Sustainability is interpreted according to the scope of knowledge, area of experience and social position. (Dresner, 2001) explores the idea that sustainability "is a contestable concept like liberty and justice". There is a common definition for SD highlighted by Norwegian Prime Minister Gro Harlem Brundtland presented in World Commission on Environment and Development (WCED, 1987) which estates that: "Sustainable development is development which meets the needs of present without compromising the ability of future generation to meet their own needs" (Brundtland, 1987).
There is another definition of SD presented by (WCED, 1987) stating: "In essence, sustainable development is a process of change in which exploitation of resources, the direction of investments, the orientation of technological development, and institutional change are all in harmony and enhance current and future potential to meet human needs and aspiration" .

These definitions like majority of definitions are based on the concept of *needs* and *limits*.
The needs embrace required conditions for all people to achieve reasonable life standards whereas limits concept discusses about the capacity of the existing resources to fulfil the required needs of the present and the future, requested by society through their expectations (Khalfan, 2001).
As found that the concept of *'Human needs'* is a very controversial term which might be interpreted differently in various societies (du Plessis, 1999). Brochner *et al.* (1999) believes that "a crucial

matter is how 'needs' are to be understood" The existing problem with such definitions lies in existence of undefined types and amount of 'needs' which turns these definitions into terms of philosophy and a framework (Brandon, 1999). Therefore it is important that in the definition of SD in each field, the range of needs and limits are clarified. As a result, Khalfan concludes that any development should help to fulfil needs and should not increase limitations (Khalfan, 2001).

2.4 Sustainable Development Review

Also there are other definitions of SD based on interest and the focus of each discipline towards the matter. Outlined below are some of these definitions;

"Positive socioeconomic change that does not undermine the ecological and social systems upon which communities and societies are dependent"

– William Rees, Defining Sustainable Development

"The deliberate effort to ensure that community development not only enhances the local economy, but also the local environment and quality of life"

– PLACE3S Planning Method, Center of Excellence for Sustainable Development

" Long term health and vitality – cultural, economic, environmental, and social"

– Sustainable Seattle Indicators, 1995

"Living on interest, not drawing down capital"

– Paul Wilson, NorthWest Report

"Development that maintains or enhances economic opportunity and community well-being while protecting and restoring the natural environment upon which people and economies depend"

– An Act from the legislature of the State of Minnesota

"Providing for a secure and satisfying material future for everyone, in a society that is equitable, caring, and attentive to basic human needs"

– William Rees, Defining Sustainable Development

"The ability of a society, ecosystem, or any such ongoing system to continue functioning into the indefinite future without being forced into decline through exhaustion"

– Robert Gilman, president of Context Institute

"The management of our resources in such a way that we can fulfil our economic, social, cultural, and aesthetic needs without permanent impairment to the resource base and the life support systems on which we all depend."

– *Environmental Council of Alberta, Conservation Strategies in Canada*

"Essentially require[ing] human societies to take into account the long-range consequences of their actions"

– *World Resources Institute, The Environmental Almanac*

Fig 2.1, below illustrates different perspectives of SD among different professions (Chaharbaghi and Willis, 1999).

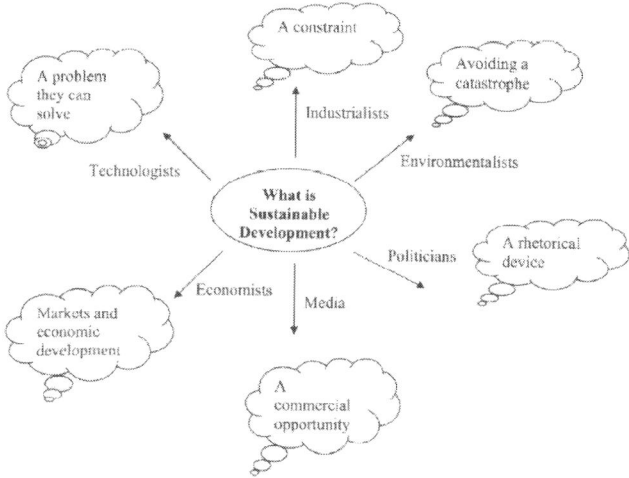

Fig 2.1 Different Perspectives of SD (Chaharbaghi and Willis, 1999).

The department of Environment, Transport and the Regions (DETR) the UK government points out that: "Sustainable development is a very simple idea. It is about ensuring a better quality of life for everyone, now and for generations to come. To achieve this, [it] is concerned with achieving economic growth, in the form of higher living standards, while protecting and where possible enhancing the environment.... and making sure that these economic and environmental benefits are available to everyone, not just to a privileged few" (DETR, 1998).

Few years later (DETR, 2000) the UK government recognised the significance of SD and made it as a pivotal item which emphasises on the environmental, social and economic criterion to gain a better quality of life for everyone for the present and the future generation through:
1. Social progress which recognises the needs of everyone.
2. Effective protection of the environment.
3. Prudent use of natural resources.
4. Maintenance of high and stable level of economic growth and employment.

2.5 Concept Focused Definitions

As aforementioned each profession seeks SD through its scope and varieties of definitions are implications of such views on SD. Here some focused definitions of SD are presented for clarification.

2.5.1 Intergenerational Equity Focus
"Development which meets the needs of the present without compromising the ability of future generations to meet their own needs" (WCED, 1987).

2.5.2 Human (Intergenerational equity), Activities and Environmental Focus
According to WCED, SD is a "development that meets the needs of the present without compromising the ability of future generations to meet their own needs". Sustainable development implies economic growth together with the protection of environmental quality, each reinforcing the other. The essence of this form of development is a stable relationship between human activities and the natural world, which does not diminish the prospects for future generations to enjoy a quality of life at least as good as our own. Many observers believe that participatory democracy, not dominated by vested interests, is a prerequisite for achieving sustainable development (Mintzer, 1992)[Online source].

2.5.3 Human Activities and the Environment (Limitations) Focus
The guiding rules are that people must share with each other and care for the earth. Humanity must take no more from nature than nature can replenish. This in turn means adopting lifestyles and development paths that respect and work within nature's limits. It can be done without rejecting the many benefits that modern technology has brought, provided that technology also works within those limits (IUCN, 1991, p8.).

2.5.4 Economy, Environment, Human Activities Focus

The term refers to achieving economic and social development in ways that do not exhaust a country's natural resources. See also, Ashford (1995) and The World Commission on Environment and Development (1987). In the Commission's words: "In essence sustainable development is a process of change in which the exploitation of resources, the direction of investments, the orientation of technological development, and institutional change are made consistent with the future as well as present needs"(WCED, 1987).

2.5.5 The Virtue of Economic Growth Focus

"Sustainable development not only suggests that economic growth is tolerable environmentally, but that growth is a necessary requisite to effective social and environmental welfare" (Jonathon Porritt, 1992).

2.5.6 Ecological Justice Focus

"The term development suggests that lessons of ecology, should be applied to economic progress... it provides an environmental rationale through which the claims of development to improve the quality of (all) life can be challenged and tested" (Michael Redclift 1987)

2.5.7 Sustainable Development and Business and Society Focus

The *Customer is always right* is one of the main principles in the business sector. Thus customer satisfaction is the pivotal objective which defines the level of success of each business effort. Since human is the customer of all activities made on the planet, considerations of a human oriented approach in all aspects of sustainability that attempt to present a systematic mechanism (as a service and business) is crucial. Hence it can be concluded that: "Business can not address the sustainable development challenges alone; it needs an active dialogue with other stakeholders in the society" (Stigson, 1999, P.430).

2.5.8 Sustainability and Mechanism of Education and Knowledge Focus

Among some researchers sustainability is considered as a mechanism like education and knowledge and it is claimed that "sustainability is about the long term... and it is difficult to capture, analyse and feedback useful data to designers at the present time" (Brandon, 1999, P.396.).

2.5.9 Sustainability and Science Focus

Redclift and Sage (1994, P.17) believe that sustainable development is achieved through application science and technology and all problems imposed on human society by the 'external limits' of nature can be sorted out.

The above descriptions show that the definitions of SD vary and are a matter of time and conditions ruling in each society based on relevant terms.

2.6 Sustainable Development Dimensions

What is derived from different definition is that; the basis for the concept of sustainable development consists of different aspects emphasising on three central dimensions namely: the environmental, economic and social dimensions (Ryding, 1998).

Fig 2.2 illustrates the fundamental principles connected to SD. It points out that SD comprises three broad topics of social, environmental and economical aspects which are often known as the 'triple bottom line'.

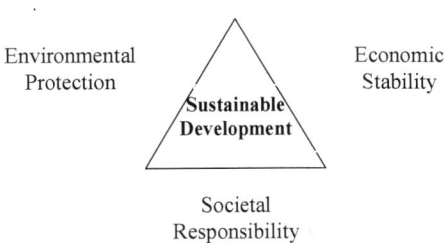

Fig 2.2 Three Fundamental Principles Connected to Sustainable Development (Ryding, 1998).

The environmental dimensions involve issues such as healthy air, water and living conditions, non-depleted resources, existing limitations in nature which are under pressure by human activities. The economic dimension deals with economic growth, financial stability and welfare issues. The social dimension embraces activities such as education, health, and societal protection objectives and the fulfilment of human expectations. Sustainability in society should be simultaneously addressed regarding all three dimensions. This fact leads to reciprocal equilibrium between environmental limits, social and economic development needs (Berggren, 1999).

2.6.1 Environmental Aspect of SD

This aspect embraces aspects such as environmental negative impacts, energy and resources consumption, biological diversity, human health and wellbeing. Other technical aspects focus on efforts made to satisfy life-cycle perspective and usually support the environmental sustainability philosophy and involves providing the planet with the conditions to preserve the earth in an appropriate shape and condition for both the existing and the future generations based on an intergenerational equity. Therefore in these scopes environmental sustainability is achieved when human activities are performed without depleting the natural resources or degrading the natural environment. This reality needs new views towards life, consumption and manufacturing culture. In other words it can be said that the problem may depend on our ability and desire to change our habits and thoughts rather than new technology and methods application (WBCSD, 1997). Hence, minimisation of natural resources and energy consumption, material degrading, reuse, recycling could be considered as panaceas to protect the environment through reducing the consumption of energy and materials by employing efficiency and waste management. This aim is achievable when a better perception of environment, its ecosystems, and existing conditions and facilities are gained. (Dasmann *et al*, 1973) considers population growth and limiting factors such as climate, soil, water and complex biotic factors as the main elements in economic development concerns. "The environmental limits to growth determine the carrying capacity for any species, which may be a subsistence level, a security level or the optimum level, which is the normal objective for human population, their domestic animals and their crops" (Ibid, p.3).

Rethinking and redesigning of available processes are two evolutionary factors which cause better conditions for the future based on primary design and intensions. The rethinking and redesigning stages are considered as a part of development towards sustainability and a reply to those environmentalists who point out that; "Sustainable development is a contradiction in terms and can be merely used as a cover for continuing to destroy the natural world" (Dresner, 2002).

2.6.2 Economical Aspects of SD

The economical aspects of SD embrace all attempts to enhance profitability based on resources, finance, labour, time and management through a sustainable economy. These activities include cost reduction through efficiency improvement and reduced energy and raw material inputs in order to create added value. Economic stability represents efforts to secure and enhance the economic conditions of various interests based on and adopting courses of action that apply and facilitate different forms of task and resource effectiveness. Also, "all economic development takes place within natural ecosystems, which may or may not have been already modified by man" (Dasmann *et al*, 1973, p.3) Thus, this dimension is assumed as an effective motivation to follow up the process of SD.

Parkin (2000) presents a model including five capitals for achieving SD in a society. Parkin's model consists of five capitals, described as following:

Natural Capital: This embraces all environment and ecological resources, including both renewable and non-renewable materials, services such as the natural waste processing system.

Human Capital: This consists of all factors related to human well-being and wealth such as: health, knowledge, safety, motivations, skills and relevant terms.

Social Capital: This is related to all societal and communication efforts; Family, community, government, business, school and other terms are considered as examples of this group.

Manufactured Capital: This indicates all existing facilities and products, manufactured by humans up to now for developing their work and life; Tools, machines, buildings, industrial products are examples of this group.

Financial Capital: This is considered as the reflection of four aforementioned categories and has no value by its own, but its value is based on other former capitals.

To develop a sustainable global economy, the attempts deal with three major challenges namely: pollution, depletion, and poverty (Hart, 1997). As it is found in Hart's concept, the interactions of poverty as a matter of social aspect and pollution and depletion as examples of environmental aspects are considered as concerns to achieve economic sustainability. Hence, it is derived that obtaining sustainability in each aspect of sustainable development requires consideration of other dimensions of sustainable development.

2.6.3 Social Aspects of SD

This dimension of SD seeks to establish sustainable communities. It focuses on efforts made to provide a worthwhile and meaningful life for everyone. Societal responsibility represents efforts made to identify and develop social functions that guarantee and improve the quality of life for people as the customer of products. The quality of life comes to the forefront in this dimension. It focuses on the potential required for major changes in established systems which attempt to introduce SD as a dynamic process which includes process of change. However, the existing SD paradigm does not deal with the time dimension of the SD the balance between needs and limitation through the life cycle of SD.

The main definition of the SD can be summarised as; "Sustainable development requires meeting the major needs of all and extending to all the opportunity to satisfy aspirations for a better life". However, "living standards that go beyond the basic minimum are sustainable only if consumption standards everywhere have regard for long-term sustainability" (World Commission on Environment and Development, p44). It seems that the majority of researchers accept that "Sustainability is about the long term... and it is difficult to capture, analyse and feedback useful data to designers at the present time" (Brandon, 1999, P.396.). Hence it is believed that SD is an evolutionary systematic mechanism which can not be obtained unless a prudent consideration towards its aspects is being held. Sustainable Development embraces development efforts such as housing which attempts to address social needs as well as taking care to minimise potential negative environmental impacts of the activity (Hill and Bowen, 1997).

Social aspects of SD can be considered as one of the crucial areas in SD which without their fulfilment achieving SD seems to be impossible. "When attempting to describe sustainability and by implication sustainable construction... it is necessary to understand the developmental priorities as well as cultural context..." (du Plessis, 2001). Culture and related social issues as a set of traditions, habits, and achievements, obtained by a society over time are respected and play a pivotal role in individual's life and fulfilment of expectations. Therefore any attempt related to human life can not be held disregarding cultural and societal aspects. (Guy and Kibert, 1998) place emphasis on a human value-driven process. In their paper they point out that: "Sustainability indicators integrate environmental, social, and economic factors such that the complex cause and effect relationships between these multiple factors can be more readily investigated. The whole systems approach of sustainable development differs from traditional environmentalism by its inclusion of economic and social factors. The selection of sustainability indicators will therefore inevitably be a human value-driven process. Environmental health will nonetheless be paramount".

The overall review of SD is presented through the definition quoted by (Shipworth, 2002); "Environmental impacts mitigation is not sustainable development. Sustainable development is a process of continual evolutionary change toward lifestyles that lie within the ecological carrying capacity of our planet, this developmental trajectory must, *at each point*, be socially acceptable, politically viable, economically feasible and technically possible. ... we need to focus not only on the product (the built environment), but also on the co-evolutionary dynamics of the systems that (re)create and consume the product (industry and society)".

The summary of what has been discussed is illustrated by Parkin in a model, consisting of five capitals. Table 2.1 presents the Parkin's model for SD.

Table 2.1 Capital stock and flows of benefits: a modernised economic model for SD. (Parkin, 2000)

Sustainable Development Aspects	Type of Capital	Stocks	Flow of Benefits
Environmental	Natural	Soil, sea, air, ecological systems	Energy, food, water, climate, waste disposal
Social	Human	Health, knowledge, motivation, spiritual ease	Energy, work, creativity, innovation, love, happiness
	Social	Government systems, families, communities, organisations	Security, shared goods, (e.g. culture, education), inclusion
Economical	Manufactured	Existing tools, infrastructure, buildings	Living/work/leisure places, access, material resources
	Financial	Money, stocks, bonds	Means of valuing, owning, exchanging other four capitals

2.7 Emergence of Sustainable Development

The emergence of SD depends on various conditions throughout the life cycle. The complexity of the emergence process is illustrated in Fig 2.3. Here it is conceptualised that SD is a dynamic system which evolves over time in existing environmental, economical and social conditions. In this work SD is viewed as a dynamic process of change searching for optimal conditions through life cycle. This concept is illustrated in Fig 2.3 as a four step model based on work by (Charter and Chick, 1997). In this figure each level is considered as the evolutionary step of the former stage.

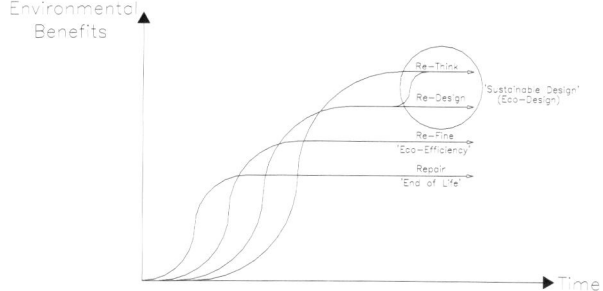

Fig 2.3 Step Model of Eco-Design Innovation (Charter and Chick, 1997)

As shown in the figure, environmental benefits are conceptualised on function of time, experience and innovation in design. In the sixties and seventies repair and disposal (end of life) were considered as solutions to product design and environmental problems whereas in the eighties and nineties an attempt to achieve eco-efficiency started to emerge through different practices in different levels through refining designs and enhancing the quality of existing designs. Despite the great efforts made by these practices, the results were unsatisfactory because the environmental impacts were not reduced to an acceptable level. In the nineties the environmental impacts motivated stakeholders and designers to review existing design practices with a view to incorporating environmental concerns. A series of efforts have been made with the objective of achieving a sustainable society through the re-thinking of products and product processing systems. Although at the moment some practices are still working based on the 'repair' conditions concept, it is obvious that users' future expectations can force designers to improve their quality of service. Current design embraces 'repair' and 'refine' (eco-efficiency) aspects but in order to achieve a sustainable society and future 'redesign' and 'rethink' of processes the quality of design will need to continue to evolve. By utilising the above analogy shown Fig 2.3, design process evolves to obtain better quality of life by adding value through the application of environmental strategies and sustainable customer satisfaction through the concept of 'gaining more from less'.

2.8 Determinant of SD

Each profession defines the problem of SD through its own perspective. Thus sustainability in each field of science has its own procedure to deal with sustainability. (Dincer and Rosen, 1999) believe that SD is achieved by a society just through application of energy resources types with no environmental negative impacts. Also a series of studies mention that SD achievement is a matter of long term (Dincer, 2000; Brandon, 1999, P.396.).

As earlier solutions to sustainability included only environmental issues, and other dimensions of SD were ignored or poorly noticed, thus the objectives proposed in SD dynamic system were not obtained and this caused partial achievements in SD. The early attempts towards SD were focused on mitigation of environmental impacts caused by production to fulfil human needs. However, over the time it has proved that the tasks, handled to reduce the impacts are needed but are not sufficient to solve the problem. Other strategies and range of efforts are required to fulfil this real need of human to sustainable life quality on the planet. Many researchers like Shipworth support the idea and state: "Environmental impacts mitigation is not sustainable development. Sustainable development is a process of continual evolutionary change toward lifestyles that lie within the ecological carrying capacity of our planet" (Shipworth, 2002). All these dissimilar thoughts about sustainability issue made it a nebulous objective up to now and this is the main reason that the process of SD is followed independently in each area of science. (Robinson, 2004, P. 379.) states that: "what can and should be done to achieve a sustainable society is not fundamentally a scientific or technical issue" and "scientific analysis can inform but not resolve the basic questions posed by the concept of sustainability". As it is understood the movement towards SD started through 'environmentalism' and then led to 'sustainability' and the followed by sustainability in each field. Hill and Bowen (1997) discuss modern technology together with increasing population as leading to rapid depletion of the earth's physical resources, and give a good coverage of the evolution of the concepts of 'environmentalism' 'sustainability' and 'sustainable construction'. Also (Khalfan, 2001) explains that "pollution, Consumption and technology are primary driving forces of environmental change".

These quotes show that the achievement of SD requires a strict level of discipline and management in controlling the production processes and efforts. Then mainstream SD has been formed by the movements and attempts towards *design for the environment* (DfE) and since the process of design is an evolutionary procedure and a function of time and conditions, then DfE develops and embraces a wider area to cover sustainability issues. There are several complementary terms frequently used to describe various aspects of DFE: design for disassembly, design for remanufacturing, design for recycling, design for reuse, and others (Kibert *et al*, 2000, P.909). Also other schools of philosophy such as dematerialisation, rematerialisation, intensity of use in materials (IOU) and eco-efficiency are applied methods in DfE. Agenda 21 suggests a series of action in order to reduce wasteful and inefficient consumption patterns and finally to set a balance between consumption and population regarding the planet's existing capacities [Concept of *needs* and *limits*]. The process of SD has a great need to rethinking rather than a set of efforts. (WBCSD, 1997) states that: the problem may depend on our ability and intention to change our minds and incorrect habits rather than on the technology. All efforts made in SD process aim at better quality of life of planet inhabitants as users. Better quality of life can be achieved through providing higher standards of life for the humans. This quality enhancement should be considered in all dimensions of human life. Quality of environment as a pivotal aspect essentially affects the quality of human life and it should be considered that without consideration of the environment all the efforts would be aimless. The emergence of DfE presupposes; "... movements must rely on natural ecology and the developments of industrial ecology as the underpinnings of this philosophy. Then this philosophy opens the door to the use of natural systems behaviour, designs, evolution and strategies as both metaphors and engineering approaches for sustainability in the built environment. Without turning to nature for its compass, the sustainable building movements are no more than a set of disconnected efforts with nothing to tie them together" (Kibert *et al*, 2000, P.915).

2.9 The Environment as the Main Determinant of the Equilibrium in SD

Nature innately behaves as a zero-waste system. (Kibert *et al*, 1999; 2000) believe that the environment as a dynamic system never produces waste and pollutions by its own and it is people and their activities that cause a large amount of harm to the system. Also (Holender, 2000) the president of seventh generation introduces the environment as a zero-waste system, mentioning "Zero Waste is the mother of environmental no-brainers."

Thus zero waste philosophy as a compatible system on the planet can be applied as one of the solutions towards the problem as Peter Montague, Editor of Rachel's Environment & Health Weekly estates; "Zero Waste poses a fundamental challenge to 'business as usual.' ... It has the potential to motivate people to change their life styles, demand new products, and insist that corporations and governments behave in new ways. This is a very exciting development". The philosophy aims at waste elimination rather than waste management. Hence it places the emphasis on the prudent exploitation of resources and the material development process regarding their whole life cycle (WLC). Besides that energy type and consumption concerning potential pollutions, emissions generation are placed in the proposed priorities. The main objective in this philosophy focuses on application of resources which generate the lowest negative impacts in the WLC. This fact can be achieved through attention towards energy resources, materials type and application of technology and specific strategies and policies (Dincer and Rosen, 1999). Thus, DfE is considered as a practice in which product development process is improved by consideration of environmental concerns based on products WLC (Keoleian and Menerey, 1994). Although DFE efforts are required for establishing SD principles but as discussed already other considerations towards different dimensions of SD is crucial to fulfil human real needs (Parkin, 2000; Shipworth, 2002).

2.10 Design for the Environment (DfE)

DfE is proposed as an approach, creating 'front-loaded' design and encountering methods that can be adapted, removed, recycled, reused and reprocessed (Wilson *et al.*, 1998). DfE focuses on input reduction methods and resource management in order to obtain efficiency. The result would lead to outputs management which causes a severe reduction in environmental impact through waste management based on the product's WLC. Hence, it can be said that DfE is a systematic integration of environmental concerns into product WLC. All in all DfE follows a pivotal aim which is minimising the impact of product over its WLC by maximising product's benefits (Ernzer et al.) [Online source].

There are several complementary terms frequently used to describe various aspects of DFE: design for disassembly, design for remanufacturing, design for recycling, design for reuse, and others (Kibert *et al*, 2000, P.909).

Cleaner production and *eco-efficiency* are assumed as two cardinal objectives of DfE.

2.10.1 Clean Production

Cleaner production is the systematic reduction in material use and the control and prevention of pollution throughout the chain of industrial processes from raw material use through product end of life (BATE, 1998). This is a type of process with the consideration of product WLC. In DfE holistic consideration of the careful use of energy and materials are employed in designed-system beside the endeavour to reduce the impacts of this use on the natural environment, over the life-cycle of the designed system from source to disposal stage (Dickson, 1997). Fig 2.4 illustrates the flow of materials in a cradle to grave approach. The holistic objective of DfE as suggested by (Miyatake, 1996) seeks to achieve sustainable building with a need to change the process of creating the built environment by modifying linear processes into the cyclic process. This means a process carrying the meaning of material flow '*from cradle to cradle*'.

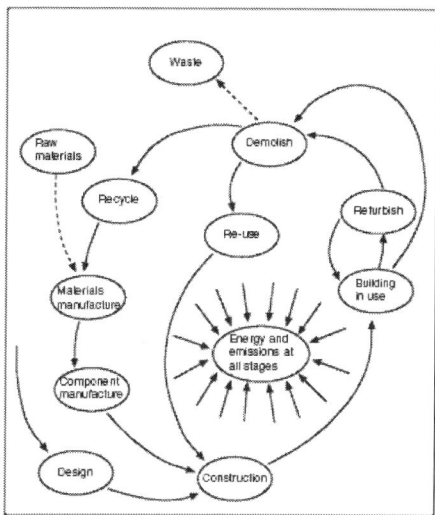

Fig 2.4 Material Flows: Cradle to Grave (today condition) (Dickson, 1997).

2.10.2 Eco-efficiency

Eco-efficiency focuses on companies' activities and aims at reducing the material and energy output of goods and services. It focuses on reducing toxic waste, making materials recyclable, maximising sustainable use of resources, increasing product durability and increasing the service intensity of goods and services (Fiksel, 1994). Eco-efficiency involves in *'gaining more from less'*. It covers concepts such as: dematerialisation, rematerialisation, selling services instead of product and behavioural retrospect regarding consumption culture.

Dematerialisation

Dematerialisation is not a new concept or approach to be applied in SD or environmental issues. Industries often attempt to lower the cost of production through intensity of use (IOU) and reduction in per unit mass consumption (Bunker, 1996). The idea can be developed beyond material and resources consumption and is capable to embrace energy amount use as well. In some cases like the building process the concept has developed to the extent of 'zero energy' which points to receiving energy requirements from on-site renewable resources (Roaf *et al.*, 2001). Generally dematerialisation discusses *'how to produce concise but efficient'*. In this concept it is seriously believed that *'less is more'* by Mies van der Rohe (Blaser, 1986). In this approach it is attempted to produce high quality goods through consumption of less material and energy. It focuses on higher efficiency in production process. The concept of dematerialisation has strong correlations with the concept of *minimisation* and covers it in all dimensions.

Rematerialisation

Resource productivity is defined in many ways; it can be presented as output per unit of energy or material. It is generally accepted that improving resource productivity is "good for the environment" (Pearce, 2001). This concept covers a large area of features such as re-use, recycle, and salvage use, repair and refurbishment. It can be considered as a sub-set of the dematerialisation concept as well because it embeds the IOU concept in dematerialisation and considers better utilisation of materials and possible services. It can be helpful both economically and environmentally. It is admired and encouraged by society as well.

Selling Services instead of Products

This is a new intension of SD and was introduced by industry to SD. Kibert *et al.* (2000) highlighted that dematerialisation is achieved through increase of resource productivity. Regarding this, optimisation might be introduced by a systematic dematerialisation which sells services instead of products which is also referred as a service economy solution concerning industrial ecology. Researchers like (Stahel, 1998; Goedkoop *et al*, 1999; White, 1999) believe that product service system (PSS) is potentially both economically and environmentally efficient. It not only gains financial benefits but also reduces negative environmental impacts in product life span or WLC and finally reduces the consumption of energy and material intensity as well (Stahel, 1994). The concept developed further and turned into *"Moving from Eco-Products to Eco-Service"* as recently presented by (Bhamra et al., 2001). The concept strongly supports DfE and moves towards zero waste generation as the key objective in both product and building design.

Consumption Retrospect

Change in the way we build or produce (Smith, 2001, preface page), seems to be a crucial issue as well as to be a long term effort; "History tells us that propagation of technology is a time consuming process. It might take more than half a century to incorporate some technological change into basic systems such as agriculture, energy and transport" (Lagerstedt, 2003). Hence, retrospect and change in consumption culture habits might solve the problem rather than technological responses to the problem (WBCSD, 1997). This aspect of DfE embraces human social and cultural dimensions which can be very difficult and time consuming. (Smith, 2001, Preface page) explains; "For change to be widely accepted there have to be convincing reasons why long-established practise be replaced". There has always been resistance towards new change from society as Smith mentions that the existence of something convictive is necessary. Rebound effect is one of the examples of the resistance faced by society caused by dematerialisation and efficiency consideration.

Rebound Effect (RE)

A rebound effect (RE), also called *take back effect* or *offsetting behaviour* is caused by the increase of consumption because of both efficiency enhancement and costs lowering (Musters, 1995; Alexander, 1997; Herring, 1998). RE is considered as a consequence of dematerialisation concept which is a '*loss due to efficient gain/s*'.

Henry Saunders (1992) states that "energy efficiency gains can increase energy consumption by two means: by making energy appear effectively cheaper than other inputs; and by increasing economic growth, which pulls up energy use"

Therefore rebound effect is a by-efficiency effect which is the reflection of customers' consumption culture. This potential fact can always cause harm to DfE's efforts and should be carefully considered in the movements towards sustainability. Denis Hayes (1978) views a sustainable world through "Material well-being almost certainly indexed by the quality of existing inventory of goods, rather than by the rate of physical turnover. Planned obsolescence would be eliminated. Excessive consumption and waste would become causes of embarrassment, rather than symbol of prestige". Here, Hays quote hints to a cultural revolution in the societies and people's beliefs.

2.11 Sustainability and Quality Concept (Overall Review)

Sustainability is an issue which is tightly linked to the concept of quality of life and its performance generated through the balance between environmental profiles and other existing dimensions discussed and presented by (Ryding, 1998; Parkin, 2000). The final goal in SD is achieving better quality of life for the human generation based on current time, existing conditions and facilities.

"...to improve the performance [and quality] ... a continuous improvement philosophy should be applied (Oakland and Aldridge, 1996). To achieve such a goal, the use of quality tools and techniques that can be used to improve performance is indispensable. Any harm to the quality has a direct effect on the process of SD achievement. In other words; because quality embraces fulfilment of human expectations concerning technical and ecological issues as the main dimensions of SD, therefore any ignorance or poor consideration of this characteristic affect the mechanism towards sustainability. In quality approach many factors affect a product creation and consequently the impacts. The results gained by a number of studies show that: Design (e.g., lack of coordination of design, unclear and missing documentation) and poor workmanship (e.g., ignorance and knowledge) were distinguished as the main factors which influence the quality (Cnuddle 1991; Hammarhund and Josephson 1991; Burati et al. 1992; Love and Li 2000). According to the results obtained by the researches it can be concluded that the design stage of a product has a pivotal role in establishing the impacts and respectively the quality and process of SD. Therefore the strategies employed in the design stage to improve the quality should be selected very prudently. A few strategies used in quality approach in DfE to achieve higher level of sustainability are presented and explained in the next section.

2.11.1 Design for Maintainability (DfM)

The military service of the United States in 1954 was the pioneer for creating and developing the concept of Maintainability (Blanchard and Lowery, 1969). Maintainability is defined as the ability of an item, under condition of use, to be retained in or restored to a state in which it can perform its required function, when maintenance is performed under stated conditions and using prescribed procedures and resources (BSI, 1984). Maintainability is "the ability to maintain in the least amount of time at the lowest cost" quoted John Rydzewski at (ASHRAE, 2000).
(NASA, 2001) views maintainability as a concept of design in sustainability to achieve ease, accuracy, safety, and economy of maintenance regarding product WLC.
Maintainability is a term that should be used beside other terms such as durability, serviceability and flexibility and does not make any sense by itself. Something which is maintainable should be able to last for a long time for receiving services and because of its long lasting there is a need to be flexible as well or maintainability does not carry its real meaning. DfM provides benefits and values for both manufacturer and end user. It affects the durability of the product regarding its WLC based on product serviceability. Durable products need more planned and non-planned maintenance during their WLC. The rate of reliability and serviceability for a product depends on its maintainability level. The dramatic impact of maintenance can be noted through overlooking product whole life cycle costing (WLCC). Maintainability is a characteristic of design, whereas maintenance is the result of it (Blanchard *et al*, 1995).

2.11.2 Design for Serviceability (DfS)

Serviceability is a subset of maintainability and deals with the potential failure of a product before its obsolescence or end of life. For handling services it is important that the product is designed to be serviced and maintained for a certain period of time. Serviceability is defined as the ability to maintain the product in the optimum conditions in order to fulfil its proposed functions regarding product performance, quality and reliability. There are two types of services for product maintenance, namely, preventive and corrective services. The first is presented in order to prevent failure and the latter is done to fix and repair a fail [Wikipedia, online encyclopaedia].

2.11.3 Design for Performance (DfP)

The performance approach is, first and foremost, the practice of thinking and working in terms of ends rather than means. It is concerned with what ... is required to do, and not with prescribing how it is to be constructed. (Gibson, 1982)

(Brochner *et al.*, 1999, pp. 369-370) also believes that the performance concept focuses "...on 'output' of technical description" and "performance should give sharper focus on quality instead of price only". Performance should be considered in the context and carries a vast area of indicators. The overall objective of product or building performance is tied with the meaning of effectiveness regarding design. Availability, reliability, maintainability and capability are components of the effectiveness equation (Berger and Herzl, 1993). Different equation formats are presented by different individuals for effectiveness (Blanchard *et al*,1995) but the main concept focus on gaining the lowest long term cost for the promoter concerning whole life cycle costing (WLCC) (Barringer, 1997) can be descried as follows:

$$\text{System Effectiveness} = \text{Effectiveness} \div \text{LCC}$$

The level of performance of a product is affected by its components quality as a function of time and current conditions.

2.11.4 Design for Durability (DFD)

Products should be designed and manufactured in a way to fulfil both manufacturer and user needs over the long term. The concept of durability is not a new concept and its consideration belongs to ancient time. Among the users durability is always a positive factor in selection of goods. The monuments remaining in different communities are good examples of durability. Although durability is an important topic regarding SD and DfE, it can not be discussed with compromising issues such as: flexibility, maintainability, serviceability and performance. There are complex interactions between components of a system. Issues relevant to durability are components of a sustainable dynamic system and the study of the system without perception of components and the existing links between them is not useful. There are other potential variables like design technological characteristics and detailing, materials selection, products exploitation and use which should be accounted while durability issue is addressed.

2.11.5 Design for Flexibility (DfF)

The adaptability to any modifications in design is referred to as flexibility of design and these modifications include changes accommodated in product characteristics such as function, capacity and flow over time (Slaughter, 2001).

"A function is defined as the set of activities or components to achieve a specific objective" (Slaughter, 2001).

"Capacity is defined as the ability of the facility to meet certain performance requirements, in either loads/conditions or volume" (Slaughter, 2001).

And "Flows are defined as the movements within and around a building [product] relating to surrounding environment and its usage population" (Slaughter, 2001).

She believes in that increasing of value is achieved through increasing of flexibility and extending the useful life of product or building. Flexibility has direct benefits to the owner as well as occupants regarding subsequent changes, and also provides the product with longer period of useful life (Slaughter, 2001).

Regarding flexibility different design approaches and strategies were employed by different researchers. *Physically Separating* (Brand, 1994; Glen, 1994), *Prefabrication* (Glen, 1994; Gann and Barlow, 1996) and *Overcapacity Design* (Iselin and Lemer, 1993; Glen, 1994; Gann and Barlow, 1996) are some of the suggested approaches for achieving flexibility in design. Many researchers have worked on design flexibility and nearly all of them accept that designing for this aspect can save costs and expenses in future based on product WLC. (Keymer, 2000) introduces the flexibility in design as an element, providing ease of accessibility, maintenance, operation, installation and simplified demolition for the system components through reducing both inter and intra-system interactions among system components.

2.11.6 Design for Deconstruction (DfD)

"Design for deconstruction (DFD) refers to the design ... with the intent to manage its end-of-life more efficiently. It ensures the easy disassembly ... in order to reduce waste generation and maximise the recovery of high value secondary ... components and materials for reuse and recycling. This process encourages designers to incorporate flexibility ... at the design stage in order to ensure efficient ... operation, maintenance and removal. By allowing for a variety of scenarios for ... management from its occupation to its decommissioning, DFD reinforces the need and advantage of considering the whole life cycle ... and its components" (Macozoma, 2002, P.118).

2.12 Conclusions

Most of the definitions presented here prove that sustainable development is a process of development which indicates a mechanism. (Pearce, 1996, P.312) concludes that sustainable development is "a process instead of a fixed destination". Hence it can be concluded that sustainable development is a systematic evolutionary mechanism and process which is held in a long term period under certain conditions as a function of time. Regarding this fact sustainability is the aim of this mechanism and it can be said: sustainable development needs to fulfil different aspects of sustainability. According to (du plessis, 1999, P. 380) there are three pillars of environmental, economic and social sustainability and a fourth overarching principle of adaptability exists which points out that sustainable development is a continual process of dynamic balance.

What is important regarding sustainable development is that it needs new ways of thinking about the development of the built environment. Systematic thinking and flexible approaches are requisite factors to keep the environment as a system with a dynamic balance. There are two main points about SD. The first point focuses on the context that development is being made in, which means in each development it is the context that sets the equilibrium's balance. The latter point which should be highlighted is that; there is a difference between degree of importance and level of significance of components in the context of SD. Perhaps a certain characteristic is a significant factor in SD but it should be considered that its importance is determined by the existing context. This fact shows that the importance of components depends on the reality and essence of the context which is a function of time, condition and facilities. Dealing with SD and its pertained issues in an evolutionary dynamic system needs prudent considerations to existing context and level of importance of its components. As the development is held in the context of the environment, thus DfE should be assumed as a type of design regarded to environmental concerns beside social and economical issues. There are many policies and strategies employed in DfE which generally aim at higher quality of life on the planet. Sustainable designs with all its subsets (eco-design, green design, value design) are important in order to fulfil human needs in various dimensions existing in SD (Parkin, 2000). Design characteristics and strategies affecting functionality and product's whole life cycle (WLC) were explained and discussed regarding SD and its aspects.

The summary of what has been described in this chapter is shown in Fig 2.5.

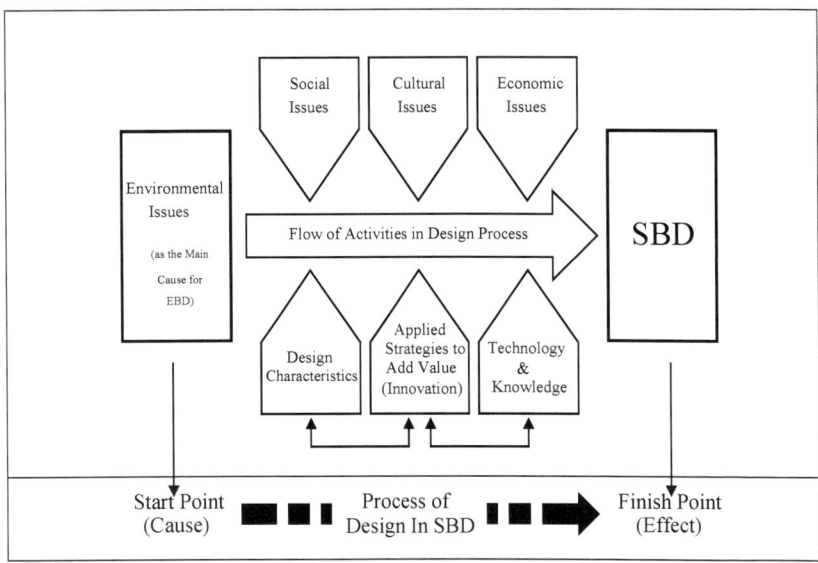

Fig 2.5 Process of Design in SD and SBD
(Here, *environmental impacts* as the *cause* and *SD* as the *effect* of process are presented.)

In Fig 2.5, environmental impacts are introduced as the main cause in process of design towards SD and respectively SBD could be the effect of this cause. In the figure it is shown that beside efforts made in design stage to apply technology and appropriate strategies, there is a severe need to consider social, cultural and economic issues in the process of design.

In this chapter it is attempted to review different individuals points of view on sustainability and SD issues and the authors' interpretation and definitions on SD will be presented in chapter four of this monograph.

CHAPTER 3

Sustainable Building; Concepts, Overviews and Scopes

3.1 Introduction

Building construction consumes 40 percent of the raw stone, gravel and sand used globally each year, and 25 percent of raw timber. Buildings also account for 40 percent of the energy and 16 percent of the water used annually worldwide (Lippiatt, 1999). This clarifies the role of the building process as the main consumer of the environment and its existing resources during the building life cycle. Naturally more consumption is followed by producing more effects and impacts. The building industry is assumed as one of the largest consumers of resources, which cause the highest rate of impacts on the environment. On the other hand, the building and construction process provide society with economic benefits and social developments. Bourdeau explains that: "On one side, the built environment constitutes one of the main supports (infrastructures, buildings) of economic development, and, on the other side, its construction has significant impacts on resources (land, materials, energy, water, human/social capital) and on the living and working environment. Hence the construction industry has significant direct and indirect links with the various aspects of sustainable development" (Bourdeau, 1999).

The aforementioned characteristics state that the building process is a mechanism which has a close link with SD. Since the building activity trends involve all aspects of SD and embraces all focused dimensions of SD, achieving sustainable building is proposed as the main objective of the building industry. The emergence of the building process in the process of SD is derived from the point of view that embraces all dimensions of SD. It involves economic, social and cultural issues, and environmental impacts and profiles based on accommodating human need. These reasons create a series of movements under the umbrella of SD, integrated in the sustainable building.

3.2 Building as a Product

A product is defined as "Something produced by human or mechanical effort or by a natural process."(American heritage on line dictionary) Also in the hyper online dictionary it is described as "the amount of an artefact that has been created by someone or some process" or "a consequence of someone's efforts or of a particular set of circumstances" (Hyper online Dictionary). According to these definitions building can be considered as a product because it is formed through a process by human efforts under particular conditions. Hence, all the regulations and rules about a product can be applied to buildings.

3.3 Building Impacts on the Environment

Industrial activities such as buildings, over the past century have caused serious ecological and environmental problems (Shrivastava, 1995). Global warming, acid rain, ozone depletion, natural resource scarcity, air pollution, toxic wastes, loss of bioversity, and industrial accidents are assumed as the negative impacts of industrial consequences over recent decades. Buildings as a multi-disciplinary industry, from pre-construction phase to post-construction phase affect the environment. (Boussabaine and Kirkham, 2004) classify the environmental impacts into two main groups, namely: atmospheric related and resources related. The atmospheric impacts embrace problems such as the green house effect and ozone layer and the resource impacts refer to air, water and earth pollution.

3.4 Sustainable Building (SB)

SB embodies vast areas and achieving it requires much effort. "The sustainable building concept has shown many developments in a relatively short period of time. However, these developments have taken place mostly at the abstract level of policy makers and research scientists, and less at the level of the practitioners. This leaves us with a sophisticated strategic concept of sustainable building. The translation of this concept into operational practices proves to be difficult" (Van Bueren, 2000).
(Pilvang and Sutherland, 1998) claim; "Environmental Management in Project Design serves as the working title for the project, whose overall objective is 'to promote the use of cleaner technology in building and construction projects'. The title also implies a strategy for achieving a gradual reduction in resource consumption and environmental impact in building and construction activities. This strategy is based on the recognition that the decisions taken before a building or construction becomes a physical reality often determine the environmental impacts throughout its life cycle". (Patermann, 1999, P.414) points out that the construction industry should address both environmental and social impacts such as: balancing reduced costs, improved performance, satisfying customer's needs, with caring for the environment and improving safety and the quality of life for society in general. As it can be seen in Patermann's concept building consists of parameters such as environmental, social and economic profiles, addressed in SD dimensions.
"Thus, the key to sustainable building and construction lies with planners, design architects and engineers. They are the ones, in consultation with clients and users, to give a project its form and to

select its design and materials. In many cases they also plan the execution of projects and supervise the works" (Pilvang and Sutherland, 1998). Hence, to improve in the field of SD and SB there is a need to develop sustainable building design (SBD) as a tool to encounter the problem of sustainability in the building industry.

3.4.1 Sustainable Building Design (SBD)

A good design is always made based on context otherwise it produces more problems rather than solutions. "When attempting to describe sustainability and by implication sustainable construction [building] ... it is necessary to understand the developmental priorities as well as cultural context..." (du Plessis, 2001). The other parameters that affect the building design as an equilibrium formed based on different variables should be counted in the process of design.

(Brandon, 1999, P.396.) explains; "The focus for construction must be on improved quality which makes it natural and/or desirable to sustain a building or group of building. This 'quality' will encompass performance, energy, waste, emissions, longevity and all the aspects of current and future 'needs'".

Since architecture and design fields embrace a vast area of subjectivities beside technical and artistic issues, SBD covers many various areas. Norman foster and partners (1999) describes sustainable building as: "creating buildings which are energy efficient, healthy, comfortable, and flexible in use and designed for long life" (ARBE 121) [Online source].

Also (BSRIA) believes that sustainable buildings are achieved through" Creation and management of healthy buildings based upon resource and ecological principles". (ARBE 121)[Online source]

The following holistic description of SD by NASA on building process seems to be one of the best ones to clarify the subject;

"Sustainability is an over-arching concept incorporating appropriate sustainable design elements into facilities planning, design, construction, operation and maintenance to enhance and balance facility life cycle cost, environmental impact, and occupant health, safety, security, and productivity. The essential elements of sustainability include:

1. Energy efficiency and water conservation
2. Site selection to minimize environmental and transportation impact
3. Sustainable materials (i.e., reused, recycled, recyclable, non-toxic, low embodied energy content, renewable)
4. Durable and efficient materials and equipment
5. A healthy environment, including indoor air quality
6. Features in support of enhanced worker productivity

7. Design for personnel safety and security
8. Design for decommissioning and disposal
9. Enhanced building operating and maintenance characteristics (i.e., Design for Maintainability, continued efficiency, and low toxicity)
10. A philosophy that defines facility operational objectives, then tests and verifies that all building systems and components have been properly installed and perform to the level intended (i.e., Total Building Commissioning, TBC)" (NASA, 2001)

Ultimately the most sustainable building is one that will last for a longer time and is reasonably flexible for changing uses. Apart from technical aspects it must be an asset that users want to keep using, whether for practicalities or pleasure.

3.4.2 Sustainable Building Principles

Kibert (1994) proposes the sustainable building principles are as follows:

1. Minimisation of resource consumption; (Conservation)
2. Maximisation of resource reuse; (Reuse)
3. Use renewable and recyclable resources; (Renew/Recycle)
4. Protect the natural environment; (Nature Protection)
5. Create a healthy and non-toxic environment; and (Non-Toxics)
6. Apply Life Cycle Cost Analysis and True Costs (Economics)
7. Pursue quality in creating the built environment. (Quality)

The first draft included 6 items (By Kibert), and then item 7 was added to the available principles by him.
Also (Fisher, 1992) highlights five principles of sustainable design and environmental architecture. These are;

1. Healthy Interior Environment [Higher Standards of Quality of Life]
2. Energy Efficiency [Best Gains from Lowest Amount of Energy]
3. Ecologically Benign Materials [Reduction in environmental Impacts regarding WLC]
4. Environmental Form [Compatibility and adaptability of form and plan to the site, region, and climate]
5. Good Design [Level of Design Standards]

Through prudent consideration of the aforementioned principles it can be concluded that SBD has a very close link with quality and *performance concept*. Since SD covers principles and strategies to aim at better quality of life for human race founded on a proposed quality for environment based on ecological, economical and social issues, therefore in SBD better quality of building providing higher standards and quality of life for its occupants precisely concentrates on performance concept and quality approach.

3.5 Performance Concept and SBD

The holistic performance outcome is a departure from the traditional approach of developing prescriptive, analytical codes and standards. Gibson (1982, p. 4) articulates that the performance approach is concerned with what a building or building product is required to do, rather than prescribing how it is to be constructed.

Hattis (1996)

It is believed that: Performance-based building (PBB) relies on a flexible and non-prescriptive concept for building design, construction and facility management (CIB, 2003).

Performance is a long-term process dealing with buildings throughout their life spans in three aspects: customer expectations, operation, and maintenance. Optimal building performance is derived from the product of a good project development, where the traditional triangle of project objectives (Barnes, 1988) stresses time, cost, and quality (Chew *et al.*, 2004). In Barnes's triangle the meaning of quality carries ambiguities. The understanding of quality relies on identification of its determinants and components.

Quality is defined in four ways:

1. Quality of conception in terms of elegance of form, spatial articulation, contribution to culture [Design issues]
2. Quality of specification for the level of finishes required and achieving technical standards set for the building [technical and technological issues]
3. Quality of realization of project [Socio-economics and feasibility]; and the
4. Quality of conformance in which the objectives set out are realized in practice [socio-economics, reality and accountability] (Winch *et al.*, 1998).

As understood from Winch *et al.*, quality deals with design, technical and socio-economic issues. Design characteristics and applied strategies in early design stages play a pivotal role in the outcome of quality. 'Building performance' has been defined in BS 5240 as behaviour of a product in use. It can also be used to denote the physical performance characteristics of a building as a whole and of its parts (Clift and Butler 1995). It thus relates to a building's ability to contribute to fulfilling the functions of its intended use (Williams, 1993). The influence of design embraces all dimensions of SBD. Embodied energy, maintain-ability, flexibility, serviceability, dismantle ability, performance, environmental impacts, risk, economical and social issues are factors that can be considered in the process of design in SBD and building design. There is a consensus agreement on the environmental issues application as the crucial parameters in DFE different features. In majority of them the efforts rely on natural ecology and the developments of industrial ecology (BATE, 1998; Kibert et al., 2000; NASA, 2001) and a number of strategies are considered into the design in order to enhance the quality of design and achieve higher standards and values based on existing context. Green building design, bio climatic building design, eco building design, eco-efficient building design are features of DfE in SBD. In each approach according to employed philosophies a set of strategies and considerations are employed to achieve DfE and finally SBD.

3.6 SBD Overviews

Based on individual perception and interpretation of reality, experience and interest, each architect defines SBD and its characteristics in a different way. As the meaning of performance, quality and quality of life varies among different individuals therefore it is expected the approaches towards SBD and proposed principles slightly differ. This fact proves the existence of subjectivity in the field of architecture. "The term 'sustainable construction' has a diversity of meanings depending on the context and background of those using term"(Larsson, 1995, P.402). Wines (2000, p. 67) regarding diversity of views in SBD state: " For certain designers, the latest advances in engineering and environmental technology are central to their objectives; while for others, it is important to return to the lessons of history and the use of indigenous methods and materials. For another group, the resource of topography, vegetation, solar energy and earth itself are the means to achieve an expanded vision of organic buildings".
In a study done by Edwards (2001) a questionnaire was sent to a number of famous architects and their points of view were asked on SD and SBD. Some of those views were:

Kaplicky notes: "Major aspects of sustainable design are choice of materials and performance of a building once it is built." (Edwards, 2001, p. 34)

Richard Rogers's view on SD focuses on "concern for the principles of social and economic sustainability as well as the specific concerns of energy use and environmental impact of buildings and cities. (Ibid, p. 36)

Whereas for Herzog SD means:
"Using renewable forms of energy-especially solar energy- as extensively as possible." (Ibid, p. 74)

And for Yeang it is;
"Design that integrates seamlessly with the ecological systems in the biosphere over the entire life cycle of the built system." (Ibid, p.60)

While Kaplicky looks at nature as a pattern:
"There is much to learn from (nature's) more efficient use of materials. (Ibid, p.34)

Regarding SD Foster believes:
"Look to human natures, Vernacular traditions that are specific to the area in which we are working." (Ibid, p. 32)

Rogers states that sustainability needs challenge through "intelligent design and building fabric which contribute to a substantial reduction in running and maintenance costs during the life cycle of a building." (Ibid, p.360)

These various perspectives on SBD makes it difficult to develop a consensus environmental and SBD assessment method for helping stakeholders in building decision making stage for WLC. "Until a consensus is attained, the ability of the architectural community to adopt a coherent environmental strategy, across all buildings types and styles of development, will remain elusive." (Brennan, 1997)

3.7 Concept of Flexibility in SBD

The variety of scopes towards SD and SBD leads to separation of efforts in this field and to avoid this, some researchers have presented the concept of *'Flexibility of Sustainability'* as a panacea for the existing crux.
Recently the flexibility of sustainability as a key characteristic is included in sustainable architecture and design by different researchers (Guy and Farmer, 2001; Guy and Moore, 2005).

3.8 Different Philosophies in SD and SBD

Man is a product of the nature. He has been created according to the laws of nature. If he is sufficiently aware of those laws, if he obeys them and harmonises his life with the perpetual flux of nature, then he will obtain a conscious sensation of harmony that will be beneficial to him.

Le Corbusier, The Open Hand

DfE in general, and Green Design, Eco-Design, Life Cycle Design (LCD), and many other classifications in particular, are considered as sub-sets of SD. The common objective of all them is gaining more efficiency from careful use of resources though better quality of design. In all of them applied design strategies and policies are used to add value to the quality of design based on contemporary design. In this research SBD is sought through eco-building design school of philosophy and mainly focuses on building design rather than ecological and environmental concerns.

3.9 Eco-design, Eco-building design (EBD) Scope

The eco-design approach was founded by industry and was applied in product design initially (Dewberry, 1996; McAloone, 1998; Van Hemel, 1998). In general, eco-design focuses on '*Environmentally Oriented sort of Design*' whereas sometimes it carries a specific term such as '*Life Cycle Design*'. Also there are different scopes about this school of philosophy. On one hand some careful researchers accept it as an evolutionary stage of contemporary design; "such as: Sustainable Product Design (Charter and Chick, 1997; Walker, 1998); EcoRedesign (Bakker, 1995; Ryan, 1996) or Design for Environment (Allenby and Fullerton, 1992; Van Hemel, 1998) for instance" (Sherwin and Bhamra, 2001)[Online source] whereas in the other hand other researcher believe that eco-building design is an independent type of design which should be integrated in the early stages of a design (Van Nes and Cramer, 1997; McAloone, 1998; Sherwin and Evans, 2000).

Eco-design in early stages of design is explained as; "A number of companies discussed this early stage of design and highlighted how important it is to ensure that the environment is considered as early as possible. There was recognition that beyond a certain point in the design process it is extremely difficult to alter certain product features that are key to the environmental performance" (Bhamra et al. 1999).

In the case of building design, the process of design is a dynamic mechanism prone to improvement and can be assumed that the design stage is an evolutionary system and the level of progress and development compared with former experiences are established in the early stages of building design through employed strategies (Eco-features) and innovations. Also, it is believed that 80-90 percent of both environmental impacts and economic consequences are established in early stages of product design (Design Council, 1997). Eco-building design begins at the global scale and gradually narrowed down to the detailed building design as well as socio-economic concerns. EBD as a subset of SBD and SD follows the same rules and aspects of sustainability. It not only contains all technical aspects of design, but also focuses on economy and particularly on social issues of design as well as environmental concerns.

Some researchers agree that: "The cold economic rationality of capitalism, in which every institution is subordinated to the calculus of profit and loss, does not answer the question posed by every human being-that there is more to life than the pursuit of economic efficiency. We are social as well as economic beings." (The Observer, 2000).

3.9.1 Key Indicators in EBD

Ecological design generally deals with consideration of prudent application of energy and materials in a designed-system and the endeavour to reduce the impacts of this application on the natural environment, regarding project's whole life cycle (Yeang, 1995). Hence, ecological building (Eco-building) is a viable economic proposition because it is formed based on enabling a building to have lower-energy operational costs through consideration of more compatible landscape-balanced design system. It could be built at ordinary building costs (or even lower initial costs) while at the same time contributing to a sustainable future.

Researches like (Roaf *et al.*, 2001; Smith, 2001, P. 205.) highlight the challenge towards SBD needs a kind of rethinking on innovation and creativity issues such as:

1. Minimising the use of fossil-based energy in terms of embodied energy concerning WLC.
2. Substitution of other cleaner, safer sources of energy and materials according to embodied energy concerns and WLC.
3. Application of cheap, renewable, clean sources of energy such as solar, wind, geothermal types usually called on-site renewable energies.
4. Use of appliances, devices and strategies in design providing higher quality of life and efficiency.
5. Consideration of socio-economic concerns during design process to meet the highest standards of technical proficiency in combination with aesthetic excellence.

A number of strategies were used in different vernacular architectures and then in modern architecture, those gains have been ignored or poorly considered. In this study they are called '*lost values*'. The objectives followed in SBD and eco-building design (EBD) generally; attempt to enhance the quality of design and eco-efficiency through employment of a certain set of strategies in design process. Innovation and creativity in design affects the quality of design through revitalise the lost values or creating new strategies. The application of wind catchers both in ancient architecture of Middle East and today architecture all around the world in order to provide natural ventilation and passive cooling is a good example of revitalising and developing a lost value in EBD. Some examples of wind catcher use for natural ventilation in the UK projects are; Coventry University Library, Manchester University Contact Theatre, Jubilee Campus in University of Nottingham, Beddington Zero Energy Development (BEDZED) in Sutton. These examples prove that innovation in design is not always dealing with a new concept but it might appear as a new method of encountering with an old issue to revitalise a lost value. In EBD innovation embraces all kinds of engagements related to problems and existing issues.

Efficiency both ecological and economical wise (Yeang, 1995), quality of design and innovation are effective parameters, employed to establish an eco-building design method in order to achieve enhanced quality of life.

3.10 Innovation in EBD

According to (Barrett and Sexton, 1998, P. 5.) a successful innovation is defined as "the effective generation and implementation of a new idea, which enhances overall organisational performance". Based on this definition the range of innovation consists of two main stages. The first is the conceptual aspect of innovation which includes quality of idea and its newness and the latter step involves the practical aspect dealing with issues such as accountability and implementation of the proposed innovation. The emphasis were placed on the aforementioned assumptions by (Barrett and Sexton, 1998; Sexton *et al.*, 2001) presented in four groups namely: idea, newness, effective generation and implementation, and overall organisational performance. In this research innovation is not merely allocated for a particular stage of building process but it is believed that mainly in the early stages of design the outcomes are established through strategies selection and applied decisions.

3.11 Role of Designer in EBD

Compromising a designer's role in DFE is impossible. The concepts presented by the designer at early stages of design are pursued in the latter stages and finally are generated as the final project in the built environment. Hence it can be argued that designers' influence can be felt from the beginning stages of building process to the obsolescence stages. Designers can effectively control the time, budget and conditions. There are different points of view about designers' role and a few of them are presented here. (McAloone and Evans, 1996) mention that despite designers have a fair knowledge about the environment and its relevant terms but overall, there is a shortage of knowledge about global issues such as green house effects and ozone layer depletion. This hints towards unlimited fields faced in the design stage.

(Luttropp and lagerstedt, 1999) believe that there are more important issues like functionality related to design rather than environmental concerns. This view indicates the main role of design to solve the consequent problems, which mean through application of reasonable design many environmental negative impacts, might be prevented. Also some designer claim for more free actions needed for them, and mention *"the best way making designers care about DFE is to let them be free and creative. They neither want too much information, nor DFE tools"*. (Lagerstedt and Grüner, 2000). The role of designer as the first actor of DfE scenario, in presenting all design requirements based on existing conditions in an artistic, technical, managerial trend has been discussed. It has been argued that the degree of innovation, creativity and knowledge of designer regarding problem solutions can guarantee the level of design success.

3.12 SBD Assessment Method and Science

The reason why there is a need for assessment methods and evaluation systems is summarised as: "Assessment methods ... facilitate and enhance dialogue, communication and story telling among and between key parties involved in a building project." (Cole, 2005, P. 464)

SBD assessments need scientific approaches for measuring the characteristics' values. It is believed that; "rational science can and will provide the understanding of the environment and the assessment of those measures which are necessary to rectify environmental bads." (Macnaghton, and Urry, 1998, P.1)

"Environmental assessment of building in the future must evolve within a wider context of local Agenda 21 sustainable development criteria" (Curwell et al., 1999, P.286).

3.13 SBD Assessment Methods

"The lack of an agreed structure that can help decision making process achieve greater sustainability is a major problem." (Brandon and Lombardi, 2005, P.76). Number of researcher such as Mark Deakin point out that a philosophical framework is essential in evaluating sustainability but it is not sufficient by itself and explains that in evaluating and assessment of sustainability values, targeted for '*in the balance*' jobs and workings are mainly left to science and technology (Deakin, 2005) rather than philosophical frameworks. Deakin says "This is because while it might be liberal democratic doctrines that give us our philosophy, aesthetic and politics, it is science and technology that provide the measures needed to objectify the value of things theses produce and in turn, standardize what they mean to us as members of the public." (ibid, P.480)

Assessments of buildings can help building stakeholders in three ways:

1. "It simulates owners to improve a building's performance.
2. It informs decision makers during the design stages and;
3. It delivers objective measurements of a building's impacts on natural systems." (Cole, 1999, P.230)

(Todd and Geissler, 1999, P.247) believe that in assessment "regional adaptation is complex, however, and raises many considerations that may be in conflict". The complexity of assessment in some cases might be derived from lack of information and existing limitations in understanding indicators and their degree of importance, significance in a certain region and their method of ranking. By providing flexibility and weighting of building assessment criteria, it is expected to create a reasonable and acceptable method of assessment based on significance of indicators instead of their importance regarding each region in particular.

There are various methods of building assessments based on different school of philosophies and applied intensions towards SBD and their own specific definitions and priorities. Due to proposed characteristics each method covers a certain area of building and design attributes. These methods might have some common points and differences on covered fields. For example (Green Building Assessment: GB- Tools) GBA is one of the most successful methods of assessment that includes resources use, environmental loadings, indoor environment, longevity, process and contextual factors. The research implications handled by (Todd and Geissler, 1999, pp. 255-256) explain and discuss respectively;

1. "Building assessment systems must reflect national, regional and local differences if they are to be accepted and used.
2. A uniform, international system has value in stimulating the building sector in different countries to improve.
3. Assessment systems can and should build in regional flexibility while retaining global priorities.
4. In thinking about weighting of importance, we should set our system boundary at the 'world' level.
5. Out standing performance levels should be fixed (not adaptable) and should be based on sustainability relevant terms.
6. Sometimes systems should be both rating systems and agent of change.
7. Additional research is needed into the implication of adaptation of assessment system to regional conditions and the most appropriate to adaptation in various contexts.

Assessment methods work as a synthesis of current environmental knowledge related to building which plays a significant role, common among variety of researches (Cole and Larsson, 1998). The majority of assessment methods in DfE are designed based on negative environmental impacts caused by building process during its WLC and none of them focuses on design and its affiliated issues or if they did it is poorly focused and mainly ignored. Methods of building assessments in SBD are introduced, presented and then compared with each other in the next section of this study.

3.13.1 BRE's Environmental Assessment Method (BREEAM)

BREEAM is a registered trademark of Building Research Establishment (BRE) in the UK. In this method management, energy use, health and well-being, pollution, transport, land use, ecology, materials and water issues are the areas that performance of a building is assessed. It is recommended to project designers and developers to consider these issues in the early stages of the process. For assessment a labelling rating system, ending to a single score is employed. "Credits are awarded in each area according to performance. A set of environmental weightings then enables the credits to be added together to produce a single overall score. The building is then rated on a scale of *Pass, Good, Very Good* or *Excellent*, and a certificate awarded that can be used for promotional purposes"[online source, http://www.breeam.org/]. BREEAM employs three scales to assess environmental impact; Global, local and indoor issues (Prior, 1993). A range of building types is covered by BREEAM. In addition to offices BREEAM has expanded to include other types of buildings like: factories and warehouses, retail stores, homes and schools both as new buildings and refurbished ones (Baldwin et al., 1991; Prior, 1993). For example *'EcoHomes'* is a specific version of BREEM which is applied to residential facilities.

3.13.2 BEPAC

"Similar to BREEM, BEPAC can be used to evaluate the environmental performance of new design and existing buildings. BEPAC results in a composite weighting of five major areas: ozone protection, environmental quality, resource conservation, and site and transportation. BEPAC is primarily used in Canada"(Crawley and Aho, 1999).

3.13.3 Leadership in Energy and Environmental Design (LEED)

LEED developed in 1998 can be considered as American version of BREEM applied in the USA, also called USGBC. LEED rating system employs a simple checklist format which facilitates its application in the design process (US Green Building Council, 2000). "In evaluating a building using the LEED criteria, there are minimum, mandatory requirements in areas such as building commissioning, energy efficiency indoor air quality, ozone depletion/CFCs, Smoking ban, comfort and water. Once the mandatory requirements are met, a building can earn 'credit' in 14 areas. Depending on the total credits, a building receives a rating level of 'bronze', 'silver', 'gold' or 'platinum'" (Crawley and Aho, 1999).

3.13.4 LCA and LCA id

Life cycle analysis or assessment (LCA) is a technique which is applied in assessment of both industrial and building projects. It is strongly recommended to consider project's life cycle rather than just its design or construction processes, which includes all costs from an investment decision and its latter terms (Ashworth, 2004). This method involves in measurement and evaluation of negative impacts as out come of building or relevant services produced in the environment. There are many softwares such as LCA id designed and developed based on characteristics of LCA. This method and its different versions formed on studying the impacts on the natural environment over WLC. Application of this method can be very time consuming and needs environmental expertise as well. Therefore, full-scale of LCAs are not suggested to building designers. *Ecotect* a computer aided design soft ware to help building stakeholders to develop the design quality is developed based on LCAid method originally in Australia.

3.13.5 GBA (Green Building Assessment) and (GB Tools)

GBA was established and developed by GBC (Green Building Challenge) in Canada. "Green building tool (GB tool) was developed as a 'second-generation' assessment method that built on the limitations of existing methods, and confronted areas of building performance assessment that were previously either ignored or poorly defined ...Unlike BREEM in the UK and BEPAC in Canada GBC Emphasised research and involved researchers and practitioners worldwide. It was not designed as a tool for any particular application or use in a commercial market; instead it was intended to contribute to the state-of-the-art of building performance assessment and provide a forum for identification and discussion of issue and testing of potential approaches" (Todd *et al*, 2001).

Today this software is considered as a reliable one in many various countries around the world and is used in order to create countries own assessment tool. "Aspects of BREEM also served as a model for the GBC Frame work" (Todd *et al*, 2001). GBC assesses building performance through comparing similarities and differences with a selection of available assessment tools (Todd *et al*, 2001). This method concentrates on criteria such as: resource consumption, loadings and environmental impacts, indoor environmental quality, quality of service, economics, and pre-operation stages (GBC, 2000). In this method of assessment each criterion is scored with a number varying from -2 to +5. Benchmarks for scores are based on typical practice, local codes or national standards. Then all scores are summed up to category level. Default weights are considered for each category and its subsets. Then the result can be presented as separate bars for each main category.

3.13.6 Checklists (Checklist 2002) & Checklist for Sustainable Development

This technique is usually based on earlier analyses or simplified consequences of a complicated method and is presented as rules of thumb to be followed in order to achieve a better result regarding eco-design. The guidelines recommended in a checklist require being adapted to the design context by the designer. Reducing materials and energy consumption, minimisation of components number, use of healthy and efficient amount of energy are all examples of efforts done in a checklist. The checklists mainly present a set of design strategies in different categories [online source].

3.13.7 Standards

Standards such as ISO 14000 series are based on environmental management systems with the specifications with guidance for use. ISO 14004 is focusing on Guidance on principles, Systems and supporting techniques whereas 14010 provides environmental auditing, and 14050 is used for environmental vocabulary. Also there are other versions of standards such as ISO/TC 207 (ISO technical Committee) which develops and maintains ISO 14000. There are few ISOs like ISO 14040:1997, ISO 14041:1998 and ISO 14042:2000 that apply life cycle assessment to the process of evaluation [Online source] .

Table 3.1 Existing SBD Methods in Building

Source	Method	Focus	Relevant Topics	Applicable for	Potential Used	When Applied?	Unit	Scoring/Weighting/Reporting results
Building Research Establishment (UK)(1993)	BREEAM & (EcoHomes for residentials)	Building (Market-focused) (Global, local, Indoor Issues)	1.Management(Site) 2.Energy Use 3.Health & Well-being 4.Pollution 5.Transport 6.Land Use 7.Ecology 8.Water	WLC stages & Decision Making	Designers Developers	New Design Existing Design	Labelling rating System (Result is a single Score)	Qualitative Bad< X< Excellent or A sunflower rating
US Green Building Council (1998)	LEED (Leadership in Energy and Environmental design) or (USGBC)	Building (Market-Based to define a green building)	1.ProductMarketing 2.Design Guidelines 3.Environmental Auditing in existing building	WLC stages & Decision Making	Designers Developers	New Design Existing Design	Labelling rating System	Qualitative Bronze<Silver<Gold<Platinum
Natural Resources Canada & University of British Colombia (1998-2005)	GBA (Green Building Assessment) GBC 2000	Building (Commercial, Multi-unit residential and Schools)	1. Resources Consumption 2.Environmental Loading 3.Indoor Environmental quality 4.Longevity 5.Process 6.Contextual Factors	WLC stages & Decision Making	Designers Developers Environmental Experts	New Design Existing Design	Numeric rating System	Quantitative (Numeric Weighting) -2<X<+5 Difficult to use because of the complexity of the framework.
University of British Colombia (1993)	BEPAC (Building Environmental Performance Assessment Criteria)	Building	1.Ozone Layer 2.Environmental-Impact of energy use 3.Indoor Environmental Quality 4.Resource Conservation 5.Site & Transport	WLC stages & Decision Making	Designers Developers Environmental Experts	New Design Existing Design	Numeric rating System	Quantitative (Composite Weighting)
DPWS Australia	LCA id	Building	1.3D Models 2.Water Consumption 3. Materials 4. Weather Data 5.LCA Analysis 6. Atmospheric, Resource and Pollution Impacts	WLC stages & Decision Making	Designers Developers Property Owner	Early Stages of Design	Scoring System	Quantities or Qualitative
SALEM	SAM (Sustainable Architecture Matrix)	Building	Human Eco-system	WLC stages & Decision Making	Designer Developer	New Design Existing Design	Numeric Rating Scores (Single Score)	Quantitative (Numeric Weighting)
(Bergendal et al., 1995) (Magnusson, 1997)	Checklist 2002 (Checklists)	Building Product	Simplified summaries from earlier analysis	Avoidance of certain undesired events	Designers	Any time depending on the type of the list	No unit	Qualitative or Quantitative

3.13. 8 Other Building Assessment Methods

There are other methods created, developed in SBD. Some of them are named here for further reading and information as follows:

HK-BEAM in Hong Kong (Edmunds, 1999), **EcoProfile** in Norway (Pettersen *et al.*, 2000), **ESCALE** developed through a PhD thesis by CSTB (Centre Scientifique et Technique du Batiment) and the university of Savoie (Chatagnon *et al.*, 1998) and **EcoEffect** in Sweden (Glaumann, 2000).

For clarification and a better view on subject (assessment methods), a comparison held by Crawley and Aho (1999) on four famous assessment methods is presented in this comparison four methods of BREEAM (The UK), BEPAC (Canada), LEED (The US) and GBA (Canada) were compared with each other and the summary was presented in Table 2, illustrated as follows:

Table 3.2 Comparison of the Four Famous Assessment Methods

Scope	Assessment method			
	BREEAM	BEPAC	LEED	GBA
Resource consumption				
Embodied energy	X	X		X
Operation energy	X	X	X	X
Land		X	X	X
Water	X	X	X	X
Materials	X	X	X	X
Environmental loading				
Airborne emissions	X	X		X
Solid	X	X	X	X
Liquid waste		X		
Other loadings				X
Indoor environment				
Air quality	X	X	X	X
Thermal quality	X	X	X	X
Visual quality		X		X
Noise and acoustics				X
Controllability of systems				X
Longevity				
Adaptability				X
Maintenance of performance			X	X
Process				
Design and construction		X		X
Building operation		X	X	X
Contextual factors				
Contextual factors				X
Loads on immediate surroundings		X	X	X

Adopted from (Crawley and Aho, 1999, p.307)

3.14 Assessment Methods in Industry

There are many aspects and characteristics in common between building and industry. The main reason for this is that building consists of various industries and should be considered as a multi-industrial. Methods applied in industry based on eco-efficiency and design can be employed in building sector as well. Few methods both in industry and building are presented in Tables 3.1 and 3.3 similar to the former methods related to building process the majority of them are concerned about environmental issues and impact and mostly ignore or poorly on the design and its characteristics. These methods are also presented in Table 3.3 in order to be applied partially in building science as there is some common part between building and industrial efforts. One of the methods which are recommended in this research to be used by building section is the '*Eco Strategy Wheel*' developed by (Brezet and Hemel, 1997).

The strategies, employed in this method are applicable in building process as well. In this approach the product design review concentrates on field such as: low impact materials, material use, production techniques, distribution system, impacts during use, initial life time and end of life system. There are many tips to be applied and adopt from industry into building process. Also it can be said that many of the concepts in building section are developed versions of industrial methods. Concepts such as dematerialisation, rematerialisation, recycling, reuse, and many other related terms are applied firstly in the field of industry, then they developed in the building processes.

Table 3.3 Existing SD and eco-design Methods in Industry

Source	Method	Focus	Relevant Topics	Applicable for	Potential Used	When Applied?	Unit	Scoring/Weighting/ Reporting results
Technical University of Delft (Neatherland)	IdeMAT	Product	Engineering Material Energy Transport	Resources Eco-System-Quality	Designer Environmental IExperts	Life Cycle Stages	Functional Unit	Qualitative
Pre-Consultant (Netherlands)	Eco-it *Based on IdeMAT	Product	Materials Environmental Impacts	Environmental Profile Materials	Designers Environmental-Experts	Design Stages (Practical Assessment)	Numeric Rating sCORE	Quantitative
Pre-Consultant (Netherlands)	Sima-Pro (System for Integrated Environmental Products) *Based on IdeMAT	Product Process Service	Materials Environmental Impacts	Environmental Profile Materials	Designers Environmental-Experts	Design Stages (Practical Assessment)	Numeric Rating Score	Quantitative (Results can be calculated using Monte Carlo analysis)
Green Design initiative at Carnegie Mellon University	EIOLCA (Economic input-output life cycle assessment) *Based on LCA *Based on Wassily Leontief economic IO model.	Product & Service	Materials Emissions Economic-Transaction	Resources Eco-system-Quality	Engineers Designers Environmental Experts	Life Cycle Stages	Service Unit Weighting Units	Quasi qualitative Quantitative

CAPTER 3: SUSTAINABLE BUILDING; CONCEPTS, OVERVIEWS AND SCOPES

Source	Method	Focus	Relevant Topics	Applicable for	Potential Used	When Applied?	Unit	Scoring/Weighting/ Reporting results
	CED (Cumulative Energy Demand)	Product	Energy Resources	Energy Consumption Calculation Material Selection	Environmental Experts Engineers Designers	Life Cycle Stages	Energy Units	Quantitative (Calculated energy demand) & (Rough Estimation Method)
Pre-Consultants & the University of Amesterdam, Leiden and Delft as well as consultancies TNO and CE	Eco-Indicators 95, 99 Methods	Product Process	1.Environmental Impacts 2.Ecosystem 3. Human Health	To Drive Product's environmental weak points in its life cycle	Environmental Experts Designers	Life Cycle Stages	Numeric Rating Scores (Single Score)	Quantitative (Rough Estimation Method)
Lindahl (2000)	EEA (Evaluate Environmental Aspects)	Company product	Resource Emissions	Environmental Loads of Materials	Multifunctional Group	Life Cycle Stages	Identification Needed	Qualitative
Holloway (1997)	EDSM Environmental Design Strategy Matrix)	Product	Identify Environmental Design Strategies	Environmental Emission Resources	Designer	Early stages of product Design	-	Qualitative & Quantitative
Schluter (2001)	LCDSM (Life Cycle Design Structure Natrix)	Product	Identify environmental sensitive points using environmental indicators	LCA & Environmental Emissions Resources	Designer	Early stages of Design	-	Qualitative & Quantitative
Brezet & Van Hemel (1997)	MET (Material, Energy, Toxicity)	Product	Material Energy Toxicity	Resources Eco-system Quality Human Health	Designers Experienced Individuals	Life cycle stages	Functional Unit	Qualitative & Quantitative
Schmidt-Bleek (1993)	MIPS (Material Intensity Per Service Unit)	Product	Material Energy Time Rebound Effect	Resources Energy Use	Designer	Life cycle stages	Service Unit	Qualitative Simple
Van Hemel & Brezet (1997)	Eco Strategy Wheel	Product	Redesign checklist with 8 strategies: 1.Optimum Function 2.Reduce Impact in use phase 3.Reduce use of materials 4.Choose right materials 5.Optimise life time 6.optimise production 7.optimise end of life 8.Optimise distribution	Life Cycle Design Resources Eco-system Efficiency	Multi-functional Team	Early stages of LC	Optimisation	Qualitative Simple Brainstorming
The Swedish Environmental research Institute (IVL) and the Swedish Federation of Industries .(1989)	EPS (Environmental Priority Strategy)	Product	Materials Processes (indicators include damage done to 5 safeguard subjects)	Resources Human Health Production Bioversity Aesthetic Values	Environmental Experts & Financial Experts	Life Cycle Stages	Environmental Load Unit (ELU) & European Currency Unit (ECU)	Quasi Qualitative & Quantitative (Totalling up the Financial sums of five safeguard subjects)

As, shown in the Tables 3.1 and Table 3.3, the majority of methods focus mainly on environmental impacts and solutions and ignore or poorly notice design issues, characteristics and strategies influences on preventing occurrence of potential impacts.

Based on this fact about capability of design strategies and characteristics to support sustainability issues, this research entitled eco-building design aims at enhancing the quality of design and performance in order to provide better quality of life for building occupants though employment of design characteristics, environmental design strategies for achieving eco-efficiency.

3.15 Eco-building Design Assessment Method

The considerations of environmental issues regarding product create a new opportunity for various eco-design methods to be formed. (Ethernfeld and Lenox, 1997) believe that: there are variety of eco-design methods but just few of them are developed, reliable or useful regarding industrial companies [and building practices].

"A common goal for these methods is to measure and describe the environmental impact of products and services ... through their life cycle by focusing on specific environmental aspects ... [which seems to be] especially effective when re-designing products and methods" (Lagerstedt, 2003).The majority of the approaches focus on a series of distinct negative environmental impacts. However the roots of what is happening are found in design and concept stages. The current eco-design methods are mostly related to development stages of design which attempt to improve the quality of design by passage of time and they support the opinion of researchers such as (Charter and Chick, 1997; Walker, 1998); Eco redesign (Bakker, 1995; Ryan, 1996) who accept eco design as a evolutional stage of design.

In this research both concepts on existence of eco-design philosophy are accepted and employed but the greater value is given to the concept which introduces the eco-design as a school of philosophy being employed in early stages of design because in the other case it tries to rehabilitate instead of to prevent the impact. Despite what have been mentioned about this research, the role of the rehabilitation and improvement of previous findings and experiences are considered when a movement towards eco-design is sought. Effort should be made in order to achieve better quality of design and higher quality of life consequently through continuous reforms on building design.

3.16 Development of Eco-indicators in the Research

Since architecture covers various fields and consideration of all aspects is essential for balancing the design process as equilibrium, therefore investigation of EBD attributes is one of the main objectives of this study. Hence, based on literature reviewed, brainstorming, interviews and author's personal experience, this research presents EBD subsets as building design, environmental, socio-economics and energy and resources factors (Langston and Ding, 2001; Smith, 2001). This classification enables the research to study and process eco-indicators prudently and precisely. To develop the eco-indicators, there is a need to investigate each sub-set characteristics and attributes. To carry out the study, each characteristic of EBD is divided and analysed based on its sub-sets and attributes (See chapter 6). The extracted attributes are used to develop a questionnaire to carry out the research.

3.16.1 Building Design Factors

Many researchers such as (Giedion, 1980) believe that design is created based on a certain function which requires a certain space which is embraced by a certain form applying existing technology. Hence in this study, this classification is used in the structure of the questionnaire (See chapter 6) in building design factor. Functional characteristics of building include many indicators. Different emphasises are placed by different researchers regarding functionality of design. functional adaptability, relations, flexibility (Glen, 1994: Slaughter, 2001), durability (Kibert, 2000: NASA, 2001), safety and health (NASA, 2001, ISO 14000 series) as well as human and building interaction (Du Plessis, 2001), building and environment interactions (Langston and Ding, 2001; Roaf, 2001; Smith, 2001) and environmental demands (Fiksel, 1994; Nicholls, 2001) are characteristics addressed by different researchers regarding function attributes in building design. Regarding space attributes both interior spaces (Nicholls, 2001) and exterior spaces (Nicholls, 2001; Roaf, 2001) are pointed out.

Also regarded to form attributes spiritual aspects of form (Author's opinion) should be considered as well as its materialistic aspects. Issues such as built-ability, flexibility (Slaughter, 2001), durability and longevity (NASA, 2001; Kibert, 2000), reliability and usability (Markeset and Kumar, 2003), disassembling (Macozoma, 2002) are those could be addressed in materialistic aspects of form. Also architectural style, fashion (Author's point of view) and society and culture (Du Plessis, 2001) are attributes which should be highlighted in spiritual aspects of form. In technology, design service life such as longevity (Kibert, 2000), maintainability (Blanchard and Lowery, 1969; Bhamra, 2001; NASA, 2001), energy efficiency (Roaf, 2001; Langston and Ding, 2001), embodied energy (Roaf,

2001), eco-efficiency and recycling (Pearce, 2001), equipment and appliances (Nicholls, 2001) and use of technology (Langston and Ding 2001; Roaf, 2001; Smith, 2001) are attributes highlighted Hence in developing eco-indicators it is attempted to place the emphasis on these attributes in building design characteristics.

3.16.2 Environmental Profile Attributes

Ecological and environmental problems like Green house effects, ozone layer depletion, acid rain, air, water, land pollution, soil deteriorations, toxic wastes, residues, loss of bioversity and industrial accidents are impacts highlighted by researchers such as Shrivastava (1995). Also (Boussabaine and Kirkham, 2004) classified environmental impacts into two main groups of atmospheric and resource related impacts. Thus, according to their opinion air, water and earth pollutions are the impacts should be addressed in developing eco-indicators.

3.16.3 Energy and Resources Profile Attributes

This group contains energy efficiency and environmental benefits attributes. Many researchers such as (Nicholls, 2001; Roaf, 2001; Smith, 2001) highlighted the consideration of the attributes that their application in building design could provide eco-efficiency and more sustainability. These indicators are: natural light, passive heating, natural ventilation, passive cooling, insulation and air tightness, water saving devices, GEO thermal benefits, sewage and landfill gas, biomass, low energy materials, environmentally adapted technology, healthier and safer type of (renewable) energy and resources, more efficient appliances and low-embodied energy materials and are the issues addressed in eco-building design.

3.16.4 Socio-economics Attributes

Building design should address social and economical aspects as well as environmental, technological, functional and energy issues. (Boussabaine and Kirkham, 2004) addressed economical aspects of building concerning facility management cost, maintenance costs, level of components replacement costs, pollution rehabilitation and prevention costs, disposal costs, risk costs, and proportion of capital costs and running costs. Also since the social aspects are involved in quality of life and customer satisfaction, thus performance concept (Gibson, 1982) in three levels of customer expectation, operation, and maintenance should be considered over long term (Winch *et al*, 1998) in order to provide the users with higher quality of life. Regarding this fact, attributes like emotional well-being, interpersonal relations, material well-being, physical well-being and health of user and the influence of building design on these aspects should be noticed.

Based on the literature reviewed, other researcher experiences, author's experience and point of view a framework for development of eco-indicators is presented in Fig 3.1 which can be used to develop a questionnaire for carrying out the survey. All detailed information is presented in chapter 6 in questionnaire design methodology. Fig 3.1 is expanded in chapters 7 and 8.

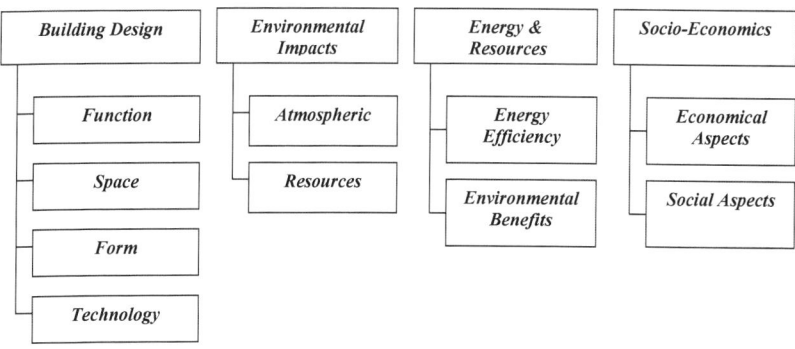

Fig 3.1 The Framework for Development of Eco-indicators

3.17 Conclusions

"A significant realignment towards possible holistic 'Sustainable' model will not be possible until the links between 'building' performance and larger scale such as community are acknowledged." It is essential to clarify and make concepts and proposed objectives explicit because the perception of performance in each class of thought is dissimilar from the other, leading to various trend of enouncement based on existing context and evaluating system (Cole, 1999, P. 244). This fact leads to different methods of assessment in different approaches founded on indicators identification and relevant systematic assessing process.

According to *flexibility of sustainability* as a key characteristic in SD, "a fundamental feature of the new environmental politics is that there is no one true, or trusted, form of expertise, no single path to the truth." (Jamison, 2001, p.27)

Diversity in design and SBD requires more efficient attempts to be made regarding sustainable architecture, involving in social and philosophical questions as well as focusing on green architecture principles (Guy and Shove, 2000).

For achieving SBD and sustainability in building sector "While acknowledging how a technical performative approach to understanding environmental design has brought undoubted benefits in terms of highlighting the issues of energy efficiency in buildings, one must fundamentally revise the focus and scope of the debate about sustainable architecture and reconnect issues of technological change with the social and cultural context within which change occurs." (Guy, 2005, p.471)

"The challenge is then for researchers to work across disciplines and engage directly in the cultural contexts of sustainability challenge order to produce situationally specific design solution" (Guy, 2005, p. 471)

Williamson et al. (2003, p.130) based on Campbell's model (1996) focus on co-existence, parity and optimisation of nature, culture and technology and look at SBD as "a construction ... that weaves together the ethical, human, scientific, aesthetic and other aspects of theses three contexts [nature, culture and technology]. If an architect can do this, she or he is performing a beautiful act."

In this chapter it is attempted to review different individuals' points of view on SBD and its relevant issues. Also a review on different assessment methods regarding SB was handled. EBD as a subset of SBD is introduced to enhance the quality of building design though application of eco-efficiency and design aspects.

Authors' interpretation and definitions on SBD will be presented in chapter 4 of this work. Then an eco-building model will be created and developed based on *Fuzzy theory* and *Fuzzy techniques* as a scientific approach instead of purely subjective available methods.

CHAPTER 4

Eco-Building Design (EBD) Conceptual Model

4.1 Introduction

The design process is a dynamic and complex system. The complexity found in design is derived from taking environmental issues, socio-economics, resources and energy consumption into consideration, in addition to the design context. Eco-building design is introduced in this chapter as a complex dynamic system which embraces many characteristics and components that play pivotal roles in the evolution of sustainable design. Thus, an understanding of the components of eco-design and their internal and external interactions might help in identifying eco-design hierarchy and structural aspects of its components.

In this chapter author's points of view on sustainability, SBD and EBD based on studied literature review and his personal experience is presented. The developed paradigm is used as a framework to carry out the research. Then based on these views a conceptual paradigm for defining eco-building design is presented.

4.2 Emergence of Sustainable Development (SD)

Industrial activities over the past century have caused serious ecological and environmental problems (Shrivastava, 1995). Creating a balance between environmental impacts and economical benefits and societal satisfaction is a complex issue. Ryding (1998) presents the sustainable development definition on function of environmental protection, economic stability and societal responsibility as shown in Fig 2.2 in chapter 2. Fig 2.2 shows that current SD paradigm is based on concepts of environmental protection, economic stability and societal responsibility. Environmental protection dimension of SD embraces aspects such as environmental negative impacts, energy and resources consumption, biological diversity, human health and wellbeing, and other technical aspects focus on efforts, made to satisfy holistic judgement, based on a life cycle point of view related to product/building processes. Economic stability represents efforts to secure and enhance the economic conditions of various interests. Whereas, societal responsibility represents efforts made to identify and develop social functions that guarantee and improve the quality of life for people as the customer of products. However, the above SD paradigm does not represent the time dimension of the SD nor deals with the balance between needs and limitation through the life cycle of SD. Because of the above limitations that are imposed by the assumption that environmental protection, economical stability and societal responsibility on SD a new paradigm need to be derived for dealing with SD complexity. This work advocates that SD is a balance between needs and limits as a function of time (life cycle), conditions, and facilities. This new concept is presented in Fig 4.1. The figure shows that the sustainability concept is integrated with the concepts of extravagancy and restriction. In the figure the outer parts of the circles are represents the limitation area and the central sections of circles show needs area whereas the area between these two parts (the black area) determines the sustainability area. The concept portrayed by the figure is that the rate of limits and needs emerge throughout the life cycle of SD.

Fig 4.1.A illustrates the conditions when the limitation area, the outer part of circle, exercises pressure on the needs area, the central part of circle. This condition generally provides many restrictions and limitations as the consequences of the existing situation. Restriction deals with the situation when the rate of limitations compared to needs is higher.

Fig 4.1.B determines the sustainable situation. The sustainability area is located between limitations and needs areas and is achieved when a balance between the needs and limitations is set. The inscribed area between needs and limitations areas is referred as sustainable conditions and sustainable development is sought through this scope. Sustainability represents the situation when the rate of limitation and needs are obeying a logical balance. It can be stated that the meaning for sustainability should be considered through moderation of needs.

Fig 4.1.C indicates the conditions that the limitations are under pressure by needs. The outcome of this condition would end in extravagancy and generally leads to a large amount of wasting including; resources, finance, time, energy and many other relevant aspects. Extravagancy represents the situation when the rate of limitation in comparison to needs is lower.

Fig 4.1 illustrates that the concept of SD should be based on a set of non-symmetric components relating to restriction and extravagancy.

Fig. 4.1 Restriction, Sustainability, Extravagancy

Since restriction and extravagancy are two terms affiliated to time, and conditions, therefore it is concluded that SD emergence depend on the aforementioned conditions throughout the life cycle.

4.3 Design Overview

Design as a dynamic process of change in building life cycle has a pivotal role in establishing many events and impacts related to building activities. Design stage can be assumed as a decision making process which has a direct impact on the quality of building and its performance over whole life cycle (WLC). Design stage is a translation of human needs, desires, and willing in an artistic, technological, economical, social, managerial, and environmental way. Design as a management process establishes the level of design quality in the early steps of project life cycle. Design also involves the question of adding values and value is a variant of time and place, therefore, values in design is a question of time and location. The importance of design stage is based on its influence on WLC of building assets. A prominent design can lead to an easier maintenance, more efficient and environmentally efficient building and better solutions for disposal stage. Design stage starts based on basic needs and ends with a concept of form. This process is presented as the model shown below by (Crawley and de Weck, 2001).

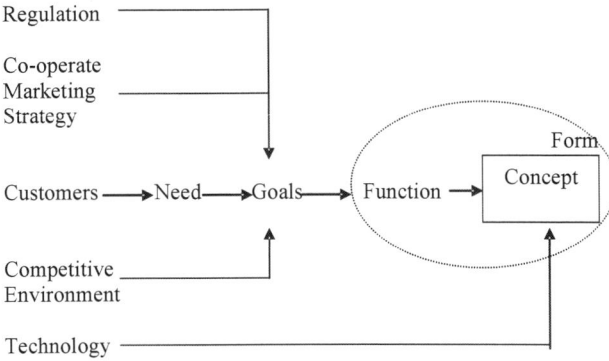

Fig 4.2 Need-Goal-Function Model, (Crawley and de Weck, 2001)

As it is seen in the model, the process of design is a balance between limitations and human needs that comes to an end by creating a concept for a certain form or product with a specific function.

4.4 Building Design and Customer Satisfaction (Kano Model Analysis)

A design which can provide a balance between environmental, economical, social, and technological aspects based on time, place, and facilities might be labelled as sustainable. The main objective for sustainable design is creating better quality of life for users, meaning that it should be a user oriented process based on building whole life cycle aspects. Therefore customer satisfaction is considered as one of the pivotal factors with high level of importance in this field. Hence, design process guarantees project success rate over its WLC. In the early 1980s, (Ullman, 1997) Professor N. Kano, presented a developed model for customer satisfaction, based on product function, often used in quality function development (QFD). Kano analysis usees a diagram for characterising customer needs shown in Fig 4.3.

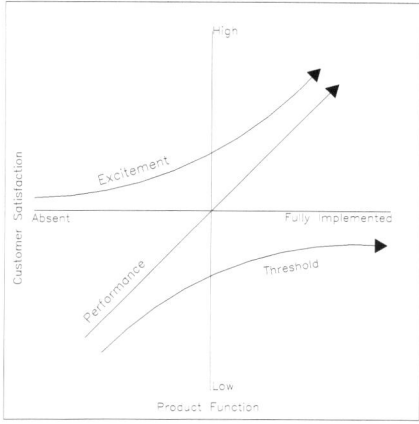

Fig 4.3 Kano Model (Ullman, 1997)

The classification, presented in this model is useful for guiding design decisions which indicates when good is good enough, and when more is better. The Kano model of customer satisfaction is illustrated in Fig 4.3. The figure presents three categories for product attributes: Threshold, performance, excitement attributes. Later in this section product can be assumed as building. A successful product or building is one which has all required basic attributes. The existence of these attributes in a product or building should be established in early design stages.

Threshold attributes: Threshold or basic attributes are aspects which their absences cause the failure for the product or building. They are assumed as the basic requirements for the basic needs. Existence of service spaces beside functional space could be an example of these attributes in buildings.

Performance attributes: The concept of *'more is generally better'* will improve customer satisfaction. These attributes encourage customers for higher demand for product or building. Higher quality will attract more customers and fulfils their satisfactions. Better performance is an exact condition for product or building success over its WLC. An example of these attributes could be efficient use of appliances in the building.

Excitement attributes: these attributes are categorised as those which are not expected and their existences lead to a dominant and delighting fulfilment of customer satisfaction. Sometimes these attributes are called as *'unknown needs'*. These attributes are pivotal factors for competitive products or buildings in the current market. An example of these attributes in building could be the use of wind energy in order to ventilate the asset or to generate energy.

Level of satisfaction and expectation are based on the rate of needs and limitations. These variants are not fixed and differ over time through the development of knowledge and technology. Therefore each new result could be evolutional version of the former one regarding new needs. Kano model attributes behave in the same way as described which means that the excitement attributes of today will be the performance or threshold attributes of tomorrow. This reality proves that both design and customer satisfactions are dynamic and evolutionary processes. This fact proves that design process and its attributes are acting based on needs and limitations on function of time, place, and facilities.

4.5 Kano Model Adaptation in Design

Since the design process is based on customer basic needs and it involves their satisfactions, thus it is interpreted that responding to customer needs requires the same strategies as shown in the Kano model. In this work Kano model and its attributes are integrated in design.

Threshold attributes including basic needs are met through an organic design, based on basic needs of user. Then performance attributes embracing added values through better quality of design followed up in order to achieve better results for higher standards of life for user. These values are those that are expected to be fulfilled and can satisfy the customer to some extents. At this level the design stage involves contemporary design. Excitement attributes are those which are unexpected by customers. These could be considered as winning factors. This fact indicates that these factors will add value to the contemporary design. Sustainable design and different schools of philosophy and available methods are examples of this category. Design for environment (DFE), eco-building design, green building design, and other similar movements are all examples to achieve buildings with higher standards of life for better quality of life. Hence Kano model based on design process is presented in Fig 4.4.

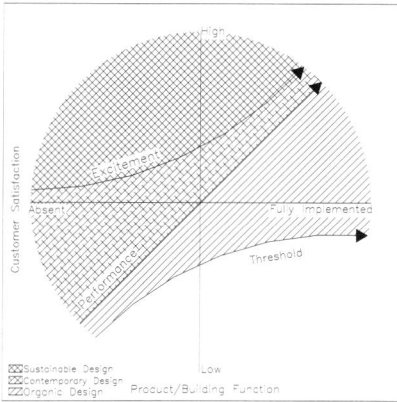

Fig 4.4 Kano Model and Design Evolution

Sustainable design attempts to add value to contemporary design through various attributes in order to gain better quality of life. In the figure above it is perceived that the evolution of design is based on development of variants. This leads to challenges held over the time to set a balance between required needs and limits.

4.6 Conceptual Paradigm of SBD

According to the above definitions the ultimate aim of SBD is a set of complex balances between human needs, ecological, environmental aspects, technological and economical aspects.
In this work the environment is assumed as a set of components which embraces three sub-sets namely: Natural Environment (NE), Imaginary Environment (IE), and built- environment (BE). Fig 4.5 shows the complexity and interaction of these components. In Fig 4.5 NE symbolises environmental aspects of sustainability, embodied natural resources, biodiversities, and all real and physical aspects. IE component deals with fantasy and myth created by human imagination including mankind's ambitions, wishes, desires, wants and spiritual needs. IE dimension is completely related to social aspect of sustainability and since there is no restriction for human's imagination and fantasy, thus no limitation rules on this aspect of sustainability. This scope can point to an unlimited range from reality to myth and from myth to fantasy. Here myth presents the meaning of something between reality and fantasy. (Paul Samson, 1995) believes that: Myth is a combination of reality and fantasy. "A myth is not a false belief of a primitive society, but rather a representation of a part-truth: a mixture of physical reality (the material world around us) and the

culturally constructed world of our minds (perceptions, beliefs, etc.)". BE is the product of integrating NE and IE. BE component of SBD at the design stage might be considered as imaginary environment with no limitation but after construction, it should be considered as a new output which is added to natural environment.

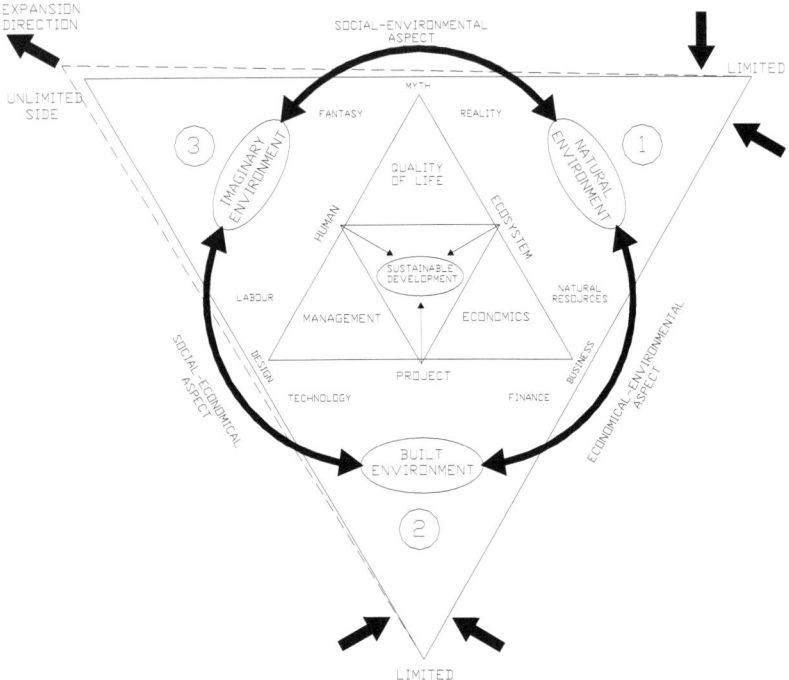

Fig 4.5 Conceptual Paradigm of SBD

If NE, BE and IE are accepted as the reflection of eco-systems, economy and society respectively, then the conjunctions of these themes will lead to the emergence of new complex interactive aspects of SBD such as: economical-environmental, social-environmental and social-economical dimensions of SBD.

Economical-Environmental component: this area is generated by integration of NE and BE, focusing on application of natural resources in economy and manufacturing. The outcome will be different projects based on certain needs and expectations in different levels with a certain range of customers.

Social-Environmental component: concentrates on both NE and IE and their yield combination. According to characteristics of each set it generates ranges, relevant to reality of NE and fantasies and expectations in IE based on society members ambitions. A myth as a consequence of this integration was discussed and explained before. Generally social-environmental aspects deal with the level of life quality and human (customers') satisfaction regarding their surroundings (eco-systems).

Social-Economical component emerges through integration of two other subsets such as IE (Society) and BE (Economy). Design as a pivotal stage which connects these two components to each other plays a main role in application of technology and resources as a consequent emergence of societal needs and ambitions.

In Fig 4.5 SD emerges when a balance among NE, BE, IE and their subsets converge. Here SD embraces human ambitions and needs, ecosystems, ecological scopes, technical innovation and economical sub-components. SD also embraces sub-set attributes such as; human's quality of life, economy, and management.

Quality of Life: embraces all physical and materialistic required aspects of life but also includes all spiritual ones as well. It focuses on all physical required needs beside their existence regarding human satisfaction.

Economy: concerns with the exploitation of resources and facilities regarding careful use of resources and strength in order to make profits in a controlled and managed process (Oxford dictionary).

Management: considered as the control and organisation of a certain task or a group in order to obtain higher efficiency due to from budget, time, labour, and resources.

4.7 An Eco-Building Design (EBD) Conceptual Paradigm

In this section a conceptual EBD model is presented. The philosophy of eco-building design is based on a set of non-symmetric eco-indicators. If these eco-indicators are incorporated in the design of building assets it will lead to sustainable building design (SBD) and ultimately to sustainable development (SD). Eco-building design embraces many aspects namely: Building design, technology management, environmental, energy and resources, socio-economical aspects. Eco-building design attempts to set a balance among design parameter subsets and basic functional needs as shown in Fig 4.6. The non-symmetry (imbalance) derives from lack of harmony between economical benefits, energy and resources consumption in SBD.

Fig 4.6 illustrates the balance among design components. Lack of knowledge about technological and environmental aspects at the design stage might lead to creation of a design which is not adapted to circumstances and project surrounding environment. This reality leads to an inappropriate consumption of materials and finally provides a large amount of emissions, pollutions, and other environmental impacts. The consequence of designing for short term can be profitable form monetary point of view but over the life cycle of the design asset a huge effort is needed to rehabilitate the pollutions and emissions outcomes. Thus, setting a balance among subsets indicators remains as one of the cardinal objectives of eco-building design in its movement towards sustainable building.

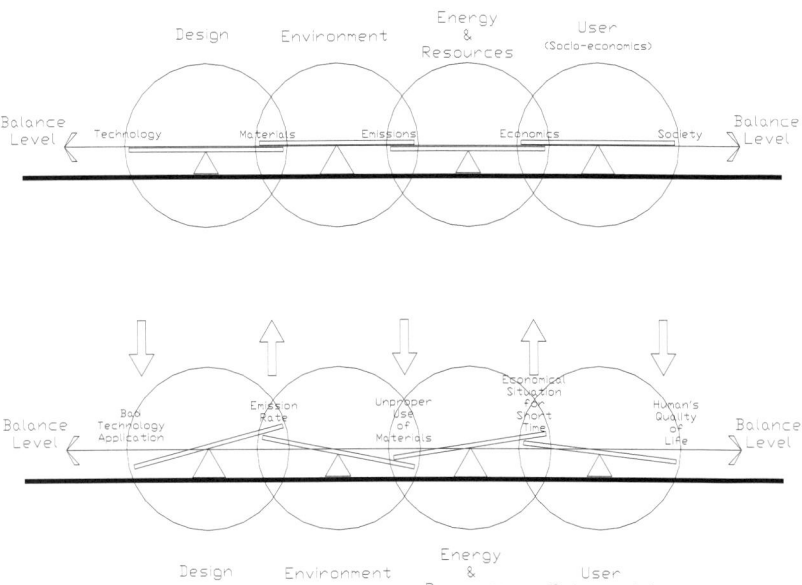

Fig 4.6 EBD Conceptual Paradigm

The balances presented in Fig 4.6 are used to develop a conceptual eco-building design model.

4.8 EBD Conceptual Model

The balances presented in Fig 4.6 are used to develop a conceptual eco-building design model. The model and its subsets are illustrated in Fig 4.7. The figure portrays the concept of well-known dictum of design "less is more" quoted by the modernist architect Ludwig Mies van der Rohe (Blaser, 1986). In this model, eco-design indicators are developed and adapted into context of design. It not only includes all attributes such as environmental impacts, materials, energy, and socio-economics issues but also life cycle design attributes. Efficient utilisation of resources to provide higher standards of life is the main objective in eco-building design.

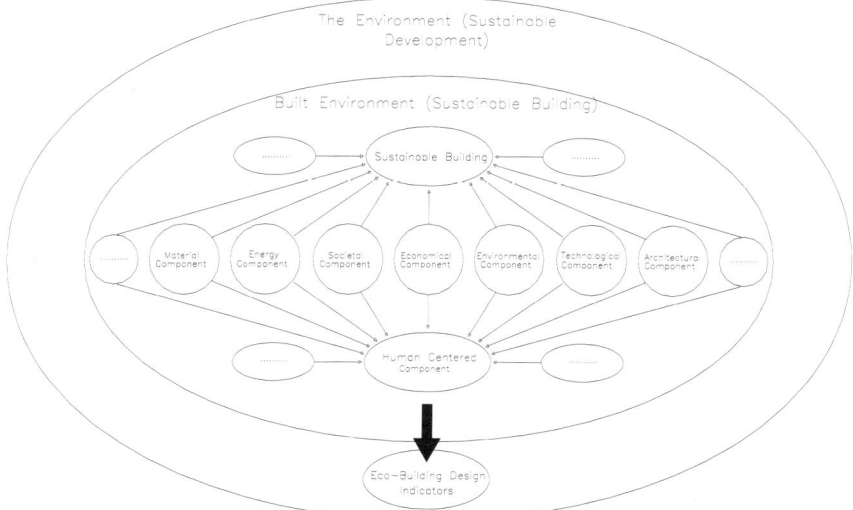

Fig 4.7 Eco-Building Design Model as a Sub-Set of SBD and SD

Fig 4.7 shows eco-building design and its indicators as a subset of SBD and SD. Here the characteristics of eco-building design regarding human centred component are presented. In eco-building design the emphasis is placed on four certain areas namely: building design, environmental profile, energy and resources consumptions and finally socio-economic aspects. As aforementioned, more efficient design is sought through adding eco-strategies and policies, oriented in a human centred approach in order to fulfil the customer's satisfaction. It is strongly believed by eco-design school of philosophy that; the level of success is determined by customer's level of satisfaction. Fig 4.7 presents how eco-building design indicators are extracted based on the required strategies for a SBD based on the human centred approach. Here human approach acts as a filter in extraction of eco-indicators. Then each eco-indicator is supposed as a factor which adds value to the quality of building design towards obtaining more efficiency through enhanced design. The approaches, employed in Fig 4.7 to achieve eco-indicators are as follow:

Architectural component focuses on basic requirements such as function, space and form of a building. In this approach architectural design translates all human needs, desires, ambitions into building design through an artistic and technical process concerning limitations and existing conditions.

Technological component in building design implies that all environmentally efficient technologies are used in order to enhance eco-efficiency. The example for this approach could be application of natural light and ventilation, passive heating and cooling, in a building which are free of charge and generate no environmental impact and pollution.

Environmental component generally places the emphasis on the environmental impacts, generated during building and other action of building assets. In this approach those strategies and techniques are sought which leave less or no emission and impact in the nature. The concept follows more eco-efficient solutions for building industries.

Economical component concentrates on monetary and financial aspects of building regarding resources, labour, time and different levels of management. It attempts to find a way to make more profit from less expenses and limitations.

Societal component is considered as one of the main factors in eco-building design and SD. As the end user should fairly feel satisfied in the building, therefore their assessments of the building are assumed as a guarantee for achieving higher level of success in design quality. Societal aspects should be considered in building design process.

Energy component focuses on application of more energy-efficient technologies and materials in building industries. The consumption of energy in WLC is addressed in here as well as the employment of healthier, safer, material with the lower embodied energy are negotiated.

Material component concentrates on the selection of materials and their availability, maintainability, supportability, durability, reusability, recycling and many concerns over WLC. In this approach application of healthier and safer materials with low embodied energy are suggested for building process which finally leads to a decrease in generation of environmental impacts.

Human component as the final crucial approach is introduced in Fig 6. This item is considered as the most important profile correlated to extraction of eco-building design indicators. Since customer satisfaction is the pivotal objective of eco-building design, therefore this approach works as a filter for extraction of eco-indicators concerning customer's expectations fulfilments. The degree of success for a building is established by level of customer's satisfaction. It is derived that: "The happier the customer is, the more successful the project is"

4.9 EBD Implications

The implications that might be achieved by application of eco-design are summarised as following:
1. Design eco-efficiency enhancement through adding value and environmental risk mitigation
2. Design for WLC
3. Better control and more efficient management of environmental impacts

4.9.1. Design Eco-efficiency Enhancement

The implication of the conceptual models presented in this chapter is shown in Fig 4.8. The figure shows how eco-building design concepts can add value to contemporary design and mitigate environmental impact risk factors in order to enhance quality of design and consequently the customer's satisfaction through better quality of life.

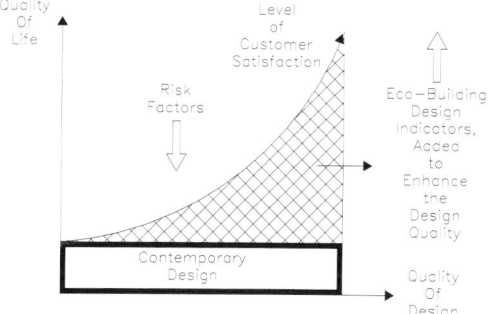

Fig 4.8 Eco-Building Design for Adding Value, and Risk Mitigation

According to Kano model (See Fig 4.4 in this chapter), the contemporary building design is considered as the basis for all types of buildings design, embracing all basic requirements at every stage of the design process. Application of eco-design strategies enhances the quality of design. This enhancement is accomplished through the application of sound environmental design strategies as well as customer's satisfaction through out the life cycle of the designed product. Environmental design strategies and deeper understanding of life cycle issues alongside sound building design principles enables the designers to deal with potential environmental impacts in a wiser manner and to mitigate the rate of risk occurrence. Better understanding of eco-building design at early stage of design will definitely reduce the rate of unknown and uncertain environmental events through out the life cycle of the designed asset.

The rectangular in Fig 4.8 assigns the contemporary design as the foundation for eco-building design, and the hatched area beneath the curve (level of customer's satisfaction) indicates that the eco-building added indicators to the design for achieving higher quality of design. This area is correlated to the level of design knowledge, innovation and creativity concerning existing conditions in the design context. As it is shown in this figure risk factors attempts to reduce the quality of design whereas in eco-building design the rate of risk severely mitigates though considerations and strategies applied in early design stages. Considerations of WLC in the eco-building design process enables designer to control risk factors more efficiently. The level of customer's satisfaction relates to the quality of life which depends on quality of designed asset. The quality of design itself relies on the level of innovation and creativity in the design process.

4.9.2 Design for Whole Life Cycle (WLC)

Miyatake (1996) has suggested that for achieving sustainable building there is a need to change the process of creating the built environment by modifying linear processes into cyclic process in construction industry. The concept is shown in Fig 4.9.

Eco-Building design emerges from the context of contemporary design to achieve sustainable buildings. The main difference of eco-building design with two former types of design (Contemporary and organic design) is related to the scope of building design. It not only efforts to extend the use stage of building but also attempts to apply strategies like reusability, recyclability, disassembling, renovations, durability and other pertained appropriate strategies causing the building life cycle to behave as a closed loop and make start and end points in building WLC process connected to each other.

This scope turns the linear WLC into a looped (Circular) WLC shown in Fig 4.9. The consequence of this concept guides designers to application of strategies in the building process such as: rematerialisation, dematerialisation, flexibility, durability, reusability, recycling, maintainability, availability, reliability, supportability, usability and other related aspects. Eco-building design as a subset of sustainable design focuses on more eco-efficient buildings through out their WLC as well as customers satisfaction.

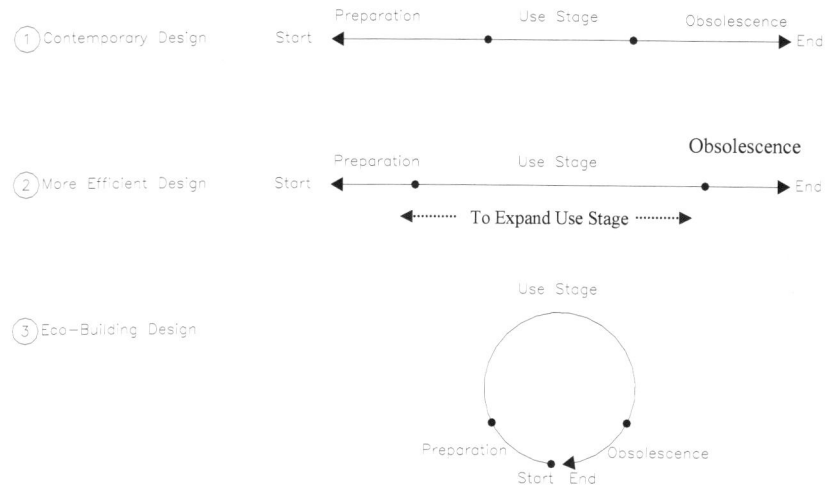

Fig 4.9 Transition or Evolution of Eco-Building Design

4.10 Conclusions

In this chapter eco-building design is introduced as an evolutional version of design which attempts to add value to the contemporary design process through application of design environmental strategies, prudent use of resources and energy in order to achieve the highest eco-efficiency over the WLC of building assets. In this approach a great consideration is given to socio-economics concerns and stockholder's satisfaction is proposed as the indicator of design success through out its WLC.

The main inspiration of eco-building design concept presented in this chapter is based on quality of life paradigm. Eco-building design concept can add value to contemporary design through fulfilment of customer's satisfaction.

CHAPTER 5

Eco-Indicators Knowledge Elicitation through Fuzzy Theory

5.1 Introduction

Sustainability of building is a difficult subject to define or measure because it is a vague and complex concept, currently there is no accurate system of measurement to assess it. This complexity caused by ambiguity and lack of knowledge, is laid in the complex systems existing in the subsets components. Sustainable building design and its relevant criteria embrace many aspects such as: production and building sustainability, ecological and environmental sustainability, and social sustainability. Each of these aspects of sustainability involves ambiguity and uncertainty. As the border between sustainability and non-sustainability is not a sharp distinct line, therefore definition and assessment of sustainability needs a lot of attempts and challenges. This means that determining exact reference values of sustainability seems to be quite unfeasible and a scientific evaluation can be held through a sustainability assessment procedure (Phillis and Andriantiatsaholiniaina, 2001). This fact is achieved through application of some types of approaches which are capable to convert subjectivity to reality. In this research fuzzy theory is employed in order to overcome the weakness related to existing subjectivity in current assessment methods.

Design decision making today involves in many objectives and data concerning economic and environmental and social issues. Each of these aspects includes a set of components with the different levels of interactions among them in their own system which cause some levels of complexity in the system. The complexity and ambiguity caused in the systems can be dealt with using fuzzy theory, which always deals with uncertainty and ambiguity of concepts. Fuzzy theory is capable to emulate skilled professionals and systematic approach to encounter vague conditions through application a natural technical tool to assess sustainability where traditional mathematics seems to be ineffective (Phillis and Andriantiatsaholiniaina, 2001). Use of linguistic variables to perform computations with words is another aspect of fuzzy theory. As it was stated by (Ducy and Larson, 1999) a rigorous and flexible approach to the problem of defining and evaluating sustainability is provided by Zadeh's fuzzy theory. Thus fuzzy theory is introduced as a tool to systematically formulate a base for quantifying information regarding sustainability and its vagueness and uncertainties which are quantitavely immeasurable (Jeganathan, 2003).

5.2 Modelling Technique for SBD

A model is defined as "a representation of something, either as a physical object which is usually smaller than the real object or as a simple description of the object which might be used in calculations" (Cambridge Online Dictionary). There are many existing methods and techniques formed and developed according to various dissimilar scopes in different studies. The proposed model should be a simplification of assumed focused aspects of study which is briefly but precisely representing the real characteristics of the subject. In other words a model focuses on certain aspects of a study. The type of a model is formed in a way to be easier to understand, interpret and apply. Mathematical models are widely used to represent measurement experiments and to analyse data. The model is an effective tool for extracting information from the measurement system, the quality of the information obtained depending directly on the quality of the model. Two stages of (1) model building and (2) model solving are the main steps of developing a model. The first stage is based on mathematical equations development. These equations deal with parameters describing the relevant characteristics of the system, including the random effects found in measurement data. The latter stage, addresses the ways to solve the model equations in a way that parameters and their associated uncertainties can be determined. Modelling behaves as a bridge between comprehensiveness and practicability. The model should reflect precisely the physical conditions of a phenomenon, and then validation is needed to confirm its correctness, while being simple enough for computations feasibility. Model should be validated and confirmed as fit for its developing purpose.

As shown in Table 3.1 in chapter 3 the available methods for assessment are mainly using subjective qualitative systems of evaluation. (Crawley and Aho, 1999, p.305) explain; "BREEAM uses three scales for environmental impact: global, local, and indoor issues (Prior, 1993). When a building has been evaluated using BREEAM, the result is a single score... and similar to BREEAM, BEPAC can be used to evaluate the environmental performance of new designs and existing buildings. BEPAC results in a composite weighting of five major areas: ozone protection, environmental impacts of energy use, indoor environmental quality, resource conservation, and site and transportation... and in LEED there are minimum mandatory requirements in areas such as building commissioning, energy efficiency, indoor air quality, ozone depletion/CFCs, smoking ban, comfort, and water. Once the mandatory requirements are met, a building can earn 'credits' in 14 areas. Depending on the total credit, a building receives a rating level of 'bronze', 'silver', 'gold' and 'platinum'... whereas in GBA each national team developed weighting for sub-criteria and criteria, which were applied and composite, weighted scores for the six criteria are used to assess. One of the weaknesses of the GBA is that individual country teams established scoring weights subjectively when evaluating their buildings. Most users found GB tool difficult to use because of complexity of framework." Also they pointed out "most methods do not meet all the identified application needs for building environmental assessment although GBA comes closest" (Ibid, p.306). Hence, in all aforementioned assessment methods the scoring is strongly based on subjectivity. As there is no sharp line as the boundaries for the subjectivity, thus finding exact scores based on precision seems to be impossible for these sorts of assessments. This weakness became a motivation of this research to employ fuzzy techniques to reduce the influence of subjectivity found in design concepts.

5.3 Measurements and Values

Data collection is handled though application of many methods. One of the existing methods is to collect data via questionnaire which was applied in this study as well (see chapter 6). In the questionnaire the respondents are asked to assess eco-indicators related to eco-building design characteristics applying measurements and values.

Assignment of numeral to objects or events based on certain rules is called measurement (Stevens, 1951). Measurement of phenmenons and events is theoretically feasible when rules can be set up on either rational or empirical basis.

There are different scales employed to evaluate different levels of measurement in classifying the subject of interest.

5.4 Scoring Methods

Measurement classification includes four types namely: nominal, ordinal, interval and ratio, all used in scaling based on the subject of interest. The nominal scale determines numerical numbers to an object without making any comparison between numbers which mean there is no consequence or order in laying them. (e.g. sport team members' numbers). The second group is ordinal scale which includes rank-ordered objects showing rank order only. The numbers do not indicate quantities and do not show if the intervals between numbers are equally set. The illustration of ordinal scales is as $S<T<...<Z$. if in ordinal type of measurement the intervals between adjacent numbers were equal that type of measurement would be called interval scale like: $3<5<7<9$. The last group of measurement is ratio scale which possesses the all characteristics of three aforementioned scales. Kerlinger (1986) believes that ratio scales are the highest level of measurement.

In this research a ratio-based scaling questionnaire, with the score from 0 to 8 was designed. The respondents were asked to give a score to each indicator based on the degree of significance of item. Figure 5.1 illustrates the scaling method employed in this research in questionnaire design. The scoring can be interpreted by verbal terms as well. Regarding this fact scores from 0 to 2 are allocated for items which are not significant in eco-building whereas scores from 3 to 5 assign indicators which are neutral eco wise and indicators scored from 6 to 8 are described as eco-indicators carrying high degree of significance regarding eco-building design.

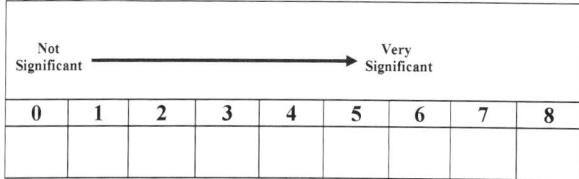

Fig 5.1 Scaling Based on Eco-Indicator Degree of Significance

In scoring part of questionnaire table, respondents are asked to score each indicator according to its influence on eco-building design. The scaling method shown graphically in Fig. 5.1 makes the process of scoring easier for respondent to read in and off whereas it is also easier for researcher to understand and interpret the results.

5.5 Fuzzy Theory Application and Scoring

Questionnaire designed and developed in this study is used to collect different individuals' points of view on eco-building indicators. Architects and building stakeholders based on their personal experience and knowledge ranked the eco-indicators. Therefore the information gathered through the questionnaire is considered as subjective qualitative data.

Since fuzzy theory (FT) also deals with subjectivity and ambiguity therefore it seems that application of FT based on mathematical rules is helpful in dealing with subjectivity in the research data. According to FT and its rules the degree of importance of each eco-indicator can be computed through indicator membership function calculation. Then weightings of indicators are considered. It can be stated that in FT the subjectivity of each indicator is translated into numeric values prepared for evaluating eco-indicator. In other words instead of dealing with a ranges and intervals between numbers the research is involved in exact numeric values which is easier and more understandable in the assessment process which is based on required accuracy.

5.6 Fuzzy Theory and Logic Application in Various Fields of Science

"Fuzzy techniques are a recognized instrument for modelling in many scientific and technical fields in the meantime" (Heine, 2001). Wherever there is a need to evaluate the degree of qualitative data, fuzzy techniques seem to be helpful and applicable. BBC [online source] introduces fuzzy logic as *'the logic which provides technique with intelligence'*. Also it claims that fuzzy logic and rules enable the systems to be either estimated or evaluated. Number of specialised literatures such as Gottwald (1993) and Zimmermann (1996) explained the theory of fuzzy set and fuzzy logic but each profession applies them according to their needs. Fuzzy techniques are not limited to a specific field or area of science. It can be used by any branch of science which involves uncertainty and subjectivity. Fuzzy logic application embraces numerous areas. Several researches applied and developed fuzzy rules for different purposes. Some examples of fuzzy logic (FL) applications are presented as followings:

5.6.1 Fuzzy Techniques and Manufacturing

(Dutta, 1993) in manufacture, stated that "Not only has fuzzy logic significantly enhanced knowledge-based/expert system technology, it has fundamentally altered the granularity of intelligence. With the help of fuzzy logic, manufacturers of home appliances are today embedding intelligence inside individual products".

5.6.2 Fuzzy Techniques and Engineering Modelling

"Fuzzy models can be a suitable solution for many modelling problems ... They are able to handle uncertainty more adequately than classical models can do. Connections of systems and processes, which normally cannot be described by classical models, can be expressed by means of fuzzy rules. The uncertainty of modelling parameters is considered by fuzzy parameters, respectively the membership functions to fuzzy sets.
[Whether] a fuzzy-model is more suitable for a special problem than classical models or not mainly depends on the modelling purpose and on the given conditions." (Heine, 2001).

5.6.3 Fuzzy Techniques and Electronics

In electronics and computer science there is a numerous application of fuzzy rules and logic. "technology harmonizes computers with humans, making it perfect for forming a mathematical model of a human in his society, building intelligent machines and vastly improving the human/machine interface" quoted by Toshiro Terano, the director of LIFE about fuzzy logic (Johnson, 1989).

5.6.4 Fuzzy Techniques and Science

(Kuswandari, 2004) employed FL and relevant rules to develop a measuring model for sustainability of forest management. Also there are many other applications of fuzzy rules in different categories of scientific researches.

5.6.5 Fuzzy Techniques and Managements

FL is used in different branches of management for various levels of measurements. (Dong and Wong, 1985) employed FL to develop a system to analyse and compute risk in earthquakes. (Bousabaine and Elhag, 1998) used FL for cash fellow analysis in construction management. There are vast applications of FL in different areas of management.

5.6.6 Fuzzy Techniques and its Overall Applications

There are many branches of knowledge that found fuzzy logic application helpful to solve their existing problems. Various methods were created and developed to solve many problems. Many defuzzification methods (method of computation and evaluation) such as centre of gravity, average of maxima, median, height, maximal height, area, and maximal area were applied in different areas. It can be stated that the capability of fuzzy rules and logics to deal with the real daily problems presents a unique feature of fuzzy technique to assist researchers to cope with uncertain and risky conditions which are beyond their knowledge and understanding.

5.7 Fuzzy Theory Method (Methodology)

Three pivotal stages should be considered in order to create an evaluation system based on fuzzy theory;

1. To calculate membership function of each eco-indicators
2. Linguistic variables (possible alternatives for assessment)
3. A method for calculation and computation (Defuzzificatin)

Each of the aforementioned stages is explained in the following sections.
"The basic structure of the type of fuzzy system [based on fuzzy logic] is a model that maps input characteristics to input membership functions, input membership function to rules, rules to a set of output characteristics, output characteristics to output membership functions, and the output membership function to a single-valued output or a decision associated with the output." Also it is believed that "Fuzzy inference systems have been successfully applied in fields such as automatic control, data classification, decision analysis, expert systems, and computer vision. The main advantage of fuzzy logic is its flexibility and tolerance to imprecise data. Fuzzy logic can model nonlinear functions of arbitrary complexity."[Online source]

5.7.1 Fuzzy Membership Functions (MBF)

Fuzzy techniques define the degrees of each component according to a certain characteristic which is called eco-indicator in this research. This degree is presented as a numeric membership belonging to interval of $0<x<1$. The full membership is also shown by 1 whereas full non-membership is presented by 0. In other words fuzzy logic is based on the theory of fuzzy sets which relates to classes of objects without sharp boundaries in which membership is a matter of degree. In this approach, the classical notion of binary membership in a set has been modified to include partial membership ranging between 0 and 1 (Zadeh, 1965). The degree of membership between 0 and 1 is defined by a membership function (MBF). The only condition a membership function must really satisfy is that it must vary between 0 and 1. Hence, fuzzy logic can be applied for the qualitative type of data which carry subjectivities. In fuzzy logic the degree of subjectivity of each eco-indicator is presented as a MBF. There are various ways to illustrate MBFs such as: graphs, numbers or other ways of presentation (See chapter 10).

5.7.2 Fuzzy Linguistic Variables

These variables are used as a rule base to control the system of evaluation or assessment. It can be said that linguistic variables are a set of rules for controlling the systematic assessment of the system. It includes different possible alternatives of conditions which provide the subjectivity leading to qualitative data. Another important aspect of fuzzy rules is its linguistic variables, in performing computation applying words. If a traditional mathematical approach towards sustainability assessment were adopted, such as cost-benefit analysis or algebraic formulas, then certain factors, which are impossible to quantify, would be left out. However, it is believed that all aspects of sustainability cannot be quantified and yet are very important as, for example, values and opinions. In this area of human thought fuzzy logic performs successfully (Zadeh, 1979; Zimmermann, 1991). Fuzzy rules help the researchers to cope with the existing weaknesses regarding subjectivity and ambiguity in a scientific trend.

5.7.3 Defuzzification (Method of Computation)

"The defzzification process (output inference) translates the linguistic outputs of the inference step into numerical values so it can be used for ranking or comparisons" (Wanous, 2000). This stage of process is merged by integration of MBFs and linguistic variables and the outcome is presented as a scoring system which enables the researcher to interpret the data and comparisons them with each other. In this research the MBFs carry the *scores* and linguistic variables carry the *weights* and defuzzification is produced through integration of both of them. Scores are weighted and divided by the sum of weights to provide a single eco-rating. The rate can be used for evaluation and comparisons. The characteristics of new rate consist of characteristics of both MBFs and linguistic variables. If the MBF is shown by S and Linguistic variable is presented by W then the computation method (R) can be illustrated as follows:

S *(MBF)* × W *(Linguistic variable)* = R *(New Rating Score in defuzzification stage)*

5.8 Advantages of Fuzzy Theory Techniques

Holistically fuzzy logic helps to have better understanding of subjectivity in a comparable sense. It makes the process of judgement easy when it seems too difficult to interpret. Overall advantages of fuzzy techniques are grouped as follows:

1. Encode knowledge at very high level of abstraction
2. Reduce the number of rules in a system; and,
3. Produce more robust and more stable system (Hurson *et al*, 1994)

In addition to the above, Fuzzy techniques provide such a flexibility which is impossible with conventional modelling approaches (Dutta, 1993).

5.9 Fuzzy Theory and Eco-Building Design (EBD)

Building design dynamism is a complex process because it includes various design indicators. Consideration of different aspects such as environment, economy and society in addition to design characteristics makes the process of design even more complex. The essence of this complexity is derived from variety of components and probable uncertain interactions that they create between each other in different levels. This fact leads to existence of complexity in design assessment process. Therefore the meaning of complexity in design processes differs over time, location, and conditions. The subjectivity in design decisions makes the process of assessment quite vague and difficult. As it was stated before, fuzzy theory is capable to cope with this weakness of qualitative evaluation.

Eco-design Indicators Knowledge Elicitation

Design knowledge elicitation requires many editions, corrections and modifications before final draft validation. In our work we used a questionnaire approach to carry out this task. Our approach to knowledge elicitation is based on closed ended questions and single response for each question was assumed which means each question has just one answer. Also it is a rating one, because the participants are requested to rate the degree of each eco-indicator regarding eco-building design. The process is presented and discussed as follows:

a. Knowledge Elicitation through the Open-Ended Questions

A draft copy of the questionnaire was shown to the interviewee (practicing architects) at the end of interview and they were requested to read through it and give any recommendation, cumulative information or any modifications needed, regarding sequences, wordings, structure, and layouts of the questionnaire. They were also asked to review the list of questionnaire eco-indicators, affecting eco-building design and suggest any necessary modifications respectively to the content and the wording. Then a set of questions are asked in order to find out about their own opinions and approaches towards eco-building design. These questions are quite general ones which make them to think about the subject and provide the researcher with some useful information.

1. What are the needs, design and environmental characteristics of a building in early phases of building development in eco-building design?
2. What are the relationships between building and its needs, design and its environmental requirements?
3. How can design and environmental issues assist building designer to improve the level of design for better quality of life?
4. What is eco-building design from your point of view?
5. How eco-building design is achieved?
6. What is your approach to improve eco-building design quality?
7. What are the main eco-indicators that possibly affect eco-building design quality?

The answers to these questions are not limited, thus each answer opens a new argument and provides new data. Since in the field of architecture individuals' views towards a certain subject verifies, therefore a set of various opinion which help to improve the questionnaire are found.

b. Refining the Knowledge Elicitation Process

One of the main objectives of this attempt is focused on providing a consensus set of eco-indicators among practicing architects. Therefore the process was carried out through asking the individuals to review the list of eco-indicators and take their suggestions for improvement of the list component in a way that the list contains the majority of eco-building design indicators. In this stage more severe emphasis on few eco-indicators was suggested according to their pivotal role that they play in eco-building design. For example, although site restrictions, landscape design, and climate could be seen in the questionnaire eco-indicators, a few interviewees suggested that the building orientation be added to the list according to its effects achieved in eco-building design quality. Thus in the list, sometimes it seems that some eco-indicators are repeated but it should be claimed that they are for more emphasizes on a few special eco-indicators. This weakness (repetition of some eco-indicators) is improved when factor analysis and data reduction are carried out in the next chapters in order to reduce the number of eco-indicators to the optimum minimum. Therefore at this stage, just establishing an exclusive consensus list of eco-indicators was the main objective of this process.

Our knowledge elicitation questionnaire was designed based on four main categories, forming eco-building design. Those four categories are:

1. **Building Design Indicators**

It is believed by the majority of interviewees and the author that eco-building design is innately the process of building design through more efficient application of facilities and existing resources in order to provide higher quality of design to present better quality of life to building occupants. This is achieved via consideration of certain and specific both building and environmental design strategies in coherence with available technology regarding consumers' needs, desires, and willing. Even some interviewees mention that the building design is responsible for higher quality of life and should embrace the eco-indicators to establish higher standards for living. Therefore it is said that eco-indicators are assumed as additive factors to the building design to add value to the quality of building and its outcome for the residents. Hence, in this study the building design is assumed as one of the most pivotal category of eco-building design respectively all individuals' points of view.

2. **Environmental Profile and Eco-efficiency Indicators**

According to the recent decades harms caused by building industry, a great emphasis is placed on environmental impacts of building process. Also it is believed by majority of the interviewees that a more conservative type of design which focuses on eco-efficiency and less pollution generation can lead to a massive reduction of environmental impacts and future risky consequences caused by building and its relevant industries. The policies and strategies employed regarding this view affects both directly and indirectly the building design outcomes. Hence, environmental profile and eco-efficiency is selected as one of the main categories of eco-building design by the author and was strongly approved by the interviewees as well for carrying out the study.

3. Energy and Resources Consumption Indicators

It is strongly believed that the amount of energy and resources in the world are limited, therefore any consideration towards this reality is admired and appreciated. Building industry as one of the main consumers of existing materials, resources and energy should be controlled based on the targeted policies based on reduction and more efficient use of resources and required energy for procedure. In this survey to accomplish this effort, energy and resources consumption are presented as a category of eco-building design.

4. Socio-Economic Indicators

Socio-economics in eco-building design plays a crucial role regarding projects level of success. In other words it can be said that consumer's satisfactions and expectations fulfilment indicates the success rate of the building design. Customers satisfactions are argued, discussed, and focused both social and economical wise. For this reason in this research socio-economic aspects are considered as one of the four main categories of eco-building design survey, and its eco-indicators are discussed in this regarding.

Our final version of the eco-indicators knowledge elicitation format was designed and developed consisting of the four aforementioned categories. Then each of categories was divided into its own characteristics and sub characteristics. At the end the questionnaire was formed based on attributes which are called eco-indicators in eco-building design. Finally 115 questions were extracted to develop the questionnaire.

Table 5.1 illustrates the eco-building design indicators included in each category for further investigation and evaluation

Table 5.1 *Categories of Eco-Building Design*

Category	Characteristic	Sub characteristic	No	Eco-indicator Description
Building Design-related	Function	Relationship	1	Logical Connections with Adjacent Functions
			2	Functional Zonings
			3	Compatibility with other Functions
		Adaptability	4	Adaptability to the New Change(s)
			5	Adaptability to the Surroundings
			6	Adaptability to the Environment
		Flexibility	7	Upgradeability and Extensions
			8	Flexibility in Use Stage
			9	Flexibility for Adding Function to the Main Function for Achieving Higher Performance
		Durability	10	Renovation and Upgradeability
			11	Performance Regarding Longevity
			12	Longevity of Function
		Safety & Health	13	Physical Aspects
			14	Psychological Aspects
		Human and Building Interactions	15	Adaptability Regarded to Indoor Quality
			16	Physical Dimensions (Ergonomics)
			17	Effect of Function on Human Behaviour
			18	Circulation And Distribution Regarding the Existing Function in Design
		Building and Environment Interactions	19	Landscape
			20	Adjacent Zones (Macro View)
			21	District (Micro View)
		Environmental Demands	22	Market
			23	Society
			24	Government
			25	Organisations (NGOs & Quasi NGOs)
			26	Control of Emissions
			27	Energy & Eco-efficiency

Table 5.1 *Categories of Eco-Building Design*

Category	Characteristic	Sub characteristic	No	Eco-indicator Description
Building Design-related	Space	Interior Spaces (Micro View) Regarding Activities, Functions, Appearance, Quality of Design, Rate of Comfort and Relief, Optimum Conditions	28	Level of Tranquillity
			29	Level of Comfort
			30	Number of Occupants (Spatial Capacity)
			31	Occupants Needs
			32	Distribution of Activities
			33	Indoor Quality Performance (Optimum Conditions)
			34	Internal Zoning Regarding Spatial Relationships in Design
		Exterior Spaces (Macro View) Regarding Activities, Functions, Appearance, Quality of Design, Landscape, optimum Conditions	35	Landscape Design
			36	Natural Physical Conditions (Topography, Underground Water Levels, …)
			37	Building Orientation
			38	Climate
			39	Outdoor Performance
			40	Adjacent Functions and Spaces (Relationship with Surroundings)
			41	Site Restrictions
	Form	Materialistic Aspects	42	Form Built Ability (Feasibility of Building)
			43	Maintainability (Ease of Maintenance)
			44	Geometry of Form (Aesthetics and stability)
			45	Adaptability and Coherence of Form
			46	Durability regarding Flexibility
			47	Components Detailing and Design
			48	Predictability of Longevity of the Form (Some Forms and Shapes Last for Longer Period of Time).
			49	Reliability and Usability Regarding to Form and its Durability and Maintenance
			50	Disassembling Regarding Building WLC and Time.
			51	Reusability and Recyclability Regarding Building WLC.
		Spiritual Aspects	52	Philosophical Values Related to Design Concepts
			53	Style of Design
			54	Fashion and Design
			55	Society and Culture Regarding Customer Satisfactions and Expectations
			56	Sense of Belonging and Place regarding Building Design
			57	Longevity of Physical Influence (Human Physical Reactions and behaviours Respectively Design)
			58	Longevity of Mental Influences (Emotions and Feelings Respectively Design)

Table 5.1 *Categories of Eco-Building Design*

Category	Characteristic	Sub characteristic	No	Eco-indicator Description
Building Design-related	Technology	Design Service Life (WLC) Structural, Mechanical, Electrical Engineering	59	Longevity Regarding WLC
			60	Maintainability Regarding WLC
			61	Energy Efficiency Regarding WLC
			62	Embodied Energy Regarding WLC
			63	Eco-Efficiency and Recyclability Regarding WLC
			64	Reliability Regarding WLC
		Equipments In a Building	65	Function Fit To Purpose
			66	Upgradeability of the Equipments Due to Future Requirements
			67	Access to the Equipments for Repairing
			68	Pollution Generation by Equipments in Building
			69	Environmental Adapted Technology in Equipments Manufacturing
			70	Noise Generation by Equipments in Building
			71	Vibration Generation by Equipments in Building
			72	Zoning and Location Of the Equipment in a Plan (Regarding Access, and Disturbance Generations)
		Use of Technology	73	Technological Innovation Application (Hybridising and Integration)
			74	Contemporary Technology Application
			75	Vernacular and Traditional Technology Application

Table 5.1 *Categories of Eco-Building Design*

Category	Characteristic	Sub characteristic	No	Eco-indicator Description
Environmental Profile and Eco-Efficiency	Environmental Impacts (Atmospheric and Resources)		76	Green House Effect
			77	Ozone Layer
			78	More Efficient Use of Water
			79	Energy Consumption Regarding the Amount
			80	Air Pollution (C02, NOx, SOx, ETC)
			81	Water Pollution
			82	Earth Pollution
			83	Ecological Deterioration Both Visually and Naturally
			84	Landfills
			85	Solid Residues

Table 5.1 *Categories of Eco-Building Design*

Category	Characteristic	Sub characteristic	No	Eco-indicator Description
Energy and resources Consumption	Energy Efficiency and Environmental Benefits		86	Natural Light through Photovoltaic and Naturally
			87	Passive Heating Through Zoned heating and Air Tightness (Heating Air and Water)
			88	Natural Ventilation
			89	Passive Cooling through Solar Shading and Ventilation
			90	Insulation and Air Tightness
			91	Water Saving Devices
			92	Geo Thermal Benefits
			93	Sewage and Landfill Gas for producing Heat and Energy
			94	Biomass for producing Heat and Energy
			95	Low Embodied Energy Materials regarding WLC
			96	Energy and Eco- Efficient Design by Consideration of Orientation, Surfaces, heat exchanges, etc
			97	More Energy Efficient Equipments and Appliances Application in Design
			98	Environmentally Adapted Technology
			99	Application of Healthier and safer Energy and Resources

Table 5.1 *Categories of Eco-Building Design*

Category	Characteristic	Sub characteristic	No	Eco-indicator Description
Socio-Economic Aspects	Social and economical Aspects	Social Aspects	100	Emotional Well-being (Safety, Happiness, Spirituality)
			101	Interpersonal Relations (Intimacy, Affection, Family)
			102	Material Well-being (Ownership, Possessions, Financial Security)
			103	Personal Development (Education Skills, Personal Competence)
			104	Physical Well-being (Health, Recreation)
			105	Self Determination (Autonomy, Choices, Personal Control)
			106	Social Inclusion (Acceptance, Status, Roles)
			107	Rights (Privacy, Due Process)
		Economical Aspects	108	Facility Management Costs Regarding WLC
			109	Maintenance Costs Regarding WLC
			110	Level of Component Replacement Costs Regarding WLC
			111	Pollution Rehabilitation Costs Regarding WLC
			112	Pollution Preventing Costs Regarding WLC
			113	Disposal Costs Regarding WLC
			114	Risk Costs Regarding WLC
			115	Capital Costs/ Running Costs (Saving Running Costs Regarding WLC)

5.10 Conclusions

This chapter is a brief review of fuzzy techniques used to develop an evaluation model for eco-building design assessment. This review can be employed to clarify the principles in which eco-building design assessment is based. Also fuzzy theory is introduces as techniques which turns the subjectivity into reality. The characteristics of the fuzzy theory have proved that this technique is considered as a reliable tool for eco-building design evaluation. Thus, it has been decided to employ fuzzy theory in order to develop an eco-building design assessment model. For achieving this objective, some statistical techniques such as, weighting, data analysis, factor reduction, ranking and relevant methods were used before development of model which are discussed and presented in the next chapters of this research in details. In this research fuzzy membership function and linguistic variables for each eco-indicator are calculated and developed in order to create an eco-building model.

"Fuzzy logic operations compensate for the lack of full knowledge of our system. Uncertainty is ubiquitous in sustainability problems, since we never have complete knowledge of the complex interrelationship of ecological systems and human society.

First, it permits the combination of various aspects of sustainability with different units of measurement. Second, it overcomes the difficulty of assessing certain attributes or indicators of sustainability without precise quantitative criteria and, third, the methodology is easy to use and interpret. Therefore, the model has the potential to become a practical tool to policy-makers whose decisions ought to contribute to sustainability and to scientists involved in the field of sustainability measurement." (Phillis and Andriantiatsaholiniaina, 2001)

CHAPTER 6

Eco-Design Indicators Extracted Knowledge

6.1 Introduction

Studying a large sample size of a population always leads to findings that reflect the characteristics of the assumed population. Our knowledge collection format was distributed among a number of practicing architects in different levels of architectural professions, involved in sustainable building design as potential respondents. The data obtained were grouped, organised in order to be analysed, discussed, and surveyed in the next section.

According to (Lupton, 2001) Royal Institute of British Architects (RIBA) job descriptions in the field of architecture are divided as:

1. Part II
2. Part III
3. Technician
4. Senior Technician
5. Architect
6. Associate
7. Director / Partner

Although in the UK the title of architect is given to the last three groups of this categorisation but in this research views of all categories towards eco-building design were gathered. Thus the aforementioned seven groups were assumed as the potential for knowledge elicitation.

The summary of all collected data, obtained through the 96 completely filled questionnaires are presented in Table 6.1 in this chapter. Fig 6.1 describes the sample size, used for this survey.

CHAPTER 6: ECO-DESIGN INDICATORS EXTRACTED KNOWLEDGE

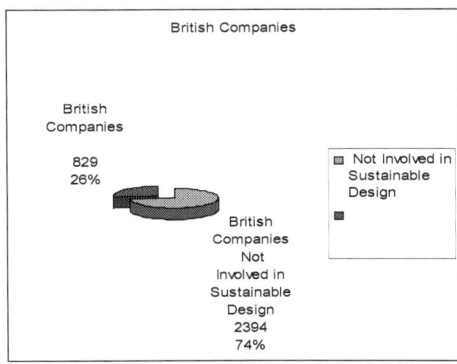

Fig 6.1 Number of Architectural Companies in the UK, Involved in Sustainable Building Design

6.2 Knowledge Extraction Findings

Overall findings of the questionnaire are presented and discussed in the next section of this chapter.

6.2.1 Respondent's General Information Finding (Questionnaire first page)

The first page of the questionnaire includes 12 questions relevant to respondent's general information. Two questions of the page asking individual's name and their companies name are designed as optional ones but the other 10 questions were asked in order to provide some statistical data about the study. The findings of respondents' general information are presented in the following section of this chapter.

1. Respondents Job Descriptions

Findings of this part show the respondents job descriptions according to RIBA. Fig 6.2 indicates participation rates based on their job descriptions. As shown in the figure, 6 partII, 5 part III, 0 Technician, 3 Senior Technicians, 56 Architects, 11 Associates, and 15 Directors participated in this study as the respondents (Totally 96 participants).

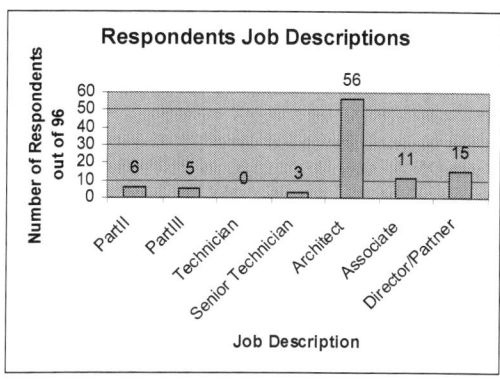

Fig 6.2 Respondents Job Descriptions

As seen, the large majority of research based on architects views embracing last three groups and part III category totalling 90.6% of the sample size.

2. Participants Job Ownership or Organisation

In this part the respondents were asked about the type of the practices that they are employed in. The data obtained is shown in Fig 6.3 reflects the findings of this part.

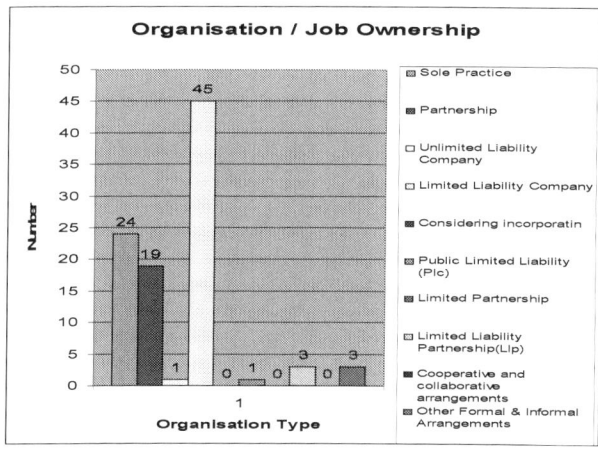

Fig 6.3 Organisation Type

The study determined that 24 participants (25%) of this research were Sole Principals, while 19 were included in Partnerships (19.7%), 1 in Unlimited Liability Company (1.04%), 45 in Limited Liability Company (46.8%), 1 in Public Limited Liability Company (1.04%), 3 in Limited Liability Partnership (3.12%), and 3 in other Formal and Informal Arrangements (3.12%). In each case an individual as a representative of the team is reflecting the point of view of the company.

3. Participants Years of Experience

Although the author believes that the experience is necessary but is not what is only needed for great point of view, this question was asked to have further statistics regarding further information possibly required. The respondents years of experience are illustrated in Fig 6.4 based on data collected through questionnaire.

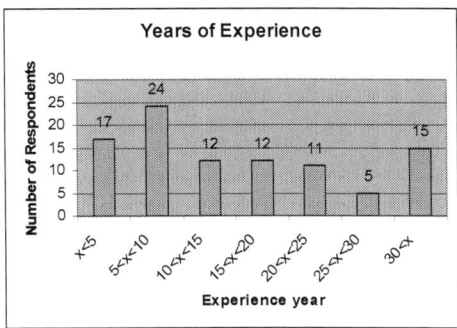

Fig 6.4 Respondents Years of Experience

As illustrated in Fig 6.4, as a practicing architect or relevant profession made up 17 (17.7%) respondents out of 96 have the experience of less than 5 years, 24 (25%) the experience between 5 to 10 years, 12 (12.5%) experience between 10 to 15, 12 (12.5%) experience 15 to 20, 11 (11.4%) have experience between 20 to 25, 5 (5.2%) of them the experience of 25 to 30 years and 15 (15.6%) individuals the experience more than 30 years.

4. Interest in Design Regarding Eco-Building Design

One of the questions regarding general information concentrates on the rate of interest of respondents regarding eco-building design. From the data obtained it is concluded the majority of the participants except one case, strongly agree on design concerning eco-indicators. The result of finding is presented in Fig 6.5 as follows:

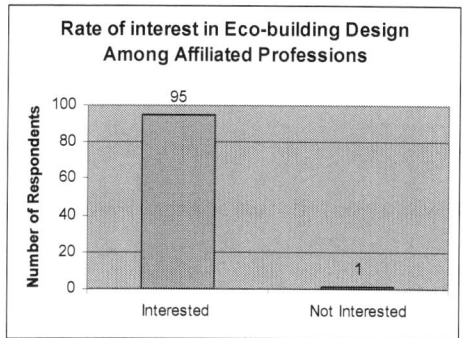

Fig 6.5 Rate of Interest in Eco-building Design among Affiliated Professions

As shown in Fig 6.5, 95 out of 96 (98.95%) do agree with design regarding eco-building design and just one out of all (1.05%) disagrees.

5. Number of Architects in Participants Company

The companies which the questionnaires were sent to are categorized according to number of employed architects in this research and the finding of this part is described in Fig 6.6 as follows:

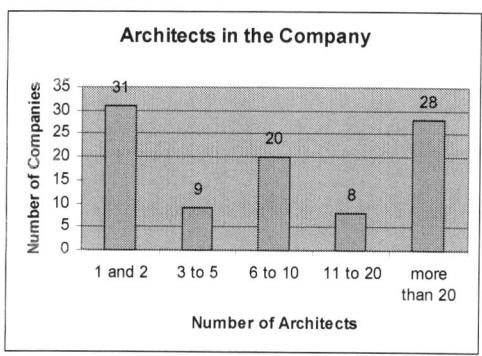

Fig 6.6 Number of Architects in the Company

As it is reported according to collected data, 31 companies (32.29%) have less than 2 architects and 9 companies (9.3%) have 3 to 5 architects. Also 20 companies (20.83%) have between 6 to 10 architects and 8 out of 96 (8.3%) have 11 to 20architects. There are 28 companies out of 96 (29.16%) that have more than 20 architects as well.

6. Number of Expertise in Eco-Building Design (Sustainable Building) in Companies

From the survey findings it can be concluded that there are 59 companies which have 1 to 2 expertises in sustainable building design, and also 15 of them have 3 to 5 expertise. Also this report announces that 8 of companies take advantage of existence of 6 to 10 expertise in sustainable design while 14 other companies have employed more than 10 experts each in this field for developing the projects regarding sustainable building. The result of survey obtained data is illustrated in Fig 6.7.

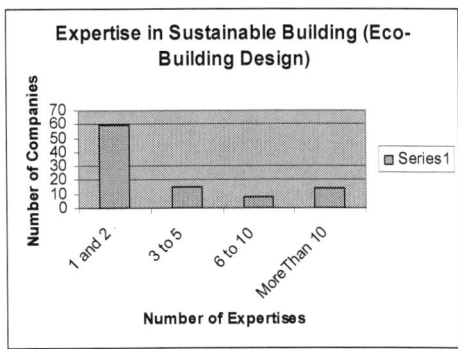

Fig 5.6 Expertise in Sustainable Building (Eco-Building Design)

7. Projects Handled in Companies Related to Sustainable Design

Each company claimed that a few or many projects based on sustainable building design were handled by them but it should be taken to account that what is the definition of sustainability? Or in other words what are the principles for assessment of sustainable building?

Fig 6.8 shows that 56 companies (58.3%) claimed that each of them have handled less than 5 projects related to sustainable building design while 14 companies (14.5%) have claimed that 5 to 10 projects were carried out by them. Also 26 companies (27.08%) mentioned that they have done more than 10 projects each related to sustainable building. Since this research attempts to be unbiased therefore these claims are neither rejected nor accepted, but are reported as a part of the findings. Hence, according to companies claiming, the obtained data are presented in Fig 6.8.

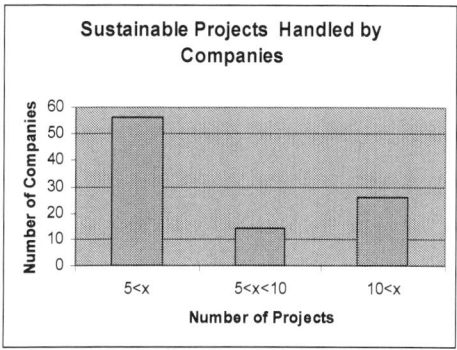

Fig 6.8 Sustainable Projects Handled by Companies

8. Training Regarding Sustainable Building Design (Eco-building Design)

The survey shows that 86 out of 96 (89.58%) respondents believe that training courses related to sustainable design and eco building design are essential for companies staff while 10 out 96 (10.42%) think otherwise.

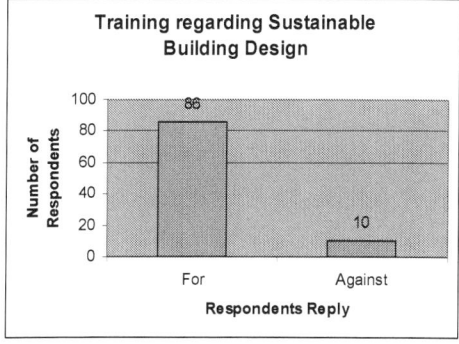

Fig 6.9 Training Regarding Sustainable Building Design

9. Computer Software or Relevant Programmes for Assessment

The companies were also asked if they employ any programme or computer software to assess the projects in sustainable building design or eco-building design. The answer to this question was a *Yes* by 23 out of 96 (23.96%) and a *No* by 73 out of 96 (76.04 %). The illustration of result is shown in Fig 6.10.

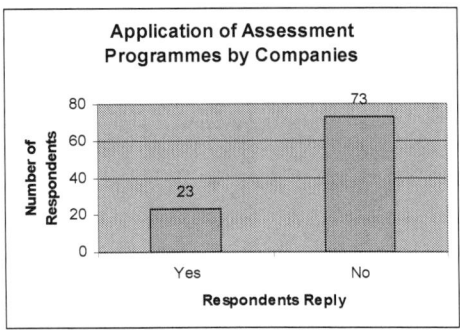

Fig 6.10 Application of Assessment Programmes by Companies.

10. Interest in Receiving a Copy of the Survey Report

All the questionnaire respondents were asked if they are interested in receiving a copy of survey report or not. If yes, they were requested to leave their contact details in order a copy of report being sent to them by the end of study. Questionnaire data collected shows that 56 (58.3 %) have requested a copy of the report to be delivered to them and 40 (41.7%) were not interested in it. Fig 6.11 describes the proportion of respondents who expressed an interest to receive a copy of the report.

CHAPTER 6: ECO-DESIGN INDICATORS EXTRACTED KNOWLEDGE

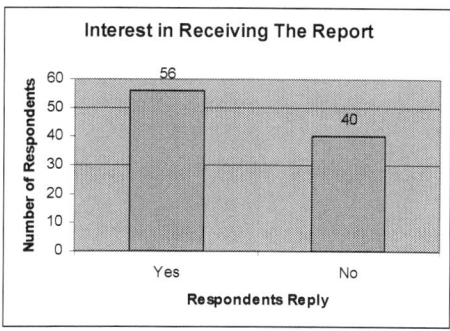

Fig 6.11 Rate of Interest in Receiving a Copy of Survey Report

At the end of the page all the participants were thanked for their time and considerable cooperation.

6.2.2 Eco-design Indicators Findings

Table 6.1, presented in this section, summarise all 96 questionnaires findings in a statistical way. Frequency of responses, average weighted mean, and standard deviation for each eco-indicator calculated by SPSS are shown in the Table 6.1. As the average weighted means of eco-indicators show; the majority of indicators except for two of them (No: 53 and 54) have means bigger than the neutral point (4.00). The fact determines that these indicators (113 out of 115) are accepted by respondents as quite important indicators in eco-building design. By considering of frequency of scores, handled by respondents, the degree of significance of each eco-indicator is understood. As mentioned in chapter 5, scores are based on a nine point scaling, from 0 to 8, present the value of the respondent's assessments. Scales from 0-2 indicate the basic needs required for building design and the range of 3-5 determines the indicators which they are not essentially eco ones but they are considered as potential indicators to develop an eco-building design. Here point 4.00 is assumed as the neutral point in scaling. Also scales from 6 to 8 are given to the indicators which play a main role in establishing an eco building design. Hence, the results shown in Table 6.1, proves that the majority of indicator have a scale (mean value) more than neutral point (4.00)which determines the indicators chosen in this survey are accepted by the selected sample population. Therefore, except for 2 the rest can be treated as eco-indicators to develop the study.

The result of knowledge extraction through descriptive information is presented in Table 6.1 in the following part of this chapter.

Table 6.1 Descriptive Information Obtained from the Questionnaire Survey

No	Eco-indicator Description	Frequency of Score									Mean	Standard Deviation
		0	1	2	3	4	5	6	7	8		
1	Logical Connections with Adjacent Functions	2	3	6	5	26	12	14	14	14	5.0833	2.03479
2	Functional Zonings	1	1	9	7	24	10	20	12	12	5.0625	1.9184
3	Compatibility with other Functions	2	2	3	7	24	15	18	13	12	5.1562	1.88249
4	Adaptability to the New Change(s)	0	0	2	1	12	11	28	21	21	6.1771	1.45815
5	Adaptability to the Surroundings	0	2	0	1	10	9	25	26	23	6.3125	1.51005
6	Adaptability to the Environment	1	0	1	0	5	3	13	30	43	6.9688	1.40265
7	Upgradeability and Extensions	0	0	1	3	13	11	30	16	22	6.1042	1.48309
8	Flexibility in Use Stage	0	0	1	5	10	12	30	22	16	6.0312	1.44698
9	Flexibility for Adding Function to the Main Function for Achieving Higher Performance	2	1	2	8	14	15	32	14	8	5.3542	1.71052
10	Renovation and Upgradeability	1	3	2	2	8	9	29	25	17	5.9896	1.76214
11	Performance Regarding Longevity	1	0	0	0	2	12	22	29	30	6.6979	1.29061
12	Longevity of Function	3	1	3	8	15	12	19	17	18	5.5	2.02614
13	Physical Aspects	1	2	4	6	12	5	22	26	18	5.8229	1.92488
14	Psychological Aspects	3	2	7	3	12	9	23	22	15	5.5208	2.08745
15	Adaptability Regarded to Indoor Quality	1	0	3	5	16	10	24	21	16	5.7708	1.72584
16	Physical Dimensions (Ergonomics)	3	1	3	8	14	11	19	20	17	5.5417	2.02051
17	Effect of Function on Human Behavior	3	0	4	4	12	9	16	29	19	5.875	1.9695
18	Circulation And Distribution Regarding the Existing Function in Design	0	0	5	2	19	8	28	17	17	5.7812	1.66198
19	Landscape	0	1	1	2	11	11	23	34	13	6.125	1.4455
20	Adjacent Zones (Macro View)	0	3	0	4	12	15	27	24	11	5.7917	1.58225
21	District (Micro View)	1	1	3	6	16	18	25	15	11	5.4375	1.69713
22	Market	0	4	5	7	18	14	17	15	16	5.3333	1.96102
23	Society	0	2	3	4	16	15	19	19	18	5.7292	1.76802
24	Government	0	1	3	6	18	15	13	18	22	5.75	1.81804
25	Organisations (NGOs & Queasy NGOs)	1	1	7	9	24	20	14	11	9	4.9063	1.78342
26	Control of Emissions	0	1	1	4	2	5	14	25	44	6.8646	1.51914
27	Energy & Eco-efficiency	0	1	0	0	1	7	10	23	54	7.2188	1.18057
28	Level of Tranquility	3	2	12	3	27	16	14	12	7	4.6562	1.96725
29	Level of Comfort	1	0	2	3	11	14	28	24	13	5.9063	1.54972
30	Number of Occupants (Spatial Capacity)	3	3	8	11	28	15	11	9	8	4.5	1.95206
31	Occupants Needs	2	1	3	3	15	9	28	17	18	5.75	1.84676
32	Distribution of Activities	0	0	6	8	24	22	17	11	8	5.0521	1.59848
33	Indoor Quality Performance (Optimum Conditions)	0	0	3	6	11	16	23	20	17	5.8542	1.61558
34	Internal Zoning Regarding Spatial Relationships in Design	0	1	5	8	21	15	23	16	7	5.2083	1.65381
35	Landscape Design	1	1	2	7	17	8	22	23	15	5.6979	1.79543
36	Natural Physical Conditions	0	1	0	3	17	11	21	26	17	6.0104	1.53893
37	Building Orientation	0	1	0	1	1	6	12	28	47	7.1042	1.22671
38	Climate	0	0	2	3	3	8	13	25	42	6.8125	1.48191
39	Outdoor Performance	2	1	5	6	18	7	25	19	13	5.4479	1.92419

CHAPTER 6: ECO-DESIGN INDICATORS EXTRACTED KNOWLEDGE

No	Eco-indicator Description	Frequency of Score									Mean	Standard Deviation
		0	1	2	3	4	5	6	7	8		
40	Adjacent Functions and Spaces	0	1	5	6	19	11	29	14	11	5.4167	1.69001
41	Site Restrictions	0	1	4	7	13	14	25	16	16	5.6458	1.73496
42	Form Built Ability (Feasibility of Building)	0	1	3	4	24	21	18	13	12	5.3646	1.61649
43	Maintainability (Ease of Maintenance)	0	0	1	1	6	13	31	27	17	6.3021	1.24917
44	Geometry of Form (Aesthetics and stability)	0	6	2	5	21	18	20	11	13	5.2083	1.86895
45	Adaptability and Coherence of Form	2	2	2	3	15	19	29	14	10	5.4375	1.72787
46	Durability regarding Flexibility	0	0	0	0	4	9	25	30	28	6.7188	1.11169
47	Components Detailing and Design	0	0	1	5	6	10	18	32	24	6.4063	1.47668
48	Predictability of Longevity of the Form (Some Forms and Shapes Last for Longer Period of Time.)	0	1	0	2	17	18	24	19	15	5.8542	1.47241
49	Reliability and Usability Regarding Form and its Durability and Maintenance	0	1	1	1	8	10	28	25	22	6.3229	1.43266
50	Disassembling Regarding Building WLC and Time.	2	2	10	9	22	14	14	17	6	4.7708	1.94925
51	Reusability and Recyclability Regarding Building WLC.	0	0	6	3	12	9	14	23	29	6.1563	1.82571
52	Philosophical Values Related to Design Concepts	2	5	10	7	22	13	13	12	12	4.7604	2.13613
53	Style of Design	11	10	10	15	14	10	13	7	6	3.7083	2.37051
54	Fashion and Design	25	6	13	11	23	5	7	3	3	2.8021	2.26469
55	Society and Culture Regarding Customer Satisfactions and Expectations	4	7	6	7	17	12	15	14	14	4.875	2.30902
56	Sense of Belonging and Place regarding Building Design	6	1	5	7	6	10	24	19	18	5.4896	2.25713
57	Longevity of Physical Influence (Human Physical Reactions and behaviors Respectively Design)	5	1	5	10	19	10	19	16	11	5.0104	2.12005
58	Longevity of Mental Influences (Emotions and Feelings Respectively Design)	5	2	2	12	24	10	15	15	11	4.9063	2.10302
59	Longevity Regarding WLC	0	0	0	0	7	13	28	29	19	6.4167	1.16679
60	Maintainability Regarding WLC	1	0	0	0	3	7	24	34	27	6.7188	1.24565
61	Energy Efficiency Regarding WLC	0	0	0	0	2	10	27	57		7.4479	0.76598
62	Embodied Energy Regarding WLC	0	0	1	1	3	7	27	19	38	6.7813	1.28311
63	Eco-Efficiency and Recyclability Regarding WLC	0	0	1	3	3	4	17	26	42	6.9063	1.35397
64	Reliability Regarding WLC	1	0	0	3	6	4	18	29	35	6.7083	1.49326
65	Function Fit To Purpose	0	2	2	1	8	15	21	20	27	6.2292	1.65739
66	Upgradeability of the Equipments Due to Future Requirements	0	1	2	2	10	17	32	22	10	5.8542	1.42148
67	Access to the Equipments for Repairing	1	0	1	2	10	13	35	18	16	6.0104	1.46894
68	Pollution Generation by Equipments in Building	0	0	0	1	4	3	14	27	47	7.1146	1.14128
69	Environmental Adapted Technology in Equipments Manufacturing	0	0	0	0	1	3	20	26	46	7.1771	0.94027
70	Noise Generation by Equipments in Building	1	1	1	2	9	11	24	28	19	6.1667	1.60044
71	Vibration Generation by Equipments in Building	1	1	4	3	16	7	32	21	11	5.6667	1.7086

No	Eco-indicator Description	Frequency of Score									Mean	Standard Deviation
		0	1	2	3	4	5	6	7	8		
72	Zoning and Location Of the Equipment in a Plan (Regarding Access, and Disturbance Generations)	0	0	3	3	16	13	15	28	18	5.9792	1.62856
73	Technological Innovation Application (Hybridising and Integration)	1	2	3	6	14	13	20	19	18	5.6667	1.88438
74	Contemporary Technology Application	5	6	7	7	23	11	19	8	10	4.5625	2.19479
75	Vernacular and Traditional Technology Application	4	6	9	12	24	12	18	5	6	4.2396	2.01439
76	Green House Effect	0	1	1	1	2	5	19	19	48	6.9792	1.38396
77	Ozone Layer	0	1	1	2	3	3	21	18	47	6.9167	1.44853
78	More Efficient Use of Water	0	0	0	1	5	10	16	22	42	6.8646	1.28653
79	Energy Consumption Regarding the Amount	0	0	0	0	0	3	16	17	60	7.3958	0.87635
80	Air Pollution (CO_2, NO_x, SO_x, ETC)	0	0	2	1	3	2	12	20	56	7.1771	1.32184
81	Water Pollution	0	0	3	1	0	3	17	21	51	7.0938	1.33833
82	Earth Pollution	0	0	3	0	3	4	17	24	45	6.9583	1.37586
83	Ecological Deterioration Both Visually and Naturally	0	1	2	2	8	2	19	28	34	6.6146	1.57861
84	Landfills	0	0	1	2	7	9	22	21	34	6.5833	1.43392
85	Solid Residues	0	0	2	2	10	10	24	20	28	6.3333	1.52638
86	Natural Light through Photovoltaic and Naturally	0	0	0	1	3	3	14	29	46	7.1354	1.09179
87	Passive Heating Through Zoned heating and Air Tightness (Heating Air and Water)	0	0	0	0	1	6	20	30	39	7.0417	0.98319
88	Natural Ventilation	0	0	0	0	1	6	14	29	46	7.1771	0.97327
89	Passive Cooling through Solar Shading and Ventilation	0	0	0	1	6	3	15	34	37	6.9375	1.18599
90	Insulation and Air Tightness	0	0	0	1	5	5	8	28	49	7.125	1.19868
91	Water Saving Devices	0	0	0	2	8	6	19	28	33	6.6875	1.34017
92	Geo Thermal Benefits	0	1	4	3	19	8	19	22	20	5.8542	1.77692
93	Sewage and Landfill Gas for producing Heat and Energy	0	2	5	5	16	17	22	13	16	5.4896	1.80055
94	Biomass for producing Heat and Energy	0	0	1	4	14	11	24	22	20	6.0729	1.52346
95	Low Embodied Energy Materials regarding WLC	0	0	2	2	8	6	21	31	26	6.4896	1.45091
96	Energy and Eco- Efficient Design by Consideration of Orientation, Surfaces, heat exchanges, etc	0	0	0	1	1	3	7	34	50	7.3125	0.94382
97	More Energy Efficient Equipments and Appliances Application in Design	0	0	1	2	3	7	13	31	39	6.8958	1.30971
98	Environmentally Adapted Technology	0	0	1	1	14	8	20	25	27	6.375	1.48146
99	Application of Healthier and safer Energy and Resources	0	0	2	2	18	5	15	27	27	6.2708	1.63822
100	Emotional Well-being (Safety, Happiness, Spirituality)	2	1	5	4	16	10	18	23	17	5.6458	1.9627
101	Interpersonal Relations (Intimacy, Affection, Family)	5	3	8	7	24	9	19	12	9	4.6979	2.14289
102	Material Well-being (Ownership, Possessions, Financial Security)	6	7	9	5	23	16	16	8	6	4.2917	2.1517
103	Personal Development (Education Skills, Personal Competence)	4	7	7	7	21	12	25	9	4	4.4896	2.04164
104	Physical Well-being (Health, Recreation)	3	1	5	6	13	11	21	16	20	5.5625	2.07142

CHAPTER 6: ECO-DESIGN INDICATORS EXTRACTED KNOWLEDGE

No	Eco-indicator Description	Frequency of Score									Mean	Standard Deviation
		0	1	2	3	4	5	6	7	8		
105	Self Determination (Autonomy, Choices, Personal Control)	4	4	5	6	20	9	25	14	9	4.9688	2.08984
106	Social Inclusion (Acceptance, Status, Roles)	7	8	6	6	22	18	13	12	4	4.2708	2.17391
107	Rights (Privacy, Due Process)	4	6	7	6	25	12	21	11	4	4.5104	2.0157
108	Facility Management Costs Regarding WLC	0	0	4	1	15	14	30	17	15	5.8333	1.52638
109	Maintenance Costs Regarding WLC	1	0	2	1	6	10	28	28	20	6.3021	1.48763
110	Level of Component Replacement Costs Regarding WLC	0	2	1	3	10	15	34	15	16	5.8854	1.54149
111	Pollution Rehabilitation Costs Regarding WLC	0	1	2	1	11	15	31	15	20	6.0208	1.52163
112	Pollution Preventing Costs Regarding WLC	0	1	2	0	12	14	29	18	20	6.0729	1.50958
113	Disposal Costs Regarding WLC	0	3	4	2	15	20	14	16	22	5.7188	1.87338
114	Risk Costs Regarding WLC	1	1	8	5	22	16	16	14	13	5.1875	1.89355
115	Capital Costs/ Running Costs (Saving Running Costs Regarding WLC)	0	1	0	2	8	7	15	26	37	6.6875	1.48899

For clarification and better perception, eco-indicators of each characteristic in its category are discussed and presented separately in the next part of the study.

6.2.2.1 Building Design-Function Characteristic Eco-indicators

As it is shown in Table 6.1, all first 27 eco-indicators (in Function characteristic) carry a score more than neutral point (4.00). This fact shows that the majority of respondents believe that all presented indicators regarding function in building design play a quite important role to achieve a sustainable building through application of eco-indicators in eco-building design. The high score of indicators (range from 6 to 8) proves that these indicators could be strongly used as eco ones in this research. In the table, 8 indicators carrying average weighted mean of higher than 6.00 are distinguished as eco-indicators by respondents regarding function in building design. The indicators with the score in the range of 3-5 are considered as potential eco-indicators in eco-building design. Here the findings for eco-indicators in function Characteristic with the scores from 6 to 8 are presented and illustrated.

1. Adaptability to New Changes

The responses for this eco-indicator show a mean value of 6.17 and S.D. of 1.45. Frequencies and distribution of responses show that 21 respondents (21.8%) gave a score of 8, 21 (21.8%) a score of 7, 28 (29.1%) a score of 6, 11 (11.4%) a score of 5, 12 (12.5%) a score of 4, 1 (1.04%) a score of 3, and 2 (2.08%) a score of 2 to this eco-indicator. This high score (more than neutral point) shows that this indicator is recognised by respondents as one which plays a main role in eco-building design. S.D. of 1.45 also indicates the level of agreements among responses regarding this indicator. Histogram and normal curve of the eco-indicator are illustrated in Fig 6.12.

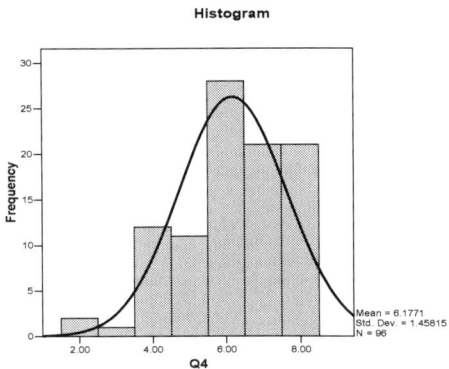

Fig 6.12 Histogram and Normal Curve for **Adaptability to New Changes (Q4)**

2. Adaptability to Surroundings and Circumstances

(23.95%) of respondents gave a score of 8, (27.08%) a score of 7, (26.04%) a score of 6, (9.3%) a score of 5, (10.34%) a score of 4, (1.04%) a score of 3, and (2.08%) a score of 1 to this eco-indicator. Also this indicator gained a mean value of 6.31 and S.D. of 1.51. A total (77.08%) of respondents assumed this indicator as an eco-indicator, and (20.8%) as a potential eco-indicator while (2.08%) as a non-eco-indicator. The distribution of responses due to their frequencies with a normal curve is presented in Fig 6.13.

CHAPTER 6: ECO-DESIGN INDICATORS EXTRACTED KNOWLEDGE

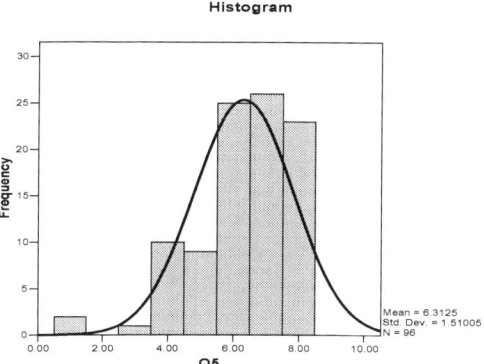

Fig 6.13 Histogram and Normal Curve for **Adaptability to Surroundings (Q5)**

3. Adaptability to the Environment

The data obtained shows that (44.79%) of respondents have given a score of 8, (31.25%) a score of 7, (13.54%) a score of 6, (3.12%) a score of 5, (5.20%) a score of 4, (1.04%) a score of 2 and (1.04%) a score of 0 to this indicator. Overall this indicator was accepted as an eco-indicator having mean value of 6.96 and S.D. of 1.40, proving the high influence of this indicator in eco-building design among respondents. Histogram and normal curve related to this eco-indicator is presented in Fig 6.14 below. The distribution of responses and frequencies are clarified by consideration of Fig 6.14. As it is shown in the Fig 6.14, there is a quite strong agreement among the rate of responses regarding this indicator. The majority of scores belong to the range of 6 to 8 which is determined as eco-indicators' range. This proves that this indicator can be assumed as an important eco-indicator in this research.

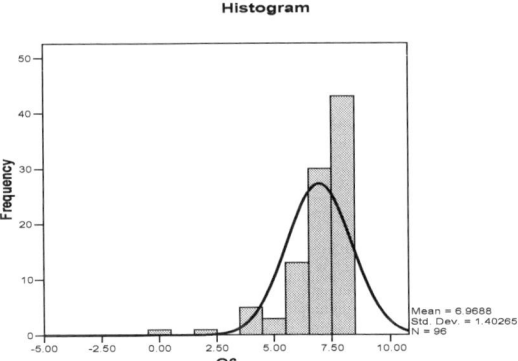

Fig 6.14 Histogram and Normal Curve for **Adaptability to the Environment (Q6)**

Concerning three questions 4, 5, and 6, it is concluded that adaptability could be one of the main items in eco-building design and its relevant cases.

4. Upgradeability and Extension

From 96 respondents, (22.9%) of them have given a score of 8, (16.6%) a score of 7, (31.2%) a score of 6, (11.45%) a score of 5, (13.5%) a score of 4, (3.12%) a score of 3, and (1.04%) a score of 2 to this indicator and totally allocate this indicator as an eco-indicator in the field of eco-building design. Also the mean and S.D. are respectively 6.10 and 1.48. From the survey findings it is derived that 68 individual out of 96 (70.83%) introduced this item as an eco-indicator and 27 (28.1%) found it as a potential eco-indicator, and just 1 of them (1.04%) assign it as a non-eco-indicator. The findings are summarised in Fig 6.15 and described through histogram and normal curve.

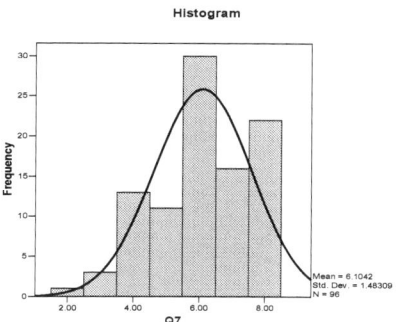

Fig 6.15 Histogram and Normal curve for **Upgradeability and Extension (Q7)**

5. Flexibility in Use Stage

16 individuals out of 96 (16.6%) gave a score of 8, 22 (22.9%) a score of 7, 30 (31.25%) a score of 6, 12 (12.5%) a score of 5, 10 (10.4%) a score of 4, 5 (5.2%) a score of 3, and 1 1.04%) a score of 2 to this indicator and finally this indicator was recognised as an eco-indicator with the mean of 6.03, and S.D. of 1.44. Overall 68 respondents (70.83%) accepted it as an eco-indicator and 27 (28.12%) assigned it as a potential eco-indicator while it was categorised as a non eco-indicator by 1 (1.04%) of them. The results are illustrated as histogram and normal curve in Fig 6.16.

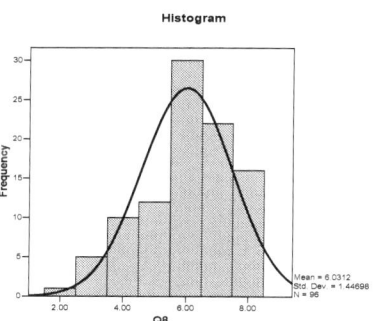

Fig 6.16 Histogram and Normal Curve for **Flexibility in Use Stage (Q8)**

6. Performance regarding Longevity

From 96 respondents, 30 gave a score of 8, 29 a score of 7, 22 a score of 6, 12 a score of 5, 2 a score of 4 and 1 a score of 0 to this indicator. A total of 81 out of 96 individuals (84.37%) believe that this indicator belongs to the eco-indicators group while 14 of respondents (14.58%) look at it as a potential eco-indicator and 1 of respondents (1.04%) assign it as a non eco-indicator. Finally this indicator with the mean of 6.69 and S.D. of 1.29 is strongly recognized as one of the main eco-indicators in eco-building design in this survey.

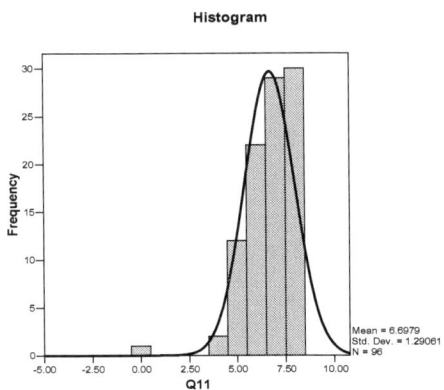

Fig 6.17 Histogram and Normal Curve for **Performance regarding Longevity (Q11)**

As shown in the Fig 6.17, there is a very strong agreement among responses in allocating this item as an eco-indicator.

7. Control of Emission

This indicator with mean of 6.86 and S.D. of 1.51 is recognised by majority of survey respondents as an eco-indicator. 44 individuals out of 96 gave a score of 8, 25 a score of 7, 14 a score of 6, 5 a score of 5, 2 a score of 4, 4 a score of 3, 1 a score of 2, and 1 a score of 1 to this indicator. Generally 83 individuals (86.45%) accepted this indicator as an eco-indicator while 11 (11.45%) assigned it as a potential eco-indicator and 2 (2.08%) grouped it as a non eco-indicator. The findings are illustrated in Fig 6.18.

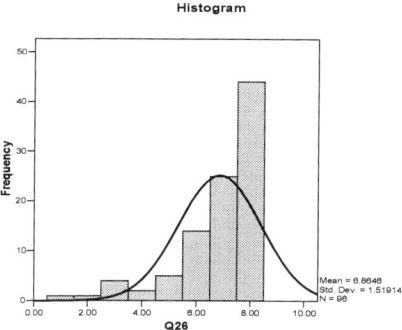

Fig 6.18 Histogram and Normal Curve for **Control of Emission (Q26)**

8. Energy and Eco-Efficiency

Consideration of energy consumption and eco-efficiency related policies, are the most important indicator among function characteristic indicators which carries a mean value of 7.21 and S.D. of 1.18 in this survey. 54 of respondents have given a score of 8, 23 a score of 7, 10 a score of 6, 7 a score of 5, 1 a score of 4 and 1 a score of 1 to this indicator. Therefore overall 87 individuals out of 96 (90.6%) have assigned this indicator as an eco-indicator and 8 individuals have accepted it as a potential eco-indicator and just 1 has looked at it as a non eco-indicator. The findings of this survey regarding this indicator are illustrated and summarised in Fig 6.19. As seen in Fig 6.19, the majority of responses are located in the range of 6 to 8. Also the peak of the normal curve in the Fig 6.19, assigns the mean value of this indicator which is equal to 7.21 in this survey.

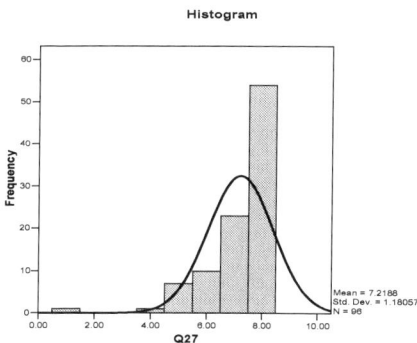

Fig 6.19 Histogram and Normal Curve for **Energy and Eco-Efficiency (Q27)**

6.2.2.2 Building Design-Space Characteristic Eco-Indicators

Indicators 28 to 41 in Table 6.1 belong to space characteristic in building design. All of these group indicators have a mean value more than neutral point (4.00). Among these indicators, three of them are distinguished as eco-indicators by respondents' assessments. The eco-indicators are introduced as follows:

1. Natural physical Conditions

17 of the respondents gave a score of 8, 26, a score of 7, 21 a score of 6, 11 a score of 5, 17 a score of 4, 3 a score of 3, 1 a score of 1 to this indicator. Results of questionnaire survey show that this indicator was selected by 64 respondents (66.6%) as an eco-indicator and as a potential eco-indicator by 31 of them (31.25%) and by 1 of them (1.04%) as a non eco-indicator. The findings for this indicator form a mean value of 6.01 and S.D. of 1.53 for this eco-indicator. The illustration of findings is presented in Fig 6.20. As it is shown in Fig 6.20 the range of scores varies from 1 to 8, and there is a variety of scaling regarding assessment of this eco-indicators which shows different point of views of the survey participants. Another point which can be seen in the histogram is that the majority of scores are in the range of 4 to 8.

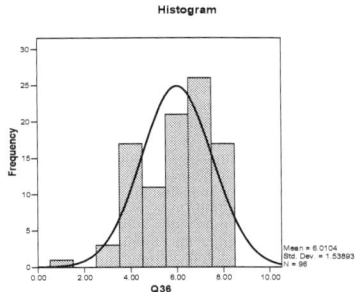

Fig 6.20 Histogram and Normal Curve for **Natural physical Conditions (Q36)**

2. Building Orientation

This indicator is also chosen by respondents as the most effective eco-indicator of this group. A total of 47 respondents gave a score of 8, 28 a score of 7, 12 a score of 6, 6 a score of 5, 1 a score of 3 and 1 a score of 1 to this indicator. Totally this indicator was selected by 87 individuals

(90.6%) as an eco-indicator and as a potential eco-indicator by 8 (8.32%) of them while 1 out of 96 (1.04%) has accepted it as a non eco-indicator. The Table 6.1 shows a mean value of 7.10, and S.D. of 1.22 which is shown in Fig 6.21 in additions to the normal distribution curve of this eco-indicator.

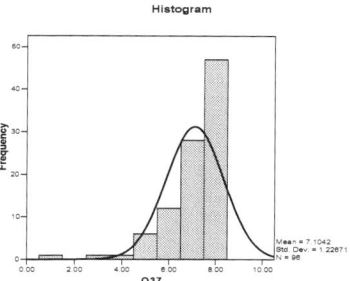

Fig 6.21 Histogram and Normal Curve for **Building Orientation (Q37)**

3. Climate

Climate influence on eco-building design was also assessed and scored by respondents as follows: 42 of them gave a score of 8, 25 a score of 7, 13 a score of 6, 8 a score of 5, 3 a score of 4, 3 a score of 3 and 2 a score of 2 to this indicator. 80 individuals chose this indicator as an eco-indicator and 14 as a potential eco-indicator in their assessments and so did two respondents as a non eco-indicator. In this study this eco-indicator presents a mean value of 6.81 and S.D. of 1.48.

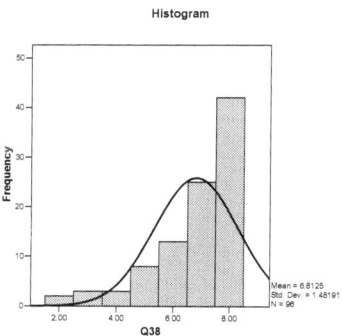

Fig 6.22 histogram and normal curve for **Climate (Q38)**

As shown in the figure the range of responses differs from 2 to 8 and the majority of responses are located between scores from 4 to 8 which confirm the importance of this indicator.

6.2.2.3 Building Design-Form Characteristic Eco-indicators

Indicators 42 to 58 belong to this group in the questionnaire. As shown in Table 6.1, all of them except for two have a mean value more than 4.00 which is the neutral point in this survey. Fashion and Style regarding design are the two indicators rejected as eco-indicators and carry mean value of 2.80 and 3.70 in this survey. The eco-indicators in this group are presented below.

1. Maintainability (Ease of Maintenance)

This indicator with the mean value of 6.30 and S.D. of 1.24 has been selected as an eco-indicator by research respondents. In this survey 17 respondents gave a score of 8, 27 a score of 7, 31 a score of 6, 13 a score of 5, 6 a score of 4, 1 a score of 3, 1 a score of 2 to this item. It is also derived from Table 7.1 that 75 individuals out of 96 (78.12%) put this indicator in eco-indicators group and 20 (20.8%) have considered it as a potential eco-indicator but 1 (1.04%) of them selected it as a non eco-indicator. Also the summary of findings is illustrated in Fig 6.23.

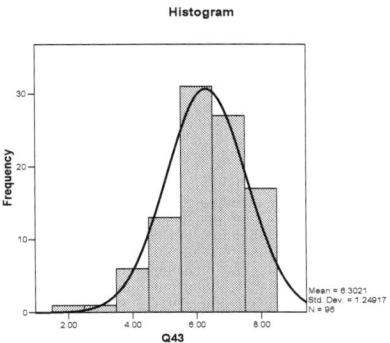

Fig6.23 Histogram and Normal Curve for **Maintainability (Q43)**

2. Durability Regarding Flexibility

This indicator is strongly accepted as an eco-indicator among the respondents. The high mean value of 6.71 and S.D. of 1.11 are proofs confirming this acceptance. In this survey 28 respondents gave a score of 8, 30 a score of 7, 25 a score of 6, 9 a score of 5, 4 a score of 4 to this indicator. No one accepted this indicator as a non eco-indicator. Overall data obtained indicate that this indicator was selected as eco one by 83 individuals and just 13 of respondents agreed that it could be a potential eco-indicator. The minimum score given to this indicator is 4.00 and the maximum is 8.00. The related information is shown as a histogram including normal distribution curve in Fig 6.24.

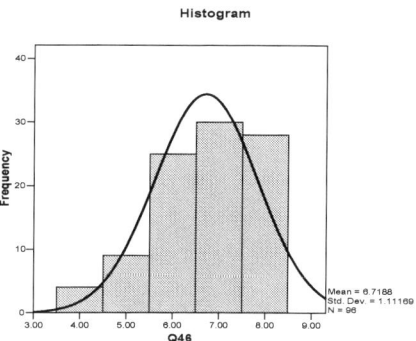

Fig 6.24 Histogram and Normal Curve for **Durability Regarding Flexibility (Q46)**

3. Component Detailing and Design

This indicator was selected as an eco-indicator according to assessments of respondents presenting a mean value of 6.40 and S.D. of 1.47 in this study. 24 individuals out of 96 gave a score of 8, 32 a score of 7, 18 a score of 6, 10 a score of 5, 6 a score of 4, 5 a score of 3 and 1 a score of 2 to this indicator. It was accepted by 64 respondents (66.6%) as an eco-indicator and by 21 (21.8%) as a potential eco-indicator and by 1 (1.04%) as a non eco-indicator based on questionnaire survey. The findings are illustrated in Fig 6.25.

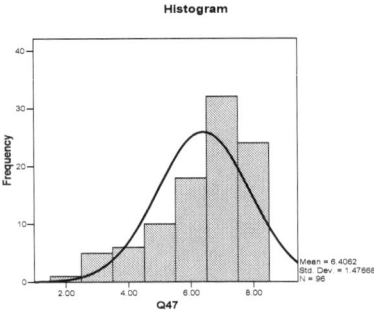

Fig 6.25 Histogram and Normal Curve for **Component Detailing and Design (Q47)**

4. Reliability and Usability

This item was distinguished by respondents of the survey as an eco-indicator, presenting a mean value of 6.32 and S.D. of 1.43. Also 22 individuals chose a score of 8, 25 a score of 7, 28 a score of 6, 10 a score of 5, 8 a score of 4, 1 a score of 3, 1 a score of 2 and 1 a score of 1 for this indicator. As a result of the findings, 75 people agreed that this indicator should be an eco-indicator while 19 other individuals believe that it is a potential eco-indicator and 2 accepted it as a non eco-indicator. Illustration of results is shown in Fig 6.26.

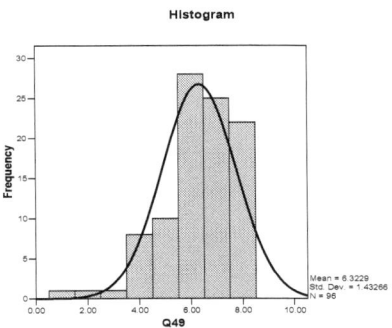

Fig 6.26 Histogram and Normal Curve for **Reliability and Usability (Q49)**

5. Reusability and Recycle ability

This indicator with the mean value of 6.15 and S.D. of 1.82 was selected as an eco-indicator of eco-building design. The questionnaire findings show that 29 responses allocated a score of 8, 23 a score of 7, 14 a score of 6, 9 a score of 5, 12 a score of 4, 3 a score of 3, 6 a score of 2 to this indicator. From Table 6.1 it is derived that 66 respondents out of 96 (68.7%) believe that this indicator is an eco-indicator while 24 (25%) of them accept it as a potential eco-indicator and 6 (6.24%) of them select it as a non eco-indicator as well. Fig 6.27 presents the related data.

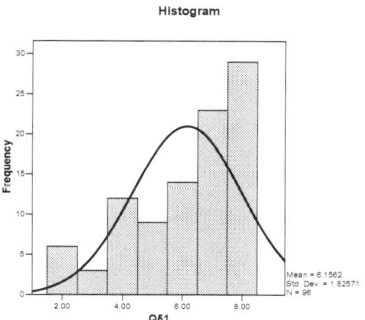

Fig 6.27 Histogram and Normal Curve for **Reusability and Recycle-ability (Q51)**

6.2.2.4 Building Design-Technology Characteristic Eco-indicators

The majority of indicators in this group are distinguished as eco-indicators based on the questionnaire survey and carries a mean value more than neutral point. Indicators 59 to 75 in Table 6.1 belong to this group. The eco-indicators of this group are introduced and described in the next section of this study.

1. Longevity Attribute over WLC

This indicator carrying mean value of 6.41 and S.D. of 1.16 was considered as an eco-indicator by data provided through the questionnaire survey. 19 respondents gave a score of 8, 29 a score of 7, 28 a score of 6, 13 a score of 5, 7 a score of 4 to this indicator. As shown in Table 7.1, 74 individuals out of 96 (77.08%) accepted this indicator as an eco-indicator and 22 of them (22.91%) found it as a potential eco-indicator. No score less than 4.00 (the neutral point) was given to this indicator which shows that there is a high level of agreement among respondents evaluations. The summary of data obtained is presented in Fig 6.28 below.

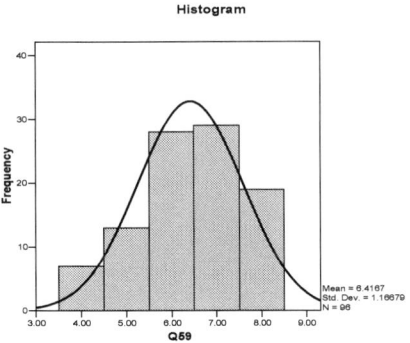

Fig 6.28 Histogram and Normal Curve for **Longevity Regarding WLC (Q59)**

2. Maintainability Attribute over WLC

This indicator with the mean value of 6.41 and S.D. of 1.24 was selected as an eco-building indicator by this questionnaire survey. 27 individuals gave a score of 8, 34 a score of 7, 24 a score of 6, 7 a score of 5, 3 a score of 4 and 1 a score of 0 to this indicator. 85 respondents out of 96 (88.54%) agreed on selecting this indicator as an eco-indicator whereas 10 of them (10.4%) accepted it as a potential eco-indicator and one person (1.04%) mentioned that it should be considered as a non-eco-indicator.

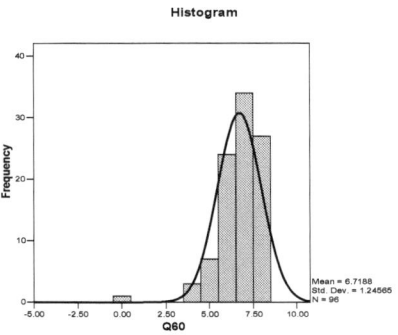

Fig 6.29 Histogram and Normal Curve for **Maintainability Regarding WLC (Q60)**

As it is shown in Fig 6.29, the majority of responses are focusing on scores 6, 7, and 8. Also Fig 6.29 shows that there is an agreement among the responses to choose the indicator as an eco-indicator by giving a score in range of 6 to 8 to this indicator.

3. Energy Efficiency Attribute over WLC

This item is one of the most effective eco-indicators both in this group and among all eco-indicators, giving a mean value of 7.44 and S.D. of 0.76. The low S.D. of this item proves that there is a high level of agreement among the respondents in selection of this indicator as an eco-indicator. Questionnaire survey shows that 57 respondents out of 96 gave a score of 8, 27 ones a score of 7, and 10 ones a score of 6, 2 a score of 5 to this indicator in their assessments. Therefore this indicator was selected as an eco-indicator by 94 individuals out of 96 (97.91%) while just two people (2.08%) assumed it as a potential eco-indicator. The range of responses regarding this indicator embraces the interval of 5 to 8 which means this indicator is strongly distinguished as an eco one by the majority of participants. This fact and other findings of research, relevant to energy efficiency eco-indicator are presented in Fig 6.30.

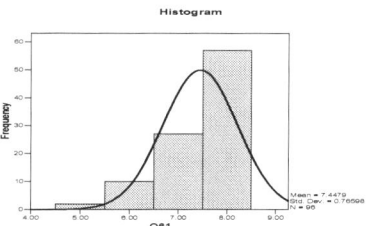

Fig 6.30 Histogram and Normal Curve for **Energy Efficiency Regarding WLC (Q61)**

4. Embodied Energy Attribute over WLC

This indicator was distinguished as an eco-indicator which presents a mean value of 6.78 and S.D. of 1.28in this study. In this research 38 people selected a score of 8, 19 a score of 7, 27 a score of 6, 7 a score of 5, 3 a score of 4, 1 a score of 3 and 1 a score of 2 for this indicator. As an outcome of the questionnaire report, 84 individuals (87.5%) supposed this indicator as an eco-indicator and 11 (11.45%) of them assumed it as a potential eco-indicator while one person (1.04%) considered it as a non eco-indicator. The basic findings of the questionnaire survey about this indicator are shown in Fig 6.31.

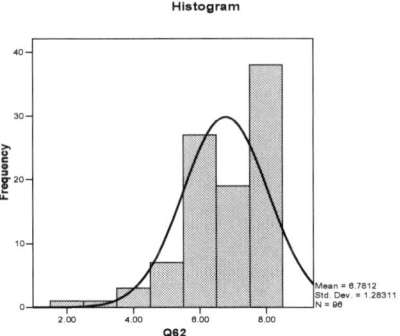

Fig 6.31 Histogram and Normal Curve for **Embodied Energy Regarding WLC (Q62)**

Also in the column of comment in the questionnaire some respondents claimed that this eco-indicator needs more consideration in the process of design and mentioned that this indicator in the procedure of contemporary design is nearly ignored. Hence existence of this item among other indicators made them somehow pleased about the questionnaire and its contents.

5. Eco-efficiency and Recycle-ability

This indicator was introduced as an eco-indicator by this research based on records of assessments handled through 96 participants. This item has a mean value equal to 6.90 and a S.D. of 1.35 which are considerable factors in this study. The questionnaire Statistical data show that 42 respondent gave a score of 8, 26 a score of 7, 17 a score of 6, 4 a score of 5, 3 a score of 4, 3 a score of 3, and 1 a score of 2 to this indicator. A total of 85 (88.54%) respondents selected this indicator as an eco-indicator and 10 (10.4%) accepted it as a potential eco-indicator and one participant (1.04%) assigned it as a non eco-indicator. The illustration of statistical data obtained is presented in Fig 6.32.

CHAPTER 6: ECO-DESIGN INDICATORS EXTRACTED KNOWLEDGE

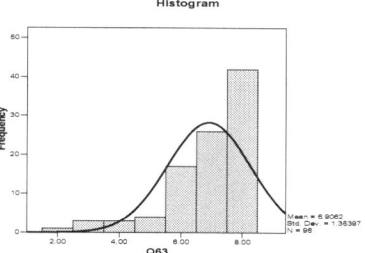

Fig 6.32 Histogram and Normal Curve for **Eco-efficiency and Recycle ability (Q63)**

As shown in Fig 6.32 the Gravity of responses are focused on score range from 6 to 8 which carry the main shares of the evaluation. This fact proves that there is a quite strong agreement among participants in considering this indicator as an eco-indicator.

6. Reliability Attribute over WLC

This indicator with a mean value of 6.70 and a S.D. of 1.49 is assumed as an eco-indicator in this research. Based on the questionnaire responses, 35 respondents gave a score of 8, 29 a score of 7, 18 a score of 6, 4 a score of 5, 6 a score of 4, 3 a score of 3, and 1 a score of 0 to this indicator. Therefore among 82 participants this indicator is assumed as an eco-indicator and among other 13 remaining ones it is known as a potential eco-indicator according to this survey statistical finding. The basic primary data extracted relevant to this eco-indicator is shown in Fig 6.33 below.

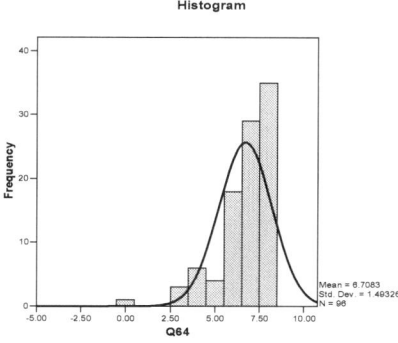

Fig 6.33 Histogram and Normal Curve for **Reliability Regarding WLC (Q64)**

As illustrated in the figure the majority of responses are located in the range of 6 to 8 which reflects the degree of eco-indicator acceptance among the participants. Also there is no response on the scores 1, and 2.

7. Function fit to Purpose Regarding Building Equipments

This item, having mean value of 6.22 and S.D. of 1.65 is assigned as another eco-indicator known by this research. The survey shows that 27 of participants gave a score of 8, 20 a score of 7, 21 a score of 6, 15 a score of 5, 8 a score of 4, 1 a score of 3, 2 a score of 2 and 2 a score of 1 to this item. Overall according to data in Table 6.1, it is derived that 68 respondents accepted this indicator as an eco-indicator while 24 of them assumed it as a potential eco-indicator and 4 of them considered it as a non eco-indicator. The outcomes of the findings are shown in Fig 6.34. As portrayed in the figure the majority of the responses are related to the range of 4 to 8 and the gravity of responses are centred in the aforementioned range. The distribution of responses proves that the majority have given a score more than neutral point to this indicator.

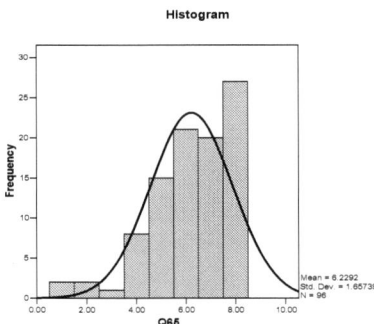

Fig 6.34 Histogram and Normal Curve for **Function Fit to Purpose** (Equipments wise) (Q65)

8. Access to Equipment for Repairing

This indicator presenting a mean value of 6.01 and S.D. of 1.46 is assumed as an eco-indicator according to participants' responses in this survey. Also findings show that 16 participants ticked a score of 8, 18 a score of 7, 35 a score of 6, 13 a score of 5, 10 a score of 4, 2 a score of 3, 1 a score of 2 and 1 a score of 0 for this indicator. This indicator was selected by 69 (71.87%) individuals as an eco-indicator, by 25 (26.04%) other ones as a potential eco-indicator and by 2 (2.08%)

individuals as non eco-indicator. The data related to this indicator, are presented and illustrated in Fig 6.35.

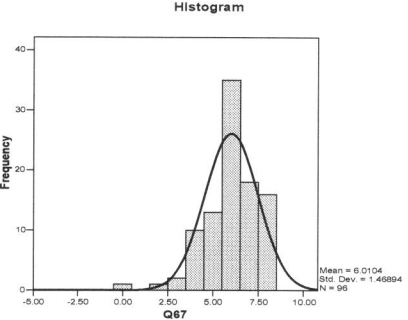

Fig 6.35 Histogram and Normal Curve for **Access to Equipment for Repairing (Q67)**

9. Pollution Generation

This indicator as a known eco-indicator carries a mean value of 7.11 and S.D. 1.14 in this research. Data obtained shows that 47 participants recorded a score of 8, 27 individuals a score of 7, 14 of them a score of 6, 3 of them a score of 5, 4 individuals a score of 4, and 1 a score of 3 for this indicator, all shown in Table 6.1. Overall this indicator is accepted by 88 participants out of 96 as an eco-indicator while 8 of them have considered it as a potential eco-indicator. Fig 6.36 as an outcome of data obtained is presented.

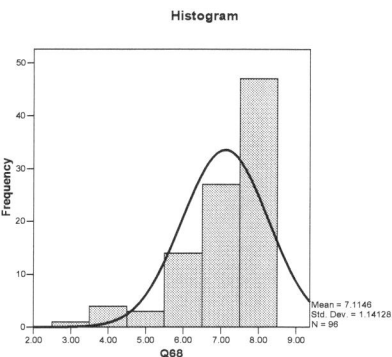

Fig 6.36 Histogram and Normal Curve for **Pollution Generation (Q68)**

As shown in Fig 6.36 the loads of responses are placed in the range of 6 to 8. The range of responses is varying from 3 (the lowest score) to 8 as the highest scores.

10. Environmental Adapted Technology

This indicator as one of the main policies in eco building design is assumed as an eco-indicator in this research. The findings determine that 46 respondents gave a score of 8, 26 a score of 7, 20 a score of 6, 3 a score of 5 and 1 a score of 4 to this indicator. None of the respondents gave a score less than neutral point to this indicator. The data shows a mean value of 7.17 and S.D. of 0.94 for this indicator. The S.D. of 0.94 shows a condensed distribution of responses and the level of agreement among respondents scaling. A total of 92 respondents out of 96 (95.83%) believe that this indicator should considered as an eco-indicator but 4 of them (4.16%) accept the item as a potential eco-indicator. The results of statistical data are presented in Fig 6.37.

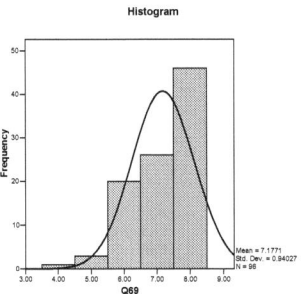

Fig 6.37 Histogram and Normal Curve for **Environmental Adapted Technology (Q69)**

11. Noise Generation by Equipments in Building

This indicator has a mean value of 6.16 and S.D. of 1.60 obtained in this survey. The collected data shows that 19 respondents gave a score of 8, 28 a score of 7, 24 a score of 6, 11 a score of 5, 9 a score of 4, 2 a score of 3, 1 a score of 2, 1 a score of 1 and 1 a score of 0 to this indicator. Overall 71 individuals assumed this indicator as an eco-indicator and 22 individuals considered as a potential eco indicator and 3 supposed as a non eco-indicator. The statistical data are shown in Fig 6.38. The range of responses differs from 0 to 8 and the majority of scores are given in the range of 4 to 8.

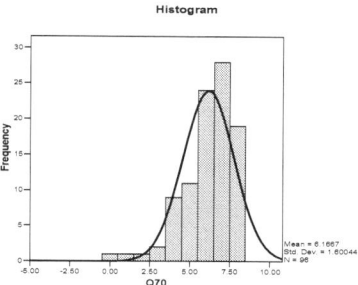

Fig 6.38 Histogram and Normal Curve for **Noise Generation by Equipments in Building**

6.2.3 Environmental Profile and Eco-efficiency

This category consists of 10 indicators which the questionnaire survey showed, are very important in establishing an eco-building design. All of the existing indicators the existing indicators in this category have an average weighted mean value more than 6.00 which proves that all of them should be considered as eco-indicators in the process of eco-building design. The findings of each indicator of this group is presented and described in following section.

1. Green House Effect

This item has a mean value of 6.97 and S.D. of 1.38 and is strongly is considered as an eco-indicator. Statistics show that 48 responses assigned a score of 8, 19 a score of 7, 19 a score of 6, 5 a score of 5, 2 a score of 4, 1 a score of 3, 1 a score of 2, 1 a score of 1 for this indicator. Overall this indicator was assumed as an eco-indicator by 86 (89.58%) respondents and as a potential eco-indicator by 8 (8.33%) of them and as a non eco-indicator by 2 (2.08%) respondents as well. The information obtained from questionnaire survey on this indicator is presented in Fig 6.39.

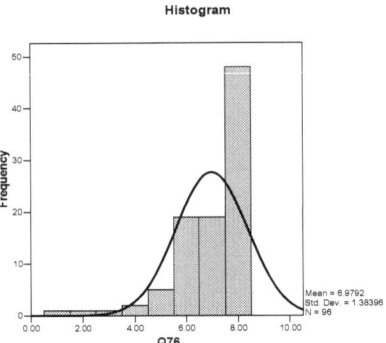

Fig 6.39 Histogram and Normal Curve for **Green House Effect (Q76)**

As shown in the Fig 6.39 the majority of responses belong to the range of 6 to 8. This fact proves that there is a strong agreement in responses rate on this eco-indicator.

2. Ozone Layer

This indicator with the mean value of 6.91 and S.D. of 1.44 according to data obtained through questionnaire survey. The data shows that 47 respondents gave a score of 8, 18 a score of 7, 21 a score of 6, 3 a score of 5, 3 a score of 4, 2 a score of 3, 1 a score of 3, 1 a score of 2 and 1 a score of 1 to this indicator. Also the study shows that a total of 86 respondents support this indicator as an eco-indicator and 8 of them considered it as a potential eco-indicator while this indicator was accepted as a non-eco indicator by 2 respondents. The relevant statistics of this eco-indicator are illustrated in Fig 6.40. The figure shows that the majority of responses belong to the range of 6 to 8 where is considered as the score for eco-indicators. S.D. of 1.44 is also considered as a quite strong agreement among the respondents points of view presented in the questionnaire survey.

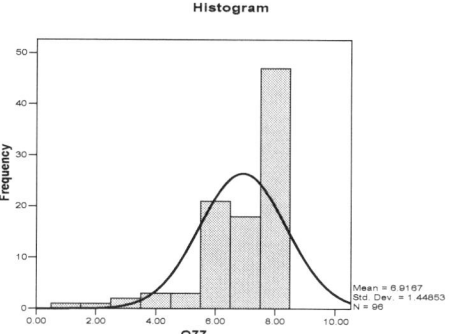

Fig 6.40 Histogram and Normal Curve for **Ozone Layer (Q77)**

3. More Efficient Use of Water

This indicator with a mean value of 6.86 and S.D. of 1.28 seems to be one of the most indicators of this group. Statistical records of survey indicates that this indicator was given a score of 8 by 42 respondents of the questionnaire, a score of 7 by 22 of them, a score of 6 by 16 respondents, a score of 5 by 10 of them, a score of 4 by 5 of them, and a score of 3 by one of them. A total of 80 (83.3%) respondents out of 96 accepted this indicator as an eco-indicator while the rest of 16 (16.6%) respondents assumed it as a potential eco-indicator. The results of survey are presented in Fig 6.41.

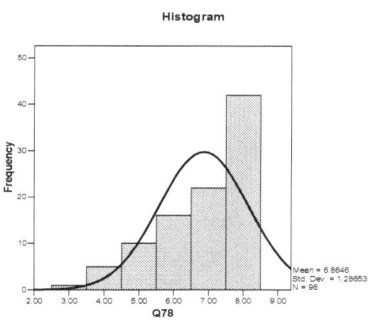

Fig 6.41 Histogram and Normal Curve for **More Efficient Use of Water (Q78)**

4. Energy Consumption

This indicator includes the mean value of 7.39 and S.D. of 0.87 in the Table 6.1, showing a high level of agreement among respondents towards this indicator. Findings in Table 6.1 mention that 60 respondents have given a score of 8, 17 a score of 7, 16 a score of 6, 3 a score of 5, to this indicator in their assessments. All the scores in scaling are more than 5. Also Table 7.1 shows that 93 participants (96.87%) assumed this indicator as an eco-indicator whereas 3 (3.12%) of them treat it as a non eco-indicator. Fig 6.42, presenting the related data is illustrated in the next stage.

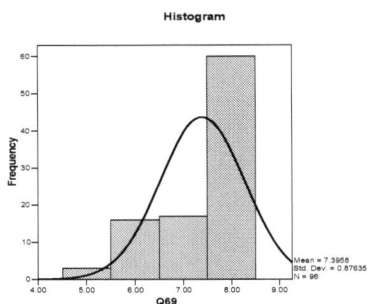

Fig 6.42 Histogram and Normal Curve for **Energy Consumption (Q79)**

5. Air Pollution

Air pollution eco-indicator has a mean of 7.17 and a S.D. of 1.32 in this survey. The statistics obtained indicates that 56 respondents gave a score of 8, 20 of them a score of 7, 12 of them a score of 6, 2 of them a score of 5, 3 of them a score of 4, 1 of them a score of 3, 2 of them a score of 2 to the indicator. A total of 88 participants (91.6%) accepted as an eco-indicator, 6 (6.25%) respondents as a potential eco-indicator and 1 (1.04%) as a non eco-indicator. The findings about this eco-indicator are presented in Fig 6.43. As it is seen in figure the range of responses differs from 2 to 8, with the score of 3 as the lowest and score of 8 as the highest in quantity. Also it is shown that the majority of responses belong to the range of 6 to 8 which is known as the area for eco-indicators.

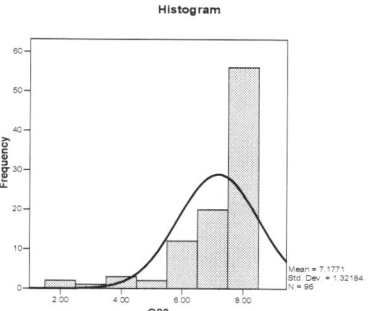

Fig 6.43 Histogram and Normal Curve for **Air Pollution (Q80)**

6. Water Pollution

This indicator has a mean value of 7.09 and S.D. of 1.33 which make it as one of the most important eco-indicators in this study. Based on questionnaire data 51 participants gave a score of 8, 21 a score of 7, 17 a score of 6, 3 a score of 5, 1 a score of 3, 3 a score of 2 to this indicator. According to information presented in Table 6.1, a total of 89 respondents (92.7%) selected this indicator as an eco-indicator and 4 (4.16%) assumed it as a potential eco-indicator while 3 (3.12%) of them accepted it as a non eco-indicator. The illustration of findings is shown in Fig 6.44.

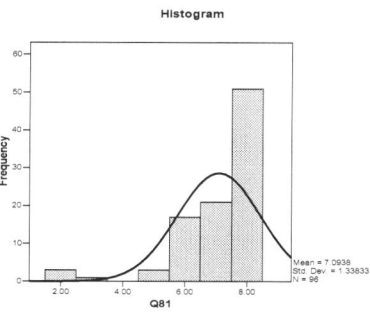

Fig 6.44 Histogram and Normal Curve for **Water Pollution (Q81)**

As illustrated in Fig 6.44, the majority of responses are related to the scores in the range of 6 to 8 which is considered as the eco-indicator zone.

7. Earth Pollution

This indicator in this study has obtained a mean value of 6.95 and S.D. of 1.37 and is recognized as one of the main eco-indicators regarding eco-building design. In total 45 respondents of the survey out of 96 gave a score of 8, 24 a score of 7, 17 a score of 6, 4 a score of 5, 3 a score of 4 and 3 a score of 2 to this indicator. This indicator was selected as an eco-indicator by 86 participants (89.58%) and as a potential eco-indicator by 7 participants (7.29%) while just 3 individuals (3.12%) accepted it as a non eco-indicator. The findings for this eco-indicator are shown in Fig 6.45.

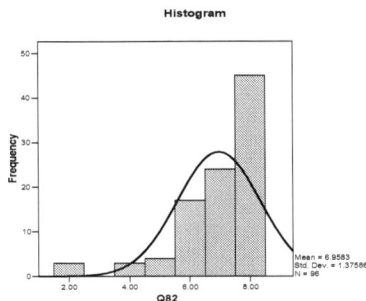

Fig 6.45 Histogram and Normal Curve for **Earth Pollution (Q82)**

As histogram shows, the majority of responses are located in the range of 6 to 8 and score 8 has the highest number among the all scores. Also the distribution of participants' responses has a strong proof in acceptance of this indicator as an eco-indicator.

8. Ecological Deterioration

This indicator has a mean value of 6.61 and S.D. of 1.37 among the other indicators and is recognized as an eco-indicator in eco-building design. The study of indicators shows that 34 respondents gave a score of 8, 28 a score of 7, 19 a score of 6, 2 a score of 5, 8 a score of 4, 2 a score of 3, 2 a score of 2 and 1 a score of 1 to this indicator which in total assign it as an eco-indicator. The overall result of the survey shows that 81 participants of research accepted this indicator as an eco-indicator and 12 participants assumed it as a potential eco-indicator while 3 of them called it as a non eco-indicator. The findings are shown in Fig 6.46 regarding this eco-indicator.

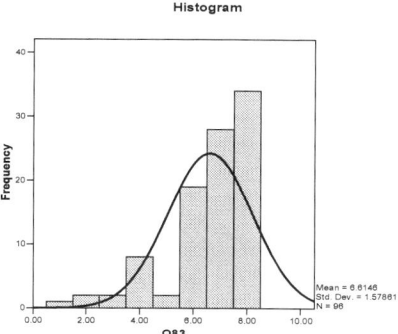

Fig 6.46 Histogram and Normal Curve for **Ecological Deterioration (Q83)**

The figure shows a big difference between the rates of responses located in the range 6 to 8 compared to other ranges of responses. As it is shown the illustration of data is also demonstrating that this indicator is accepted by majority of participants as an eco-indicator.

9. Landfills

This indicator has gained a mean value of 6.58 and S.D. of 1.47 among the research indicators and was assigned as an eco-indicator for this research. The survey demonstrates that 34 respondents gave a score of 8, 21 a score of 7, 22 a score of 6, 9 a score of 5, 7 a score of 4, 2 a score of 3 and 1 a score of 2 to this indicator. As an overall this indicator was selected by 77 respondents (80.20%) as an eco-indicator and as a potential eco-indicator by 18 (18.75%) of them and was either by one of participants (1.04%). The findings for this eco-indicator are illustrated in Fig 6.47.

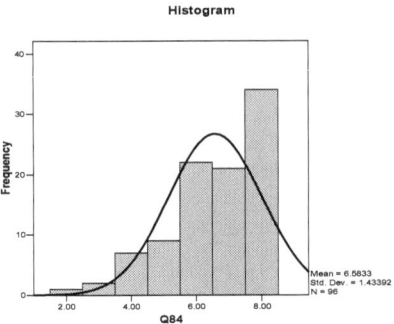

Fig 6.47 Histogram and Normal Curve for **Landfills (Q84)**

10. Solid Residues

Solid residues are considered as an eco-indicator which carries a mean value of 6.33 and S.D. of 1.52 in this survey. 28 respondents gave a score of 8, 20 a score of 7, 24 a score of 6, 10 a score of 5, 10 a score of 4, 2 a score of 3, and 2 a score of 2 to this indicator. Overall this indicator was selected by 72 respondents as an eco-indicator and by 22 of respondents as a potential eco-indicator while 2 respondents chose it as a non eco-indicator in their responses. The summary of findings is demonstrated in Fig 6.48.

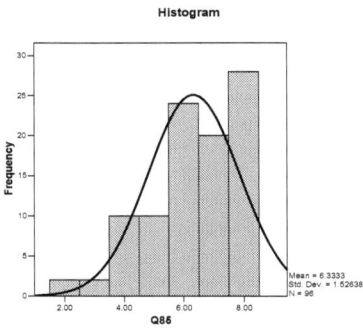

Fig 6.48 Histogram and Normal Curve for **Solid Residues (Q85)**

As illustrated in the figure the majority of responses belong to the range of 4 to 8, and score 8 has the highest number of respondents among other scores. The figure shows that this indicator is accepted as an eco-indicator among respondents concerning the demonstration of bars related to range of 6 to 8 in the figure.

6.2.4 Energy and Resources Consumption

This category embraces 14 indicators and as it is presented in Table 6.1, all of its indicators carry a mean value more than 5 and totally 12 indicators out of 14 which have the mean value of bigger than 6, are considered as eco-indicators of this category. The findings about this group's indicators are presented and reported in the following sections.

1. Natural Light

This indicator including mean value of 7.13 and S.D. of 1.09 is introduced as an eco-indicator in this category. A total of 46 respondents gave a score of 8, 29 a score of 7, 14 a score of 6, 3 a score of 5, 3 a score of 4 and 1 a score of 3 to this indicator. In total this indicator was accepted as an eco-indicator by 89 participants (92.7%) and as a potential eco-indicator by 7 of them (7.29%). The findings are illustrated in Fig 7.49. In Fig 6.49 the distribution of data shows that the majority of responses belong to the range of 6 to 8.

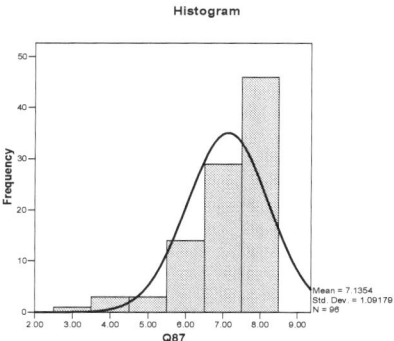

Fig 6.49 Histogram and Normal Curve for **Natural Light (Q86)**

2. Passive Heating

Passive heating is another eco-indicator found in this group with the mean value of 7.04 and S.D. of 0.98 according to survey data obtained. A total of 39 respondents out of 96 gave a score of 8, 30 a score of 7, 20 a score of 6, 6 a score of 5 and 1 a score of 4 to this indicator. This indicator was distinguished as an eco-indicator by 89 (92.7%) respondents in this research and was selected as a potential eco-indicator by 7 of them (7.29%) as well. The high mean and S.D. of 0.98 are the proofs that show there is a strong agreement among responses of participants. Also the aforementioned S.D. demonstrates a condensed distribution of responses in the range of 6 to 8. These facts are presented and shown in Fig 6.50.

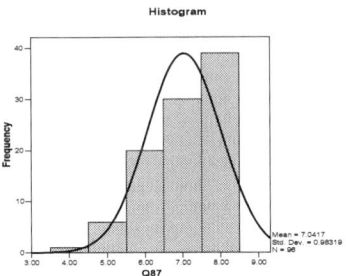

Fig 6.50 Histogram and Normal Curve for **Passive Heating (Q87).**

3. Natural Ventilation

This indicator has a mean value of 7.17 and S.D. of 0.97 and is considered as another eco-indicator of eco-building design. The survey shows that a total of 46 respondents gave a score of 8, 29 a score of 7, 14 a score of 6, 6 a score of 5 and 1 a score of 4 to this indicator. Also none of respondents selected a score of less than 4 for this indicator. As an overall the research indicates that 89 individuals (92.7%) accepted this indicator as an eco-indicator whereas 7 (7.29%) respondents assumed it as a potential eco-indicator. The Fig 6.51 shows the findings of the study.

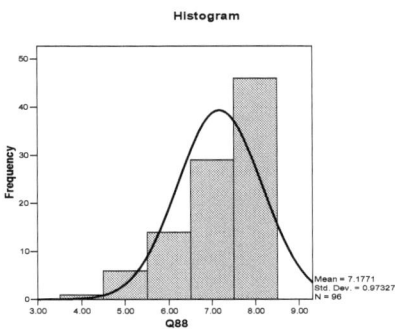

Fig 6.51 Histogram and Normal Curve for **Natural Ventilation (Q88)**

4. Passive Cooling

This indicator carries a mean value of 6.93 and a S.D. of 1.18 in this survey. Table 7.1 also shows that 37 respondents gave a score of 8 and 34 a score of 7, 15 a score of 6, 3 a score of 5, 6 a score of 4 and 1 a score of 3 to this indicator. As an overall it is shown that a total of 86 (89.58%) of respondents accepted this indicator as an eco-indicator and 10 respondents (10.41%) considered it as a potential eco-indicator. The result of findings is graphically presented in Fig 6.52. As shown, the majority of responses are placed in the range of 6 to 8 in this questionnaire survey.

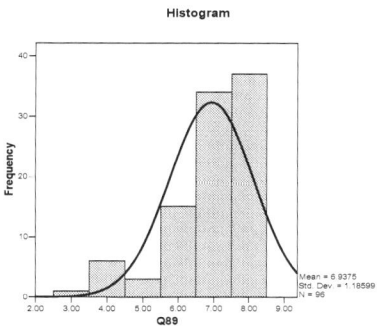

Fig 6.52 Histogram and Normal Curve for **Passive Cooling (Q89)**

5. Insulation and Airtight ness

Another eco-indicator of this group is insulation and air tightness indicator with the mean of 7.12 and S.D. of 1.19 based on the questionnaire survey findings. Table 6.1 shows that 49 respondents gave the score of 8, 28 the score of 7, 19 the score of 6, 6 the score of 5, 8 the score of 4 and 2 the score of 3 to this indicator. In summary it is concluded that a total of 85 participants (88.53%) selected this indicator as an eco-indicator while it was assumed as a potential eco-indicator by 11 respondents (11.45%) in this research. Fig 6.53 illustrates the findings.

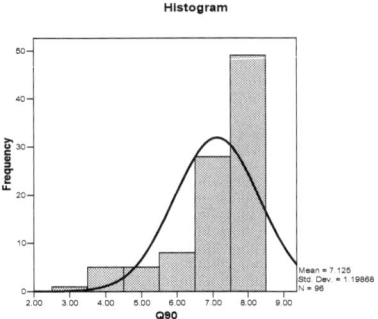

Fig 6.53 Histogram and Normal Curve for **Insulation and Airtight ness (Q90)**

6. Water Saving Devices

This indicator is distinguished as an eco-indicator in its group, presenting mean value of 6.68 and S.D. of 1.34 due to questionnaire responses. 33 of respondents have given a score of 8, 28 a score of 7, 19 a score of 6, 6 a score of 5, 8 a score of 4 and 2 a score of 3 to this indicator. Totally it can be seen in table 6.1 that a total of 80 respondents out of 96 (83.3%) agreed that this indicator should be considered as an eco-indicator and 16 of them (16.7%) accepted it as a potential eco-indicator. Fig 6.54 illustrates the related data.

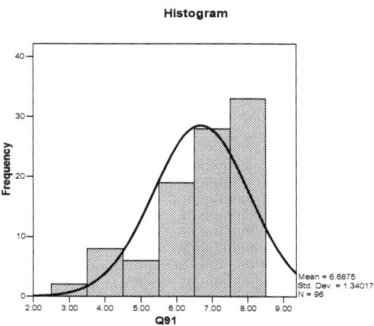

Fig 6.54 Histogram and Normal Curve for **Water Saving Devices (Q91)**

7. Biomass

Biomass is one of the eco-indicators of this group which has a mean value of 6.07 and S.D. of 1.52 based on data obtained through this survey. Also the study indicates that 20 of respondents gave a score of 8 whereas 22 a score of 7, 24 a score of 6, 11 a score of 5, 14 a score of 4, 4 a score of 3 and 1 a score of 2 to this indicator. As a result of report this indicator was selected by 66 respondents of survey (68.75%) as an eco-indicator and by 29 respondents (30.20%) as a potential eco-indicator and by 1 respondent (1.04%) as a non eco-indicator. Fig 6.55 illustrates the findings of the survey.

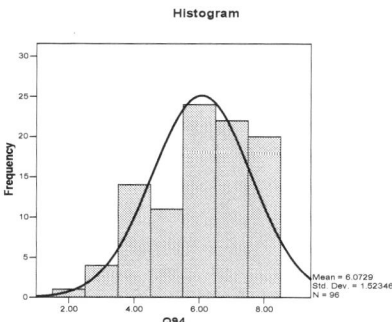

Fig 6.55 Histogram and normal Curve for **Biomass (Q94)**

8. Low Embodied Energy

This indicator with the mean value of 6.48 and S.D. of 1.45, extracted from Table 6.1 is one of the eco-indicators presented by this group. The data shows that 26 respondents gave a score of 8, 31 a score of 7, 21 a score of 6, 6 a score of 5, 8 a score of 4, 2 a score of 3 and 2 a score of 2 to this indicator. As an overall this indicator was selected as an eco-indicator by 78 participants out of 96 (81.25%) and as a potential eco-indicator by 16 (16.6%) participants and as a non eco-indicator by 2 respondents (2.08). Fig 6.56 illustrates the findings of the survey.

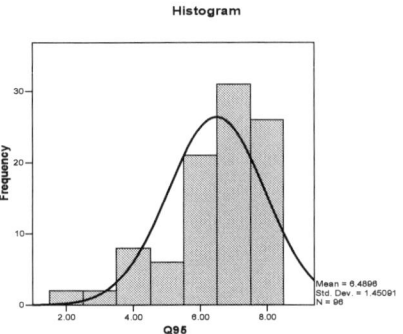

Fig 6.56 Histogram and Normal Curve for **Low Embodied Energy (Q95)**

9. Energy and Eco-efficient Design

This eco-indicator has a quite high mean value of 7.31 and S.D. of 0.94 which means it is supported by majority of the respondents as an eco-indicator in this research. The survey shows that 50 respondents gave a score of 8, 34 a score of 7, 7 a score of 6, 3 a score of 5, 1 a score of 4 and 1 a score of 3 to this indicator in their questionnaires. In total 91 participants selected this item as an eco-indicator whereas 5 respondents chose it as a potential eco-indicator. Fig 6.57 illustrates the distribution of responses and shows the normal curve related to this eco-indicator.

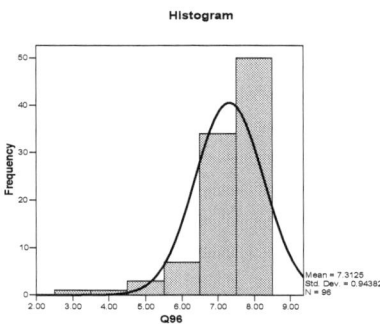

Fig 6.57 Histogram and Normal Curve for **Energy and Eco-efficient Design (Q96)**

Fig 6.57 shows that there is a strong agreement among respondents this eco-indicator. Also as shown, the majority of scores belong to the range of 6 to 8.

10. More Energy Efficient Equipments and Appliances

This indicator was selected as an eco-indicator by a total of 83 respondents (86.45%) in this survey and was also chosen as a potential eco-indicator by 12 of respondents (12.5%) and as a non eco-indicator by 1 of them (1.04%). Data in Table 6.1 shows that 39 participants gave a score of 8, 31 a score of 7, 13 a score of 6, 7 a score of 5, 3 a score of 4, 2 a score of 3 and 1 a score of 2 to this eco-indicator. In Total this indicator was chosen as an eco-indicator which has a mean value of 6.89 and S.D. of 1.30 due to data obtained through the questionnaire survey. Fig 6.58 presents the statistical results of this study.

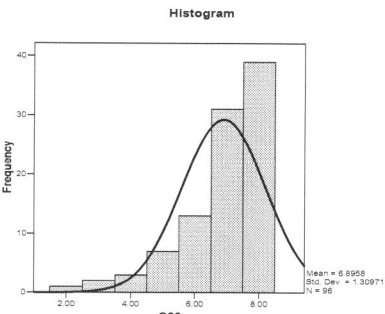

Fig 6.58 Histogram and Normal Curve for **More Energy Efficient Equipments and Appliances (Q97)**

11. Environmentally Adapted Technology

This indicator was selected as an eco-indicator by a total of 72 individuals out of 96 who participated in this research. Other 23 individuals selected this indicator as a potential eco-indicator and just one participant accepted it as a non eco-indicator. From Table 6.1 it is derived that 27 of respondents gave a score of 8, 25 a score of 7, 20 a score of 6, 8 a score of 5, 14 a score of 4, 1 a score of 3 and 1 a score of 2 to this indicator in their assessments when filling in the questionnaires. This indicator was distinguished as an eco-indicator with mean value of 6.37 and S.D. of 1.48 (See Table 6.1). More statistical illustrations are presented in Fig 6.59. In this figure the majority of responses belong to the interval between score 4 to 8.

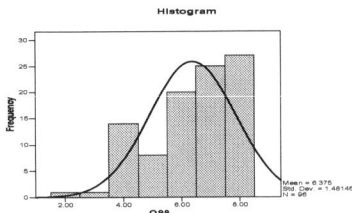

Fig 6.59 Histogram and Normal Curve for **Environmentally Adapted Technology (Q58)**

12. Healthier and Safer Energy and Resources

This indicator with the mean value of 6.37 and S.D. of 1.48 based on data gained is considered as an eco-indicator in this category. The survey shows that in total 69 individuals selected this indicator as an eco-indicator and 25 selected it as a potential eco-indicator but 2 people accepted it as a non eco-indicator. Details in Table 6.1 is also showing that 27 individuals gave a score of 8, 27 a score of 7, 15 a score of 6, 5 a score of 5, 18 a score of 4, 2 a score of 3, 2 a score of 2 to this indicator. Findings presented in Fig 6.60 illustrate the results of the questionnaire survey on this indicator.

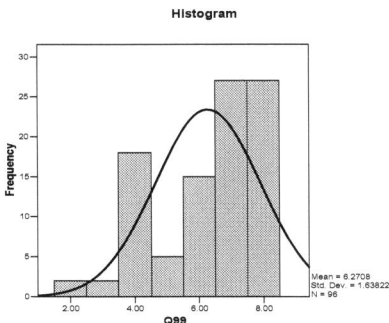

Fig 6.60 Histogram and Normal Curve for **Healthier and Safer Energy and Resources (Q99)**

6.2.5 Socio-Economics

In this category the range of mean values of indicators varies from 4.27 to 6.68 which show that this category is based on subjective assessments of participants. This fact proves that finding a consensus strategy in this category seems to be difficult. Findings and pertained data regarding the eco-indicators of this category are discussed and presented in the next stage of this research.

1. Maintenance Costs Regarding WLC

This indicator was selected as an eco-indicator of socio-economics category which has a mean value of 6.30 and S.D. of 1.48 based on data collected. 78 respondents of this survey gave scores from 6 to 8 to this indicator and selected it as an eco-indicator, and 17 of them gave a score between 3 to 5 to this indicator and assigned it as a potential eco-indicator while 3 participants looked at this indicator as a non eco-indicator and ticked a box giving scores from 0 to 2. Details of Table 6.1 also indicate that the scaling for this indicator is reported as follows:
20 individuals gave a score of 8, 28 ones a score of 7, 28 respondents a score of 6, 10 individuals a score of 5, 6 of them a score of 4, 3 individuals a score of 3, 2 a score of 2 and one a score of 0.
Fig 6.61 presents the relevant basic statistics obtained for this indicator through the questionnaire survey.

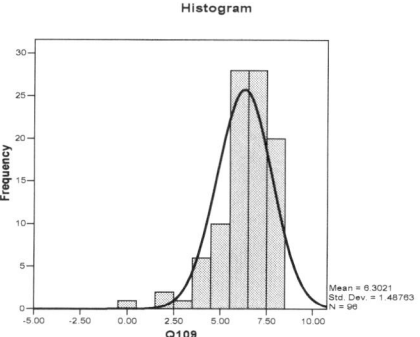

Fig 6.61 Histogram and Normal Curve for **Maintenance Costs Regarding WLC (Q109)**

2. Pollution Rehabilitation Costs Regarding WLC

This indicator was selected, as an eco-indicator by 66 respondents (68.75%) and by 27 of them (28.12%) as potential eco-indicator while 3 (3.12%) respondents accepted it as a non eco-indicator. According to details in table 6.1, 27 respondents gave a score of 8, 15 a score of 7, 31 a score of 6, 15 a score of 5, 11 a score of 4, 1 a score of 3, 2 a score of 2 and 1 a score of 1 to this indicator. This indicator was determined as an eco-indicator which has the mean value of 6.02 and S.D. of 1.52 in this research. Fig 6.62 shows the relevant data about this eco-indicator.

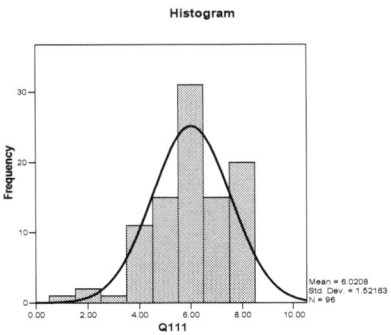

Fig 6.62 Histogram and normal Curve for **Pollution Rehabilitation Costs (Q111)**

3. Pollution Preventing Costs Regarding WLC

This indicator was selected by majority of participants as an eco-indicator in this research and carries a mean value of 6.07 and S.D. of 1.50 in this study. Overall 67 respondents selected it as an eco-indicator and 26 of them as a potential eco-indicator while 3 of respondents assigned them in non eco-indicators category. Details, shown in Table 6.1, also indicate that 20 individuals gave a score of 8, 18 a score of 7, 29 a score of 6, 14 a score of 5, 12 a score of 4, 2 a score of 2 and 1 a score of 1 to this indicator. The data are presented, and illustrated in Fig 6.63.

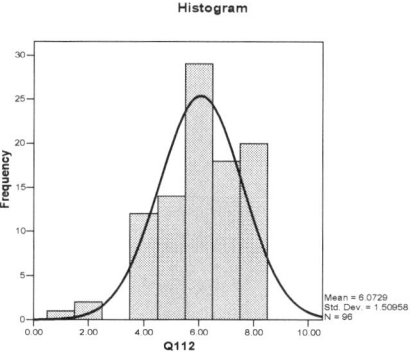

Fig 6.63 Histogram and Normal Curve for **Pollution Preventing Costs (Q112)**

4. Capital Costs/ Running Costs (Saving Running Costs)

This indicator is the most important eco-indicator in socio-economics presenting a mean value of 6.68 and a S.D. of 1.48. The survey reveals that a total of 78 respondents (81.25%) selected this indicator as an eco-indicator and 17 of them (17.70%) as a potential eco-indicator while one of them (1.04%) accepted the indicator as a non eco-indicator. Details presented in Table 6.1 also indicate that 37 participants gave a score of 8, 26 a score of 7, 15 a score of 6, 7 a score of 5, 8 a score of 4, 2 a score of 3, and 1 a score of 1 to this indicator. The Fig 6.64 presents the basic findings about this indicator through questionnaire survey.

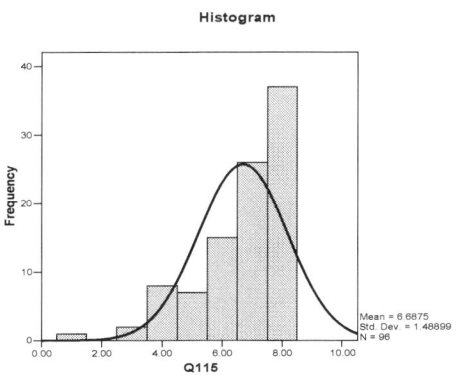

Fig 6.64 Histogram and Normal Curve for **Saving Running Costs (Q115)**

As shown in the figure the majority of scores belong to the range of 4 to 8, but the high level of effects are made by the scores in range of 6 to 8. Also 38.54% of survey population accepted that this indicator should be given a score of 8.

6.3 Conclusions

The eco-indicators were introduced, discussed and described based on the findings through the questionnaire survey handled in this work with participation of 96 representatives of different architectural practices in the UK. According to statistical data obtained based on practicing architects and related professions the indicators of the eco-building design were assessed and scaled based on practicing architects points of view regarding their experience in building design towards sustainable building. The results provided in this chapter have distinguished how many and which of the indicators are assumed as eco-indicators and should be taken into account. The data obtained are applied for development of study in the next stages such as data ranking, factor analysis and data reductions and the development of a model for eco-building design assessment in the next chapters. The gained information through this vast questionnaire survey establishes a great and reliable foundation for development of the study. The credit of research is based and set on findings obtained in this section and the overall results of this study are criticised, evaluated on this part of study. Hence, the existence of a set of reliable data and findings in this section can guarantee the success of the work.

CHAPTER 7[*]

Eco-Design Indicators Knowledge Organisation

7.1 Introduction

Identification of eco-building design indicators and evaluation of their level of influence play an essential role in sustainable building design. Ranking is related to having a list of eco-indicators which are ranked in order based on their importance, so that a user or researcher does not need to search entire set of data to follow the trend of survey. The obvious need to ranking is when researchers are faced with huge set of the data. Ranking provides researchers with both saving time and analysing accurately the findings from their research. It might also help researchers in making decision to select between similar eco-indicators. Ranking plays a pivotal role in this study because of the large number of eco-indicators involved in this research.

This chapter examines how to use statistical techniques to rank the data obtained from a questionnaire, embracing 115 questions in four different categories (See chapter 6), distributed among experienced experts in the field of sustainable building design. Statistical methods were employed to analyse the questionnaire. In this research the method of evaluation and ranking is based on statistical features such as: average weighted mean, standard deviation, coefficient of variance, and severity indices. To carry out the ranking task, SPSS and Microsoft Excel programs are used. Eco-indicators are ranked within each category, sub-category and overall. The process findings and discussions are presented in following sections.

7.2 Methodology of Study

Priority ranking is carried out, based on a questionnaire survey which was commissioned among practicing architects based in the UK. The questionnaire used in this study was designed based on literature review, authors' experience and brainstorming. 115 indicators were extracted and used to develop a questionnaire. The questionnaire on *eco-building design indicators* consists of four clusters. Each cluster is divided into subcategories and attributes as illustrated in Fig 7.1 and Fig 7.2. The cluster and their subcategories are presented as:

---

[*]**Note**: *The main part of this chapter was published in the journal of Architecture by Routledge (Vakili-Ardebili and Boussabaine. 2007).*

1. **Building Design Factors**
   - Function
   - Space
   - Form
   - Technology

2. **Environmental Profile and Eco-Efficiency Factors**
   - Atmospheric Environmental Impacts
   - Resources Environmental Impacts

3. **Energy and Resources Factors**
   - Energy Efficiency
   - Environmental Benefits

4. **Socio-Economic Factors**
   - Social Aspects
   - Economical Aspects
   -

The hierarchy and structure of the questionnaire are presented in Fig 7.1, and Fig 7.2.

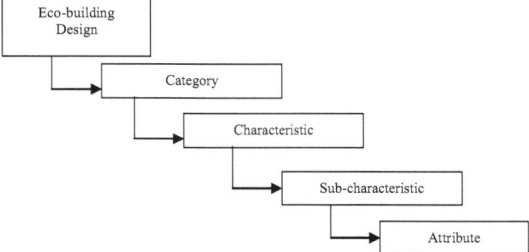

Fig 7.1 Hierarchy in the Questionnaire

Fig 7.1 illustrates the questionnaire's hierarchy. Eco-building design is divided into four main categories. Each category consists of a number of eco-characteristics containing a number of sub-characteristics which may include some attributes. For example performance is an attribute related to durability whereas durability is a sub-characteristic of function. Function itself is a characteristic of building design category.

Fig 7.2 illustrates the existing hierarchy and structure of eco-building design indicators in detail. In Fig 7.2 eco-building design category is divided into four main groups namely: building design, environmental profile, energy and resources and socio-economics.

As shown in Fig 7.2, building design profile consists of 75 indicators divided into four characteristics; function, space, form and technology. The second category relates to the environmental profile and embraces 10 attributes divided into two main sub-characteristics of atmospheric and resources impacts. These are parts of environmental impacts characteristic. The third category in eco-building design is energy and resources consumption profile embracing 14 attributes. This is part of the main characteristics of energy efficiency and environmental benefits. The fourth category of eco-building design is related to socio-economical with 16 attributes. The category includes two main characteristics of social aspects and economical aspects, each containing 8 attributes.

The classification of attributes, characteristics and their categories are presented in Fig 7.2. Based on this classification, a questionnaire and data were formed and collected to carry out this research (See chapter 5).

CHAPTER 7: ECO-DESIGN INDICATORS KNOWLEDGE ORGANISATION

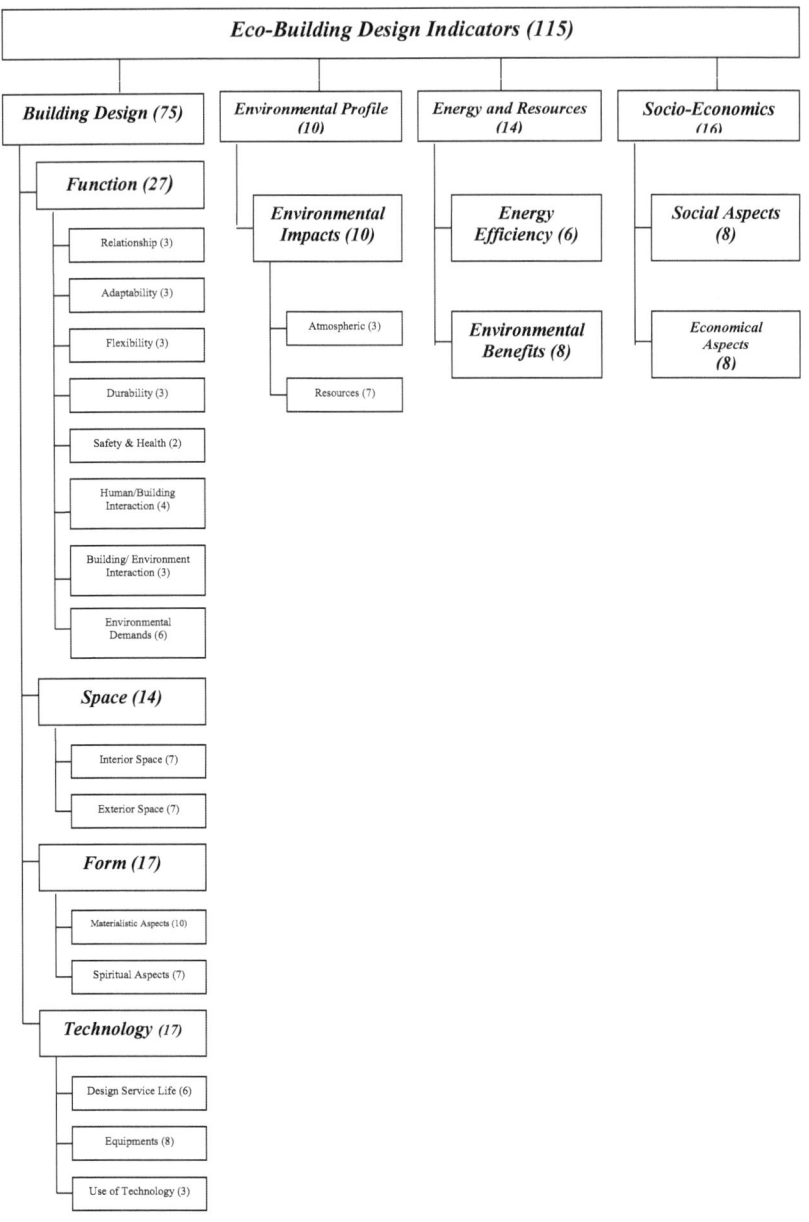

Fig 5.2 Eco-Indicators Questionnaire Structure

For assessing the degree of influence of each variable a nine-point scale (See Fig 5.1 and Chapter 5) is used.

The degree of significance varies form 0 (not significant) to 8 (very significant).
Scores 0, 1, 2 stand for *not eco significant*
Scores 3, 4, 5 stand for *moderately eco significant* (Point 4 is the neutral point)
And scores 6, 7, 8 stand for *highly eco significant.*

7.3 Analysis and Ranking of Eco-indicators

A mean weighted rating for each eco-indicator is computed to indicate the importance of each indicator, using equation (7.1). Since the rating range varies from 0 to 8, therefore point 4 is assumed as the neutral point.

Mean weighted rating = $(\sum R \times F) \div n$ equation (7.1)
Where:
         R = Rating of each indicator (0, 1, 2, ..., 6, 7, 8)
         F = Frequency of responses
         n = Total number of responses (in this research n = 96)

Severity index (S.I.) measure is employed in order to rank the indicators according to their significance. Equation (7.2) presents how S.I. is calculated:

$S.I. = [(\sum W \times F) \div n] \times 100\%$ equation (7.2)
Where:
         W = Weight for each rating (0, 1/8, 2/8, ..., 6/8, 7/8, 8/8)
         F = Frequency of responses
         n = Total number of responses (in this research n = 96)

The calculations of weighted mean and severity indices of indicators are presented in Tables 7.1 to Table 7.7.

7.4 Measuring Architects Concordance

Expression of standard deviation (SD) as a percentage of the mean, is called Coefficient of Variation (COV), and is helpful for comparing relative variability of various responses. It is computed through equation (8.3).

$COV = (S \div M) \times 100\%$ equation (7.3)

Where:

S = Standard Deviation

M = Weighted mean of sample

The calculations of COVs are presented in Tables 7.1 to Table 7.7.

Kendall's coefficient of concordance (W): it is described by SPSS 12.0.1 (2003); "Kendall's W is interpretable as the coefficient of concordance, which is a measure of agreement among raters. Each case is a judge or rater and each variable is an item or person being judged. For each variable, the sum of ranks is computed. Kendall's (W) ranges between 0 (no agreement) and 1 (complete agreement)." Also Kendall's W can be computed via equation (7.4) as following: (Siegel and Castellan, 1987)

$W = 12 \times S \div K^2 \times n \times (n^2 - 1)$ equation (7.4)

Where:

S = sum of squares of deviations of eco-indicators

K = number of quantity surveyors groups

n = number of eco-indicators in each category

SPSS software was used to carry out kendall's concordance test. The results are shown in Table 7.8. Also the correlation between different eco-indicators within each category can be computed through techniques in SPSS such:

Pearson correlation, Spearman's rho, and Kendall's tau_b.

7.5 Ranking Based on Statistical Data

Tables 7.1 to 7.7 illustrate statistical ranking results based on mean and standard deviation of eco-indicators. In the tables attribute, characteristic, category and overall rankings of each eco-indicator are presented. The ranking in this research is based on the magnitude of severity indices. The discussions and results of ranking are explained in the following sections.

7.5.1 Building Design

This category contains four characteristics namely: function, space, form, and technology. Each of these characteristics is separately scored and ranking is carried out on each eco-indicator. The first 30 ranked eco-indicators (a quarter of indicators) are selected from overall ranking column and presented in Table 7.8. The table shows the most important indicators of eco-building design out of the 115 indicators.

7.5.1.1 Function

Table 7.1 portrays function attributes. Function as a characteristic of building design category consists of 8 sub-characteristics and embraces 27 eco-indicators (See the questionnaire). The average weighted mean in this group varies from 4.90 to 7.21. This score is higher than neutral point (4.00). Also the severity indices vary from 61.32% to 90.23%, which indicates their level of importance. As it can be seen in Table 7.1 four eco-indicators (Q27, Q6, Q26, and Q11) are the highest ranked amongst this group. Q27 (*Energy and Eco-efficiency* indicator, part of Environmental Demands characteristic) with an overall ranking of 4 and severity index of 90.23% is the highest ranked indicator in this cluster. An overall examination of the table indicates that all eco-indicators carry a value more than neutral score, meaning that all of them seem to be important in eco-building design as viewed by respondents.

Table 7.1 *Building Design Category – Function Attributes*

Question	Mean	Std. Deviation	Coefficient of variation	Severity index	Attribute Ranking	Characteristic Ranking	Category Ranking	Overall Ranking
Q1	5.0833	2.03479	40.02891822	63.54125	2	25	61	95
Q2	5.0625	1.9184	37.89432099	63.28125	3	26	62	96
Q3	5.1562	1.88249	36.509251	64.4525	1	24	60	94
Q4	6.1771	1.45815	23.60573732	77.21375	3	6	21	44
Q5	6.3125	1.51005	23.92158416	78.90625	2	5	18	39
Q6	6.9688	1.40265	20.12756859	87.11	1	2	6	15
Q7	6.1042	1.48309	24.29622227	76.3025	1	8	25	48
Q8	6.0312	1.44698	23.99157713	75.39	2	9	26	51
Q9	5.3542	1.71052	31.94725636	66.9275	3	22	56	89
Q10	5.9896	1.76214	29.41999466	74.87	2	10	29	55
Q11	6.6979	1.29061	19.26887532	83.72375	1	4	14	28
Q12	5.5	2.02614	36.83890909	68.75	3	20	49	81
Q13	5.8229	1.92488	33.05706778	72.78625	1	12	36	65
Q14	5.5208	2.08745	37.81064339	69.01	2	19	48	80
Q15	5.7708	1.72584	29.90642545	72.135	3	15	39	68
Q16	5.5417	2.02051	36.46011152	69.27125	4	18	47	79
Q17	5.875	1.9695	33.52340426	73.4375	1	11	32	59
Q18	5.7812	1.66198	28.74801079	72.265	2	14	38	67
Q19	6.125	1.4455	23.6	76.5625	1	7	24	47
Q20	5.7917	1.58225	27.31926723	72.39625	2	13	37	66
Q21	5.4375	1.69713	31.21158621	67.96875	3	21	52	85
Q22	5.3333	1.96102	36.76935481	66.66625	5	23	57	90
Q23	5.7292	1.76802	30.85980591	71.615	4	17	42	71
Q24	5.75	1.81804	31.61808696	71.875	3	16	40	69
Q25	4.9063	1.78342	36.34959134	61.32875	6	27	65	100
Q26	6.8646	1.51914	22.13005856	85.8075	2	3	8	21
Q27	7.2188	1.18057	16.35410318	90.235	1	1	2	4

The overall ranking of this indicator (Q27= energy and eco-efficiency indicator) is 4 out of 115, in category ranking it is 2 out of 75 (number of indicators in building design category), in characteristic ranking is 1 out of 27 (number of indicators in function characteristic), and in attribute ranking is 1 out of 6 (number of indicators in function sub-characteristic; here *Environmental Demands* is considered as a sub-characteristic of function characteristic in the questionnaire). This indicator carries a severity index of 90.23%, a coefficient of variation of 16.35%, standard deviation of 1.18 and average weighted mean of 7.21. Accordingly this indicator is deemed to be the most important eco-indicator in the design process of sustainable buildings.

7.5.1.2 Space

Space is the second characteristic of building design category, includes 2 sub-categories and 14 attributes. *Interior Spaces* and *Exterior Spaces* are the two main sub-characteristics associated with this group. Table 7.2 presents all statistical results and rankings of this group.

As shown in Table 7.2, the range of average weighted mean changes from 4.50 to 7.10 (all attributes present a mean higher than neutral point = 4.00). Severity indices range from 56.25% to 88.80%. The highest ranks belong to Q37 (Building Orientation) and Q38 (Climate), presenting severity indices of 88.80% and 85.15% with an overall rank of 11 and 23 out of 115. In category ranking, they are ranked 5 and 9 out of 75, in characteristic ranking, ranked of 1 and 2 out of 14. The high means and severity indices illustrated for these two eco-indicators in the table are strong proofs for their importance in eco-building design. The finding in this part confirms the points quoted by researcher such as Roaf et al. (2001), smith (2001) and Langston and Ding (1997 and 2001) in their books that building orientation and design according to climate characteristics are significantly important in sustainable design.

Table 7.2 *Building Design Category – Space Attributes*

Question	Mean	Std. Deviation	Coefficient of variation	Severity index	Attribute Ranking	Characteristic Ranking	Category Ranking	Overall Ranking
Q28	4.6562	1.96725	42.25011812	58.2025	6	13	70	106
Q29	5.9063	1.54972	26.23842338	73.82875	1	4	31	57
Q30	4.5	1.95206	43.37911111	56.25	7	14	72	109
Q31	5.75	1.84676	32.11756522	71.875	3	6	40	69
Q32	5.0521	1.59848	31.63991212	63.15125	5	12	63	97
Q33	5.8542	1.61558	27.59693895	73.1775	2	5	33	60
Q34	5.2083	1.65381	31.75335522	65.10375	4	11	58	91
Q35	5.6979	1.79543	31.51038102	71.22375	4	7	43	73
Q36	6.0104	1.53893	25.60445228	75.13	3	3	27	53
Q37	7.1042	1.22671	17.26739112	88.8025	1	1	5	11
Q38	6.8125	1.48191	21.75280734	85.15625	2	2	9	23
Q39	5.4479	1.92419	35.31984801	68.09875	6	9	51	84
Q40	5.4167	1.69001	31.19999262	67.70875	7	10	54	87
Q41	5.6458	1.73496	30.73010025	70.5725	5	8	46	76

7.5.1.3 Form

Form is also a characteristic of building design category consists of 2 sub-characteristics and embraces 17 indicators. *Material Aspects*, with 10 eco-indicators, and *Spiritual Aspects* with 7 eco-indicators make up the *Form* characteristic in *building design*. Ranking results in Table 8.3 show that there is just one attribute with high ranking among these 17 attributes. In Table 8.2 Q46 (Durability of form and materials) with the mean of 6.71, and severity index of 83.98% is considered as the highest ranked indicator in the group. An overall ranking of 25 out of 115, category ranking of 11 out of 75, characteristic ranking 1 out of 17, and attribute ranking 1 out of 10.

The result obtained in this part proves that design for durability has always been value for designers and the majority of architects and designers believe that durable buildings are those which conserve design values for longer time. Durability in design deals with technological characteristics and detailing, materials selection, components exploitation and use which should be tackled by architects while addressing durability issue.

Table 7.3 *Building Design Category – Form Attributes*

Question	Mean	Std. Deviation	Coefficient of variation	Severity index	Attribute Ranking	Characteristic Ranking	Category Ranking	Overall Ranking
Q42	5.3646	1.61649	30.13253551	67.0575	8	9	55	88
Q43	6.3021	1.24917	19.82148808	78.77625	4	4	19	40
Q44	5.2083	1.86895	35.88406966	65.10375	9	10	58	91
Q45	5.4375	1.72787	31.77691954	67.96875	7	8	52	85
Q46	6.7188	1.11169	16.54596059	83.985	1	1	11	25
Q47	6.4063	1.47668	23.05043473	80.07875	2	2	16	35
Q48	5.8542	1.47241	25.15134433	73.1775	6	6	33	60
Q49	6.3229	1.43266	22.65827389	79.03625	3	3	17	38
Q50	4.7708	1.94925	40.85792739	59.635	10	14	68	103
Q51	6.1563	1.82571	29.65596219	76.95375	5	5	23	46
Q52	4.7604	2.13613	44.87290984	59.505	5	15	69	104
Q53	3.7083	2.37051	63.92443977	46.35375	6	16	74	114
Q54	2.8021	2.26469	80.82116984	35.02625	7	17	75	115
Q55	4.875	2.30902	47.36451282	60.9375	4	13	67	102
Q56	5.4896	2.25713	41.11647479	68.62	1	7	50	82
Q57	5.0104	2.12005	42.31298898	62.63	2	11	64	98
Q58	4.9063	2.10302	42.86366508	61.32875	3	12	65	100

7.5.1.4 Technology

This group contains three sub-characteristics, namely: Design Service Life with 6 attributes, Equipments with 8 attributes, and use of technology with 3 attributes. In Table 8.4, there are 7 eco-indicators in the group which are ranked among the first 30 indicators namely: Q60 (Maintainability), Q61 (Energy- Efficiency), Q62 (Embodied Energy), Q63 (Eco-Efficiency and Recycle ability), Q64 (Reliability), Q68 (pollution Generation), and Q69 (Environmentally Adopted Technology). These eco-indicators' means range from 6.70 to 7.44. Also their severity indices vary from 83.85% to 93.09%, presenting the highest range of severity index in the total set. Q61 (Energy efficiency, an attribute of technology characteristic) has highest mean and severity index as well as the highest overall ranking within this group.

The results obtained from this survey show that technical characteristics affecting design service life over WLC of building assets should be considered in the early design phases in order to add values to the design and building assets. The obtained results are in accordance with authors' point of view on using design strategies to add value and mitigate environmental impact risks.

Table 7.4 *Building Design Category – Technology Attributes*

Question	Mean	Std. Deviation	Coefficient of variation	Severity index	Attribute Ranking	Characteristic Ranking	Category Ranking	Overall Ranking
Q59	6.4167	1.16679	18.1836458	80.20875	6	8	15	34
Q60	6.7188	1.24565	18.53976901	83.985	4	6	11	25
Q61	7.4479	0.76598	10.28450973	93.09875	1	1	1	1
Q62	6.7813	1.28311	18.92129828	84.76625	3	5	10	24
Q63	6.9063	1.35397	19.60485354	86.32875	2	4	7	19
Q64	6.7083	1.49326	22.25988701	83.85375	5	7	13	27
Q65	6.2292	1.65739	26.60678739	77.865	3	9	20	43
Q66	5.8542	1.42148	24.28137064	73.1775	7	13	33	60
Q67	6.0104	1.46894	24.43997072	75.13	5	11	27	53
Q68	7.1146	1.14128	16.0413797	88.9325	2	3	4	10
Q69	7.1771	0.94027	13.10097393	89.71375	1	2	3	7
Q70	6.1667	1.60044	25.95294079	77.08375	4	10	22	45
Q71	5.6667	1.7086	30.15158734	70.83375	8	14	44	74
Q72	5.9792	1.62856	27.23708857	74.74	6	12	30	56
Q73	5.6667	1.88438	33.2535691	70.83375	1	14	44	74
Q74	4.5625	2.19479	48.1049863	57.03125	2	16	71	107
Q75	4.2396	2.01439	47.51368054	52.995	3	17	73	113

7.5.2 Environmental Profile and Eco-Efficiency

Since most of environmental impacts, are caused by building processes which employ 40% of the outputs from other industries thus in this category the focus is on environmental impacts as the main motivation for the existence of eco-building design. In this study, environmental profile and eco-efficiency are definitely considered as important attributes. According to (Boussabaine and kirkham, 2004) environmental impact clusters are related to atmospheric and resources impacts. Table 7.5 presents the eco-indicators included this category. As it is illustrated in the Table 7.5, this category includes 10 eco-indicators. The score of average weighted mean for all of these indicators are very high in comparison with other categories and carry a score range from 6.33 to 7.39. Also the severity indices of this group are very high, ranging from 79.16% to 92.44%. This is a very high range in the overall ranking of eco-building design indicators. As it can be observed, the majority of attributes in this category (7 out of 10) belong to the first 30 eco-indicators out of

115 indicators. Q76 to Q82 embracing; *Green House Effect, Ozone Layer, More Efficient Use of Water, Energy Consumption, Air Pollution, Water Pollution, And Earth Pollution*, are all considered as the most important indicators within this category. The finding of this section focuses on atmospheric and resource impacts in the environment, highlighted by researchers such Langston and Ding (1997; 2001), Boussabaine and Kirkham (2004). All identified eco-indicators in this category could be clustered into three main groups. They are air, water and earth pollutions.

Table 7.5 *Environmental Profile and Eco-efficiency Category*

Question	Mean	Std. Deviation	Coefficient of variation	Severity index	Attribute Ranking	Characteristic Ranking	Category Ranking	Overall Ranking
Q76	6.9792	1.38396	19.82977992	87.24	1		4	14
Q77	6.9167	1.44853	20.94250148	86.45875	2		6	18
Q78	6.8646	1.28653	18.74151444	85.8075	5		7	21
Q79	7.3958	0.87635	11.84929284	92.4475	1		1	2
Q80	7.1771	1.32184	18.41746666	89.71375	2		2	5
Q81	7.0938	1.33833	18.86619301	88.6725	3		3	12
Q82	6.9583	1.37586	19.77293304	86.97875	4		5	16
Q83	6.6146	1.57861	23.86553987	82.6825	6		8	31
Q84	6.5833	1.43392	21.78117358	82.29125	7		9	32
Q85	6.3333	1.52638	24.10086369	79.16625	8		10	37

7.5.3 Energy and Resources

One of the main categories of eco-building design embraces the rate and type of energy and resources used in the construction of building assets. It is believed that by application of reasonable passive design strategies, energy and resources consumptions can be controlled. To do so prudent considerations of all indicators within this category is essential for achieving SBD. The category of *Energy and Resources* consists of 14 eco-indicators, divided into two main groups of *Energy Efficiency* and *Environmental Benefits*. Through observation in Table 7.6, it is perceived that 12 indicators out of 14 have the mean equal or higher than 6.07. Also it can be seen that the severity indices in this group range from 68.62% to 91.40%. Results in Table 8.6 indicate that 8 attributes out of 14 are ranked within the first 30 eco-indicators in the overall ranking. Questions Q86, Q87, Q 88, Q89, Q90, Q 91, Q96, and Q 97 namely; *Natural Light, Passive Heating, Natural Ventilation, Passive Cooling, Insulation and Air tightness, Water Saving Devices, Energy-Eco-Efficient Design, and More Energy-Efficient Equipments and Appliances*, are determined as the most significant indicators in this category. The extracted indicators are all related to environmental design strategies. The above findings confirm the view that architects think of eco-design rules in term of environmental aspects. The eco-indicators identified in this group approves that if both active and passive environmental design strategies are employed in the design phase, it might lead to a high influence on quality of design and eco-efficiency of building assets. The selected eco-indicators are also advocated by other researchers (Langston and Ding, 2001; Roaf et al. 2001, and Smith 2001).

Table 7.6 *Energy and Resources Category*

Question	Mean	Std. Deviation	Coefficient of variation	Severity index	Attribute Ranking	Characteristic Ranking	Category Ranking	Overall Ranking
Q86	7.1354	1.09179	15.30103428	89.1925	2		3	8
Q87	7.0417	0.98319	13.96239544	88.02125	4		5	13
Q88	7.1771	0.97327	13.56076967	89.71375	1		2	5
Q89	6.9375	1.18599	17.09535135	86.71875	5		6	17
Q90	7.125	1.19868	16.82357895	89.0625	3		4	9
Q91	6.6875	1.34017	20.03992523	83.59375	6		8	23
Q92	5.8542	1.77692	30.35290902	73.1775	8		13	60
Q93	5.4896	1.80055	32.79929321	68.62	9		14	82
Q94	6.0729	1.52346	25.08620264	75.91125	7		12	49
Q95	6.4896	1.45091	22.35746425	81.12	3		9	33
Q96	7.3125	0.94382	12.90694017	91.40625	1		1	3
Q97	6.8958	1.30971	18.99286522	86.1975	2		7	26
Q98	6.375	1.48146	23.23858824	79.6875	4		10	36
Q99	6.2708	1.63822	26.12457741	78.385	5		11	42

7.5.4 Socio-Economical Aspects

Socio-economical category embraces two main characteristics of eco-building design, and includes 16 eco-indicators which are shown in Table 7.7. In the overall ranking just one of these category indicators belong to the first 30 ranked eco-indicators. The highest ranking is related to Q115 (Saving Running Costs of the building). It is ranked 29 out of 115. The second important indicator in this groups is Q109 (Maintenance Costs) with an overall ranking of 40. The mean range in this category varies from 4.27 to 6.68. The severity index range changes from 50.90% to 83.49%. The result in Table 7.7, regarding socio-economical aspects indicates that there is a very superficial perception of social and economical aspects of design among surveyed architects. These could be due to their lack of understanding the impacts of these indicators on design. This might be a weakness which may cause many ambiguities, uncertainties and potential risks in SBD practices.

Table 7.7 *Socio-economic Category*

Question	Mean	Std. Deviation	Coefficient of variation	Severity index	Attribute Ranking	Characteristic Ranking	Category Ranking	Overall Ranking
Q100	5.6458	1.9627	34.76389528	70.5725	1		8	76
Q101	4.6979	2.14289	45.61378488	58.72375	4		12	105
Q102	4.2917	2.1517	50.13630962	53.64625	7		15	111
Q103	4.4896	2.04164	45.47487527	56.12	6		14	110
Q104	5.5625	2.07142	37.23901124	69.53125	2		9	78
Q105	4.9688	2.08984	42.05924972	62.11	3		11	99
Q106	4.2708	2.17391	50.9017046	53.385	8		16	112
Q107	4.5104	2.0157	44.69004966	56.38	5		13	108
Q108	5.8333	1.52638	26.16666381	72.91625	6		6	64
Q109	6.3021	1.48763	23.60530617	78.77625	2		2	40
Q110	5.8854	1.54149	26.19176267	73.5675	5		5	58
Q111	6.0208	1.52163	25.27288732	75.26	4		4	52
Q112	6.0729	1.50958	24.85764626	75.91125	3		3	49
Q113	5.7188	1.87338	32.75827097	71.485	7		7	72
Q114	5.1875	1.89355	36.50216867	64.84375	8		10	93
Q115	6.6875	1.48899	22.26527103	83.59375	1		1	29

7.6 Summary of the Findings from the Overall Ranking

The result of ranking has been presented in former parts of this chapter. Here the most important eco-indicators are extracted based on the overall ranking. Table 7.8, introduces 30 eco-indicators which are considered as the most significant ones in eco-building design based on ranking techniques used in this study. In this research severity index is considered as the best tool for ranking because of its capabilities of using average weighted mean, standard variation, and distribution of data which make it more reliable for ranking eco-indicators. The 30 extracted eco-indicators are considered as the most significant ones among 115 existing eco-indicators in this study. From the statistical average weighted mean of each indicator, it can be stated that all mean values except for 2 indicators carry values of more than 4.00 (above the neutral point) which indicates that the majority of selected indicators could be considered as eco-indicators.

The eco-indicators presented in design service life part of technology characteristic of design were confirmed by majority of the sample of surveyed architects in this research. This indicates that the degree of importance of theses indicators in the designing of eco-efficient buildings. Also functionality indicators which strongly affect the quality of building over WLC are addressed in this research. Some of the eco-indicators confirmed by surveyed architects are named as: performance, flexibility, longevity and adaptability attributes.

The results obtained are summarised in Table 7.8 below.

Table 7.8 The *30 Most Important Ranked Indicators Extracted* for Eco-Building Design

Question	Mean	Std. Deviation	Coefficient of variation	Severity index	Attribute Ranking	Characteristic Ranking	Category Ranking	Overall Ranking
Q6=Adaptability to the Environment	6.9688	1.40265	20.12756859	87.11	1	2	6	15
Q11= Performance according to Durability & Longevity	6.6979	1.29061	19.26887532	83.72375	1	4	14	28
Q26= Control of Emission	6.8646	1.51914	22.13005856	85.8075	2	3	8	21
Q27=Energy & Eco-Efficiency	7.2188	1.18057	16.35410318	90.235	1	1	2	4
Q37= Building Orientation	7.1042	1.22671	17.26739112	88.8025	1	1	5	11
Q38= Climate	6.8125	1.48191	21.75280734	85.15625	2	2	9	23
Q46= Durability (Form wise)	6.7188	1.11169	16.54596059	83.985	1	1	11	25
Q60= Maintainability	6.7188	1.24565	18.53976901	83.985	4	6	11	25
Q61= Energy Efficiency	7.4479	0.76598	10.28450973	93.09875	1	1	1	1
Q62= Embodied Energy	6.7813	1.28311	18.92129828	84.76625	3	5	10	24
Q63= Eco-Efficiency & Recylability	6.9063	1.35397	19.60485354	86.32875	2	4	7	19
Q64= Reliability	6.7083	1.49326	22.25988701	83.85375	5	7	13	27
Q68= Pollution Generation	7.1146	1.14128	16.0413797	88.9325	2	3	4	10
Q69= Environmentally Adapted Technology	7.1771	0.94027	13.10097393	89.71375	1	2	3	5
Q76= Green House Effect	6.9792	1.38396	19.82977992	87.24	1		4	14
Q77= Ozone Layer	6.9167	1.44853	20.94250148	86.45875	2		6	18
Q78= More Efficient Use of Water	6.8646	1.28653	18.74151444	85.8075	5		7	21
Q79= Energy Consumption	7.3958	0.87635	11.84929284	92.4475	1		1	2
Q80= Air Pollution	7.1771	1.32184	18.41746666	89.71375	2		2	5
Q81= Water Pollution	7.0938	1.33833	18.86619301	88.6725	3		3	12
Q82= Earth Pollution	6.9583	1.37586	19.77293304	86.97875	4		5	16
Q86= Natural Light	7.1354	1.09179	15.30103428	89.1925	2		3	8
Q87= Passive Heating	7.0417	0.98319	13.96239544	88.02125	4		5	13
Q88= Natural Ventilation	7.1771	0.97327	13.56076967	89.71375	1		2	5
Q89= Passive Cooling	6.9375	1.18599	17.09535135	86.71875	5		6	17
Q90= Insulation & Air-tightness	7.125	1.19868	16.82357895	89.0625	3		4	9
Q91= Water Saving Devices	6.6875	1.34017	20.03992523	83.59375	6		8	29
Q96= Energy-Eco-Efficient Design	7.3125	0.94382	12.90694017	91.40625	1		1	3
Q97= More Energy Efficient Equipments & Appliances	6.8958	1.30971	18.99286522	86.1975	2		7	20
Q115= Saving Running Costs	6.6875	1.48899	22.26527103	83.59375	1		1	29

7.7 Kendall's Concordance Analysis Employing SPSS

In this research *Kendall's* coefficients indicate the level of agreement between the respondents to the questionnaire on the ranking of factors influencing eco-building design. If the computed value of significance level is less than 0.05 it indicates that the null hypothesis (there is no agreement between respondents) has to be rejected (P<0.05).

The alternative hypothesis that, there is a significant agreement between respondents is acceptable with confidence of (P>95%). The statistical results of calculated coefficient of variation indicate that there is a large variation in architects' responses. Also in Table 7.9, Kendall's concordance analysis employing SPSS is presented. According to the results shown in Table 7.9 the data are reliable because the significance value is less than 0.05. Therefore there is a strong agreement between the surveyed architects.

Table 7.9 Kendall's Concordance Analysis employing SPSS

Category	Degree of Freedom (D.F.)	Chi-square	Kedall's Coefficient (W)	Asymp. Significance
Building design	74	1678.187	0.236	0.000
Environmental Profile and Eco-Efficiency	9	124.055	0.144	0.000
Energy and Resources	13	319.943	0.256	0.000
Socio-economic	15	283.741	0.197	0.000

7.8 Average Severity Indices of Eco-Building Design Category

In this work, ranking is carried out based on severity indices of attributes and their related sub-characteristics, characteristics, and categories. As it was mentioned before that there are four categories of eco-indicators, being considered in this survey, therefore in Fig 7.3 the average severity indices of each category is calculated and presented.

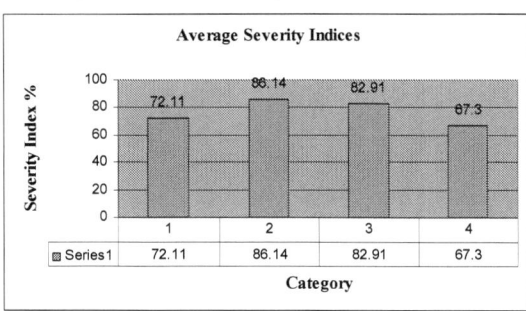

Fig 7.3 Average Severity Indices of Eco-Building Design Category

In Fig 7.3, in horizontal axis of figure, numbers 1, 2, 3, and 4 present eco-building design categories (Building Design, Environmental Profile and Eco-Efficiency, Energy and Resources, and Socio-Economic Aspects categories). The highest severity index in eco-building design belongs to category 2 (*Environmental Profile and Eco-Efficiency*) with the severity index of 86.14%, which is a significant result. The lowest one, is related to category 4 (*Socio-Economical Aspects*) with a severity index of 67.30%. The other two categories (*Building Design* and *Energy and Resources*) with severity of indices of 72.11% and 82.91% are still significant. Generally it can be said that the high range of severity indices in eco-building design attributes show that all of these categories viewed as highly significant in SBD. The lower average severity index of category 4 (*Socio-Economical Aspects*) in comparison with other categories could be because of ambiguity and uncertainty, and lack of understanding of how socio-economic factors contribute to SBD in improving the quality of life of the user. The design communities need to investigate these aspects further. The majority of attributes in this category are evaluated based on individual subjective views. The findings, illustrated in Fig 7.3, prove that all categories in eco-building design are considerably important in the design of sustainable buildings through adding eco-values.

7.9 Average Severity Indices of Building Design Characteristics

Building Design as one of the main categories, embracing 65% (75 out of 115) of total attributes, plays a pivotal role in eco-building design. Since, this category consists of four main characteristics, therefore the influence of its characteristics on eco-building design should be considered separately. Here, Fig 7.4 illustrates the influence of each characteristic based on the calculated severity indices of each building design characteristics.

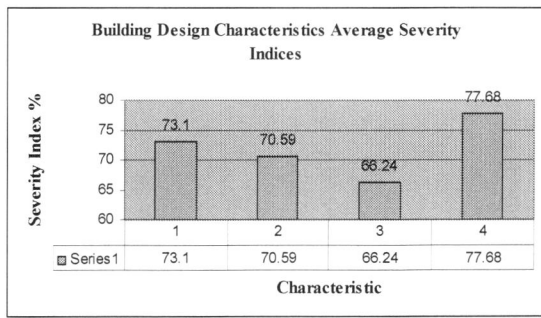

Fig 7.4 Average Severity Indices of Building Design Characteristics

Characteristics 1, 2, 3, 4, on the horizontal axis of Fig 7.4, respectively are representatives for *Function, Space, Form*, and *Technology* Characteristics in eco-building design indicators. As it is shown in the figure, the highest influence is related to characteristic 4 (*Technology*) with severity index of 77.68% while in other hand the influence of characteristic 3 (*Form*) on the building design is viewed somehow less important, with the severity index of 66.24%. In Fig 7.4 the severity index ranges from 66.24% to 77.68%. It should be stated that these values are quite high and confirms the view that these attributes are very important in the design of SB.

It can be concluded that the results shown in Fig 7.4 state that; the majority of architects rely on technology (the severity index of 77.68% for *technology* characteristic) and active design strategies to improve the eco-efficiency of building assets and rarely use passive design solutions (the severity index of 66.24% for *form* characteristic) in building design.

5.10 Conclusions

Ranking helps researchers to indicate which eco-indicators are more important. In this chapter, ranking based on severity index, average weighted mean and standard deviation of each eco-indicator were used in order to determine the degree of significance of eco-indicators in the context of eco-building design. The results of ranking are presented in Tables 7.1 to 7.8 which show the ranking of each eco-indicator. The first 30 ranked eco-indicators were presented in Table 7.8. The ranking, carried out in this research confirms that the majority of selected questions (indicators) in the designed questionnaire could be considered as eco-indicators. The majority of responses average weighted means are above the neutral point. In addition to this, the correlations between different indicators in ranking are discussed and investigated. More discussions on eco-indicators will be presented in factor analysis and data reduction chapter (8). These extracted eco-indicators will be used in factor analysis and data reduction chapter to select a set of clusters for developing an eco-building design model. (See chapters 8 and 9)

CHAPTER 8[*]

Eco-Design Indicators Combination

8.1 Introduction

The degree of significance of each eco-indicator in building design varies according to its influence on the eco-efficiency of building assets. Based on data processing and ranking in chapter 7, it is concluded that some indicators are more influential in comparison with others. A number of eco-indicators with the highest degree of significance might be considered as representative of whole set of data. Consequently the most important indicators are extracted and are treated as representative of the whole set of indicators. To achieve this aim, factor analysis and data reduction techniques are used for reducing a large number of factors into a more easily understood framework (Norusis 2000). Factor analysis is often used in data reduction to identify a small number of factors that explain most of the variance observed in a much larger number of manifest variables (SPSS 12.0.1). The outcome of this attempt is presented in a few new clusters that consist of the most important factors of the original large group (here the group is referred to the questionnaire 115 indicators). The clusters, containing the main indicators are composed based on the indicators relationship and correlations. A clear understanding of new clusters and their implications will be instrumental in the assessment of sustainable building design.

In this chapter, methodology for factor analysis and data reduction process are discussed and presented.

8.2 Research Methodology

To carry out the research the collected data were processed by two statistical procedures, namely, ***scale ranking***; presented in chapter 7 based on the mean value, Standard Deviation, coefficient of variation, and Severity index of factors in their category and in whole eco-building design indicators set. For undertaking these analyses on the data, Statistical Package for the Social Science (SPSS) and Microsoft Excel were used. The existence of 115 questions in this survey makes it difficult to handle the analysis, therefore factor analysis and data reduction are considered as an important process to decrease the number of indicators in order to handle the task more efficient.

---

[*]**Note**: *The main part of this chapter was published in the journal of Architectural Engineering and Design Management by Earthscan (Vakili-Ardebili and Boussabaine, 2010).*

This aim was achieved through application of SPSS software and as a result the redundant data is removed from the list of questions in order to obtain a manageable subset of the indicators that present the majority of eco-building design indicators. After elimination of redundant data, just 32 indicators remained, that can be presented as the representative of eco-building design indicators. They have been categorised in 6 pivotal clusters. In the next step, all evaluations and related tasks including principal component analysis, extraction of rotated component matrix, factor analysis, data reduction and categorisation are carried out on these 32 extracted indicators.

The process of the analysis is shown in Fig 8.1. The figure shows that through use of data reduction in SPSS, 115 indicators in 4 categories of eco-building design factors are reduced to 27 components. The correlations and interactions of indicators with each other are computed. Components are extracted and compared by their initial Eigen values. In the next stage, SPSS helps to analyse the factors, and categorises the indicators according to their relationship and correlations to each other. The outcome of factor analysis can be illustrated in 6 main clusters, embracing the most important 32 indicators, for assessing building design eco-efficiency.

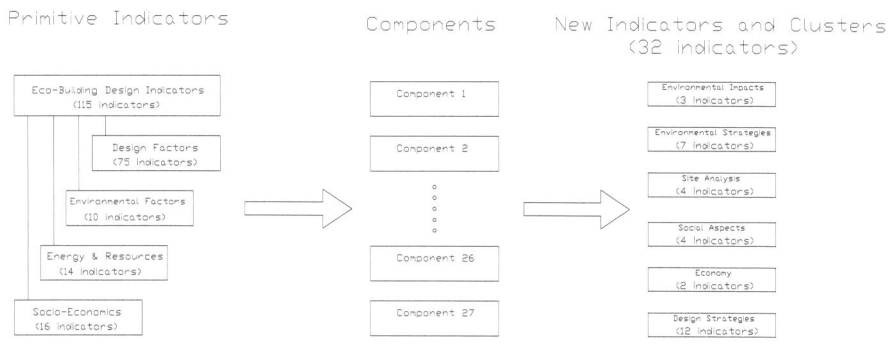

Fig 8.1: the process of data reduction and factor analysis

The process, findings, and discussions of the data analysis are presented in the following sections.

8.3 Factor Analysis

This study identified and ranked the indicators of eco-building design according to their level of significance, based on sustainable design expert views. The purpose of using factor analysis method is to reduce data and to remove redundant (not highly correlated) variables from the survey. Factor analysis is often used in data reduction to identify a small number of factors that explain most of the variance observed in a much larger number of manifest variables (SPSS 12.0.1 for Windows).

Factor analysis can be used either in hypothesis testing or in searching for constructs within a group of variables (Bartholomew and Knott 1999). It is a series of methods for finding clusters of related variables and hence an ideal technique for reducing a large number of factors into a more easily understood framework (Norusis 2000). It is used to investigate if there is an underlying relationship between the different indicators within the questionnaire. In SPSS, the principal components method is used to extract the latent components and variables. Components are a set of matrixes that present the correlations between different variables.

The process begins by finding a linear combination of variables (a component) that accounts for as much variation in the original variables. It then finds another component that accounts for as much of the remaining variation as possible and it is uncorrelated with the previous component. The process continues in this way until there are as many components as original variables. Usually, a few components will account for most of the variation, and these components can be used to replace the original variables (SPSS 2003). Hence, the outcome, presented in the following section will be a few variables that present the characteristics for eco-building design indicators.

8.4 Analysis of the Findings

These stages are needed in order to carry out factor analysis;
The first stage of the factor analysis is to determine the strength of the relationship among the variables (Shen and Liu, 2003). A *matrix of correlation coefficients* should be extracted, and then *components*, carrying Eigen value of bigger than 1 should be extracted from matrix of correlation coefficient (the most common extraction method is based on principal component analysis). In the third phase, a *rotated component matrix* should be generated in order to determine which indicators have more effective influence in each component.

Hence it can be said that the process begins with consideration of factors in the questionnaire (Eco-building design indicators in questionnaire), then a series of components are generated based on indicators in the second stage, and their correlations are investigated. In the third stage a set of more influential factors (indicators) are selected and are considered as the representative of the research for following up the study (See Fig 8.1). The results of factor analysis are presented in Table 8.1.

Table 8.1 Total Variance Explained

Component	Initial Eigenvalues			Extraction Sums of Squared Loadings			Rotation Sums of Squared Loadings		
	Total	% of Variance	Cumulative %	Total	% of Variance	Cumulative %	Total	% of Variance	Cumulative %
1	28.347	24.649	24.649	28.347	24.649	24.649	8.703	7.567	7.567
2	8.598	7.476	32.125	8.598	7.476	32.125	7.939	6.903	14.471
3	5.272	4.584	36.709	5.272	4.584	36.709	5.474	4.760	19.230
4	4.877	4.241	40.950	4.877	4.241	40.950	5.200	4.522	23.753
5	4.387	3.815	44.765	4.387	3.815	44.765	5.037	4.380	28.132
6	3.452	3.002	47.767	3.452	3.002	47.767	4.689	4.077	32.210
7	3.391	2.948	50.715	3.391	2.948	50.715	4.482	3.898	36.107
8	3.186	2.771	53.486	3.186	2.771	53.486	4.391	3.819	39.926
9	3.103	2.698	56.184	3.103	2.698	56.184	3.632	3.158	43.084
10	2.908	2.529	58.713	2.908	2.529	58.713	3.289	2.860	45.944
11	2.651	2.305	61.019	2.651	2.305	61.019	3.254	2.829	48.774
12	2.352	2.045	63.064	2.352	2.045	63.064	3.167	2.754	51.528
13	2.220	1.931	64.995	2.220	1.931	64.995	3.081	2.679	54.207
14	2.045	1.779	66.773	2.045	1.779	66.773	2.953	2.568	56.775
15	2.013	1.750	68.523	2.013	1.750	68.523	2.859	2.486	59.261
16	1.893	1.646	70.169	1.893	1.646	70.169	2.767	2.406	61.667
17	1.846	1.605	71.775	1.846	1.605	71.775	2.648	2.302	63.969
18	1.651	1.436	73.211	1.651	1.436	73.211	2.612	2.271	66.240
19	1.565	1.361	74.572	1.565	1.361	74.572	2.567	2.232	68.472
20	1.499	1.304	75.875	1.499	1.304	75.875	2.450	2.130	70.602
21	1.432	1.245	77.120	1.432	1.245	77.120	2.433	2.116	72.718
22	1.325	1.152	78.273	1.325	1.152	78.273	2.416	2.101	74.819
23	1.217	1.058	79.331	1.217	1.058	79.331	2.101	1.827	76.645
24	1.144	.995	80.326	1.144	.995	80.326	2.083	1.811	78.457
25	1.107	.963	81.289	1.107	.963	81.289	1.838	1.598	80.055
26	1.100	.956	82.245	1.100	.956	82.245	1.792	1.558	81.613
27	1.063	.924	83.170	1.063	.924	83.170	1.790	1.556	83.170
28	.962	.837	84.006						
29	.936	.814	84.820						
30	.872	.758	85.578						
...									
113	-5.227E-16	-4.545E-16	100.000						
114	-5.806E-16	-5.048E-16	100.000						
115	-8.206E-16	-7.135E-16	100.000						

Extraction Method: Principal Component Analysis.

In Table 8.1, each component is set according to a series of correlations between different indicators. Thus, it shows how correlated an indicator could be to other indicators. The first column of three sections in Table 8.1 labelled as initial Eigen values related to Eigen value of the correlation matrix and indicates which components of the table remain in analysis. To carry out the factor analysis just components with Eigen values more than 1 are selected and those with Eigen value of less than 1 are excluded. In the current context, an Eigen value is the amount of the total test variance that is accounted for by a particular factor, the total variance for each test being unity (100%). For example, the Eigen value of the first factor in Table 8.1 is 28.347. Since the total test variance that could possibly be accounted for by a factor is 115 [i.e. 100% × (number of tests)], the proportion of the total test variance accounted for by the first factor is 28.347: 115 = 24.649%, the figure given in *% of variance* column. In this analysis just 27 components carry eigenvalue of more than 1 and account for nearly 83.170% of the variance as shown in the *cumulative %* column. This means that the selected components (first 27 factors of analysis in Table 8.1) present 83.17% of the whole variance which statistically includes 95% of all data (according to data distribution, average weighted mean, and standard deviation). Therefore the 27 components can be considered as the representative of 115 indicators employed in this study. The next block of columns (Extraction Sum of Squared Loadings) are the sum of the squared loadings for the unrotated factor solution and the last block in the table (Rotation sums of Squared Loadings) are those for the rotated factor solution.

8.4.1 Scree Plot

Another way of presenting the most important factors of a study can be obtained through presentation of a scree plot of data as shown in Fig 8.2.

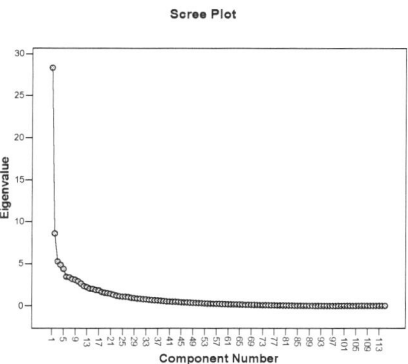

Fig 8.2 Scree Plot of 115 Eco-indicators of the Study

The purpose of a scree plot is to provide a graphic picture of the Eigen value for each component extracted in SPSS. As it is shown in the figure, the slope of scree is reducing, while moving towards components with Eigen value less than 1. The point of interest is defined between components 27 and 28, where the figure curve connects to the points, starting to get horizontal. Therefore in a scree plot the place where a sharp change in angle occurs, can be considered as the exact point that Eigen values of less than 1 are placed. On the sharp slope of curve the Eigen values bigger than one are located, while in the flatten part of the curve the Eigen values smaller than 1 are plotted.

From principal component analysis 27 components which have the Eigen value of more than 1 are selected. Next step is the extraction of rotated component matrix for finding out which indicators are contributing the highest level of influence on eco-building design. Table 8.2 presented below shows the degree of influence of each indicator in the whole survey. As it can be seen in Table 8.2 each component's correlation with all indicators of research are computed.

From Table 8.2 (Rotated Component Matrix) the indicators with the highest rate of influence can be distinguished. For example, in Table 8.2, the most important indicators for component 1 embrace range of questions (indicators) from Q76 to Q85 which carry scores from 0.569 to 0.876 presented the highest numerical value based on significance of each factor in component 1. Also the near intervals (numeric values) among indicators from Q76 to Q85 illustrate a level of affiliation in this set. The same method is used for the rest of components to extract the most effective indicators of each component as indicated in Table 8.2. The indicators with the highest scores and correlation values are chosen for each component. The result of this analysis is presented in Table 8.3.

Table 8.3 illustrates the result of factor reduction based on rotated component matrix presented in Table 8.2.

CHAPTER 8: ECO-DESIGN INDICATORS COMBINATION

Table 8.2 Rotated Component Matrix(a)

Questions	1	2	3	4	5	6	7	8	9	10	11	12	13	14	15	16	17	18	19	20	21	22	23	24	25	26	27
Q1	.133	.260	.120	-.100	.057	.232	.147	.022	.136	.945	.035	.066	.016	.154	.066	-.085	.034	.060	-.029	.007	.126	-.160	.202	.065	.065	-.061	-.148
Q2	.071	.109	.047	.015	.052	.134	-.027	.077	.082	.818	.116	.120	.124	-.026	-.032	.009	.066	-.003	-.051	.143	.092	.092	.028	-.052	.057	.037	.102
Q3	.146	.080	.292	-.049	-.033	.171	.234	.012	.014	.702	.307	.197	.032	.093	.066	.154	.004	-.005	-.031	-.090	.056	-.033	.067	.010	.005	-.033	.000
Q4	.083	-.007	.624	.066	.226	.074	-.027	.086	.134	.944	.064	.102	.061	-.019	-.020	-.154	.030	-.022	.037	.120	-.042	.022	.190	-.210	-.197	-.051	.143
Q5	.246	.153	.566	.094	.137	.154	.292	-.026	.296	.139	.094	-.024	.150	.012	-.041	-.075	.017	-.131	.024	.000	-.020	-.133	.056	-.298	.019	-.101	.222
Q6	.175	.074	.571	.037	.078	.315	.267	.032	.156	.020	.022	-.196	.203	.007	-.086	.046	.133	-.228	-.044	-.102	-.061	-.100	-.019	-.084	-.130	-.036	.234
Q7	.237	.015	.679	-.139	.029	.049	-.026	-.009	-.127	.027	.007	.043	.037	-.007	.150	.039	.254	.017	.199	.126	.135	.084	-.064	-.041	-.029	.138	-.195
Q8	.113	.044	.658	-.053	.126	.101	-.099	.082	.129	.026	.192	.036	-.013	.155	-.065	.011	-.055	-.101	.101	.307	-.003	-.100	.246	.206	.150	-.028	-.154
Q9	.066	.179	.815	-.017	.064	.051	.105	-.007	.009	-.052	.063	.067	-.021	.048	.132	.122	.005	-.036	.076	.008	.051	.077	-.015	.017	.202	-.032	-.254
Q10	.122	.151	.771	.040	-.031	.137	.016	.059	-.019	.170	-.040	.016	-.107	.113	.003	.012	-.044	.102	.022	-.184	.096	.054	-.005	.000	-.029	.094	.061
Q11	-.002	.070	.065	.029	.178	.075	.125	-.041	.109	-.057	.096	.078	.061	.078	-.036	.000	.322	-.015	.675	-.014	-.005	.117	.171	.173	-.058	.007	.001
Q12	.109	.019	.238	-.030	.050	.010	.053	.143	-.032	-.009	.052	.085	-.019	.049	.032	.171	-.068	.106	.917	.073	-.082	.016	-.055	-.033	.091	.003	.019
Q13	.100	.297	.241	.151	.174	.661	.266	.172	-.149	.054	-.020	.114	.098	-.105	.025	-.044	.066	.007	.108	.039	-.036	.001	.009	-.032	.039	-.076	.047
Q14	-.079	.319	.122	.011	.146	.577	.114	.201	.074	.262	-.066	-.014	-.140	.006	.032	.154	.161	-.020	.052	.065	.123	.074	.150	.236	-.028	-.144	.060
Q15	.128	.297	.408	.038	.102	.403	.052	.045	.091	.118	.145	.009	.256	-.001	-.013	-.182	.031	.236	.130	.031	.209	.040	.139	-.100	.141	.020	-.154
Q16	.100	.176	.274	.048	-.063	.645	-.025	-.102	.215	.175	.023	.106	.105	.132	.143	.040	.016	.158	.008	.212	-.079	.093	-.120	-.032	.175	-.002	-.194
Q17	.108	.180	.066	.120	-.077	.761	.051	-.129	.178	.134	.101	.115	.070	.193	.034	-.032	.034	.015	.005	.166	-.014	.011	-.055	-.063	-.008	.092	.044
Q18	.167	.025	.132	.016	.043	.426	-.080	-.005	.102	.198	.302	.525	.013	.180	.023	.016	.223	.156	.067	.039	-.054	-.054	.080	.070	-.001	.091	-.121
Q19	.097	.003	.009	.103	.074	.182	.181	.005	.779	.017	.024	.122	.117	.166	-.103	.137	.033	.020	.066	-.135	.054	-.019	.007	.125	.066	-.019	-.134
Q20	-.043	.127	-.007	.291	.063	.372	.012	.292	.566	.158	.003	.103	.015	.161	-.044	.182	.011	.023	-.045	.294	.096	.055	.066	.028	-.021	.124	-.033
Q21	.210	.178	.203	.022	-.039	-.015	.072	.032	.800	-.015	.117	.191	.082	.072	-.122	.230	.114	.115	-.041	.211	.232	.033	.280	-.058	-.082	.067	.104
Q22	.159	.116	.056	-.019	-.049	.058	.054	.153	.035	.110	.089	.535	-.021	.222	-.052	.069	-.071	.018	-.028	.069	.480	.132	-.098	-.066	.226	.171	-.094
Q23	.145	.241	.076	.073	.006	.139	.129	.126	.197	.139	.078	.218	-.005	.201	.096	.112	-.050	.093	-.069	-.004	.617	-.047	.025	-.154	-.099	-.097	-.257
Q24	.182	.024	.093	.047	.106	-.109	-.085	.115	-.015	.098	.016	.047	.112	.043	.149	.002	.039	-.027	-.057	-.044	.809	.085	-.007	.009	-.031	.026	.062
Q25	.165	.135	.054	.369	.086	.267	-.011	-.009	.137	-.025	-.099	.006	-.210	-.164	.038	-.021	-.049	.070	.012	-.049	.539	.093	-.140	.145	.035	.297	.207
Q26	.260	.085	-.042	.793	.083	.172	-.036	.098	.158	-.057	-.012	.077	.025	.650	.037	-.012	.028	-.100	.011	.130	.128	-.072	.032	.002	.002	.067	-.008
Q27	.294	.136	-.033	.798	.051	.037	.089	.080	.024	-.049	.100	-.041	-.017	.081	.077	.055	.149	-.111	.086	.082	-.003	-.084	.067	-.081	-.008	.065	-.012

CHAPTER 8: ECO-DESIGN INDICATORS COMBINATION

Q28	-.037	.359	.219	.027	.099	.342	-.160	-.075	.315	.098	.417	-.141	-.070	.102	.181	-.086	-.086	-.093	.152	.090	-.074	.202	.056	.192	-.017	.081	.117		
Q29	-.096	.188	-.179	.254	.300	.428	-.147	-.158	.146	.139	.367	-.150	.249	.020	.150	.099	-.142	.023	-.038	.099	.058	.125	-.066	.123	-.065	.028	-.128		
Q30	.263	-.054	.044	-.038	-.067	-.076	.175	-.015	.012	.120	.622	-.012	-.027	.042	.230	.186	.136	.015	.284	-.037	.086	-.087	.070	-.151	.005	.255	.066		
Q31	.061	.264	.039	.115	.151	.425	.150	.075	.024	.107	.540	-.076	-.039	.084	.041	.086	-.020	.046	-.042	.020	.159	-.250	.215	.101	-.098	-.100	.043		
Q32	.079	.073	.255	-.023	.217	-.047	.080	.109	.105	.204	.666	.331	-.067	.099	.077	.050	.152	.075	-.013	.091	.024	-.017	-.041	-.069	.120	-.038	.069		
Q33	.028	.270	.016	.109	.229	.220	.181	.004	.029	.080	.552	.262	.233	-.124	-.078	-.044	.165	.096	.167	-.021	-.015	.062	.197	-.041	.072	-.045	-.161		
Q34	-.094	.051	.181	-.005	.142	.060	.184	.202	.145	.287	.378	.430	-.077	.044	-.003	.040	.223	.100	-.022	-.041	.004	.181	-.081	-.038	.279	.108	.015		
Q35	.151	.027	.149	.046	.286	-.012	.101	.129	.872	.182	.132	.039	.023	.005	.065	-.002	.271	.192	-.017	-.146	-.036	.150	.103	-.033	.042	.093	.138		
Q36	.129	.004	.058	.197	.266	.001	.009	.147	.371	.037	.105	.193	-.023	.123	.122	.148	.539	.087	.231	.087	.048	-.146	.019	.004	.133	-.013	.067		
Q37	.146	.072	.053	.364	.356	.135	.068	.120	.276	.056	.167	.021	.073	.037	-.112	.005	.579	.134	-.067	.007	-.024	-.025	.016	.034	-.029	.030	-.017		
Q38	.151	-.142	.029	.245	.166	.181	.174	.071	.092	.113	.147	.132	.205	.131	.081	.053	.663	.017	.150	.039	-.023	.086	-.023	.106	-.003	.006	.086		
Q39	.118	.225	.240	.014	-.033	.204	.388	.241	.285	.060	.467	.092	-.007	-.011	-.111	.166	.103	.145	-.076	-.043	-.184	-.027	.029	.158	-.017	-.086	.042		
Q40	.230	.233	.219	-.033	.166	.070	.248	.325	.396	.239	.291	.143	.021	.065	-.036	.114	.213	.178	-.012	.077	-.075	.117	.022	-.125	.016	-.114	.090		
Q41	.017	.043	-.013	-.013	.113	-.005	.198	.002	.057	.099	.164	.353	.046	-.033	.158	.122	.223	.287	.156	.164	-.020	.019	.223	.114	-.115	.136	.506		
Q42	.016	.068	-.021	-.105	-.003	.095	.014	.053	.131	-.017	.057	.170	.130	.207	.058	.106	.133	.783	.037	.107	.038	.038	.063	.051	.043	.005	.056		
Q43	.130	.170	.243	.166	.085	.212	-.257	.204	.056	.107	.105	-.188	.135	.002	.000	-.167	.132	.381	.142	.155	.098	-.045	.067	.388	.058	.138	.071		
Q44	-.031	.107	.174	.049	.066	.011	.022	.046	.165	.161	.122	.007	.030	.133	.098	.136	-.006	.090	.094	-.044	-.082	.167	.780	-.004	.001	.081	.047		
Q45	.060	.136	.549	.077	-.004	-.028	.145	-.073	.171	.061	.105	-.016	.027	-.008	.038	.170	-.062	.378	.114	-.193	-.063	.278	.163	.132	-.125	.000	-.102		
Q46	.138	.139	.049	.227	.324	.108	-.016	-.198	-.017	.088	.064	.000	.051	.080	-.180	.103	.249	.323	.391	-.322	-.116	.017	.193	.176	.169	.089	-.039		
Q47	.231	.000	-.024	.073	.258	.427	.205	.002	-.128	.139	.134	.091	-.051	.138	.174	.219	.207	.276	-.091	-.058	-.003	-.067	.328	.053	.272	.124	.170		
Q48	.238	.180	.198	-.042	.199	.137	.214	.098	-.108	.406	.008	.040	.129	.176	.044	.129	-.054	.090	.357	.063	-.091	.15	-.016	-.219	.354	-.092	.055		
Q49	.381	.048	.142	.049	.227	.117	.075	-.035	.144	.172	.110	.055	.270	.105	.111	.147	.037	.158	.139	-.021	-.051	.107	.060	.069	.620	.058	-.024		
Q50	.163	.078	.122	-.029	-.123	-.025	.074	.120	-.006	.051	-.021	.063	.008	-.016	.022	-.014	-.016	-.002	.102	.041	.080	.854	.055	-.079	.061	.013	-.038		
Q51	.113	-.013	-.014	.283	.212	.216	.037	.167	.184	-.007	-.062	-.065	.002	.050	.045	-.082	.113	.087	-.046	.062	.125	.591	.308	.173	.068	.138	.192		
Q52	.135	.366	.077	-.009	.099	.380	-.063	.013	.019	-.031	.100	.061	.130	.523	.160	.081	.204	.011	.133	-.021	.018	.065	.101	.229	-.060	-.002	.033		
Q53	.109	.199	.123	.013	-.042	.098	-.001	.171	-.077	.031	.061	.115	.002	.199	.786	.129	-.014	.031	.026	-.017	.066	-.142	.101	.063	.016	-.021	.062		
Q54	.067	.224	.023	.044	-.016	.069	.041	.077	-.060	.037	.037	.065	.008	-.072	.830	.105	.012	.018	-.002	.113	.086	.157	-.025	-.101	.041	.039	-.038		
Q55	-.048	.399	.060	.083	.136	.051	.045	.087	.022	-.007	.216	.007	.110	.212	.493	.061	.206	.192	-.142	-.035	.291	.045	.281	-.003	.032	.180	-.040		
Q56	.009	.513	.074	.096	.070	.326	.009	.039	.195	.115	.066	.081	.124	.563	.105	.035	.037	.058	-.127	-.059	.153	-.131	.141	.014	-.003	.055	-.001		
Q57	-.021	.465	.110	.133	-.070	.158	.161	.163	.156	.001	.026	.023	-.092	.560	.177	.014	-.032	.208	.150	-.093	.048	-.034	.047	-.091	.127	.086	-.193		
Q58	-.012	.498	.182	.108	.012	.238	.074	.180	.111	.008	.122	.025	-.097	.569	.187	.026	.100	.061	.036	-.023	.072	-.061	.125	.005	.141	.087	.004		

167

CHAPTER 8: ECO-DESIGN INDICATORS COMBINATION

Q59	.161	-.116	.065	.216	.223	-.086	-.028	-.144	.145	.145	-.038	.116	.236	.845	-.082	-.033	.103	.124	.107	.008	.070	.080	.008	.146	-.002	.079	.061
Q60	.163	.002	.029	.140	.044	.061	.066	.110	.053	.041	.026	-.018	.814	.241	.005	.039	.187	.104	-.044	-.013	.011	.019	.103	.019	.076	.106	-.080
Q61	.149	-.066	-.027	.581	.076	.023	.114	.104	-.217	.236	.102	.061	.194	.196	.044	.130	.317	.198	-.028	-.105	-.026	.071	.043	.159	.052	-.106	-.004
Q62	.238	-.007	.009	.384	.242	.086	.458	.207	.128	.068	.054	.200	-.071	.024	-.160	-.097	.146	.161	-.134	-.134	.066	.178	.037	.095	.104	.019	.216
Q63	.315	-.023	.058	.547	.184	.158	.224	.214	.067	-.009	-.093	.064	.031	-.026	-.075	.279	-.035	.031	-.028	.092	-.143	.344	-.094	.042	-.156	.101	-.087
Q64	.365	.067	.099	.039	-.050	.076	.106	.122	.154	.111	.024	.006	.524	.026	.134	.386	.032	.008	.067	.034	.020	.087	-.022	.160	.496	-.105	-.046
Q65	.154	.134	.107	-.061	.267	.099	.046	-.058	.115	.147	.111	.327	.096	-.065	.078	-.010	-.156	.463	.250	.238	-.019	-.094	-.015	.142	.157	-.284	-.037
Q66	.271	.318	.499	.052	.066	-.141	.175	.090	.151	-.035	.101	.013	.056	-.057	.049	-.106	-.126	.241	.066	.066	.023	.029	-.051	.209	.056	-.154	.236
Q67	.156	.279	.008	.076	-.053	.193	-.085	.337	.074	.114	-.029	.056	.495	-.121	.033	.299	-.215	.321	.050	.075	.035	.134	.017	.023	.003	-.049	.216
Q68	.352	.098	.148	.379	.122	-.015	-.086	.403	-.119	.020	.013	.076	.052	.061	.001	.266	.111	-.014	-.165	.014	.051	.126	-.006	.137	.129	-.100	.253
Q69	.295	-.117	.141	.475	.266	-.030	.158	.197	.058	.041	-.030	.035	.236	.056	-.071	.073	.142	-.023	-.166	-.045	.078	.146	-.057	.312	-.065	-.090	.079
Q70	.148	.143	.029	.200	.379	.216	.033	-.033	.065	.165	-.060	.069	.016	-.045	.036	-.015	.021	.094	.858	.704	-.113	-.006	.048	.040	-.086	.098	-.018
Q71	.247	.122	.022	.133	.066	.198	.180	.173	-.122	.015	.072	.039	-.020	-.044	.091	.124	.052	.106	.034	.747	.013	.098	-.085	-.018	.064	-.010	.054
Q72	.093	-.008	-.053	.004	.334	.046	.194	.294	.066	.257	.101	.265	-.093	-.009	.112	.140	.250	.155	.003	.259	.024	-.110	.098	.227	.198	.205	-.030
Q73	.173	.058	.017	.062	.066	.019	.103	.106	.214	.024	.125	.013	.077	-.025	.154	.745	.066	.075	.142	.023	.029	-.075	.152	.009	.085	.056	-.032
Q74	-.021	.338	.140	.084	.007	.038	.103	.112	.147	.106	.113	-.077	.020	.179	.347	.569	.092	.083	.171	.103	.091	.014	.049	.087	.056	.176	.120
Q75	-.080	.161	.032	.138	.107	.027	.034	.205	.107	-.031	.067	.197	.086	.242	.097	.158	.029	-.037	.048	.065	.134	.139	.181	.023	.033	.860	.049
Q76	.616	.149	-.092	.326	.015	.053	-.053	.175	-.075	-.559	.168	.102	-.104	.140	-.092	.222	.062	-.147	.106	-.033	.164	.111	.068	.014	2.734E-05	-.340	.029
Q77	.730	.177	-.023	.331	.075	.025	.041	.141	.041	-.029	.152	.016	-.002	.105	-.030	.104	-.002	-.156	.066	-.011	.108	.100	.109	.066	.022	-.223	-.040
Q78	.569	.017	-.038	.207	.165	.009	.134	.186	.069	-.057	.015	.150	.299	-.037	.059	.314	.099	.094	-.033	.047	.130	-.033	-.064	-.010	-.186	.047	-.313
Q79	.654	-.021	.191	.331	.224	-.565	.086	.065	-.129	.075	-.103	.047	.065	.087	-.027	.092	.133	-.051	.058	.105	.077	.049	.013	.215	-.066	-.049	-.025
Q80	.623	.115	.191	.269	.113	.020	.037	.107	.070	.065	.010	.051	.010	.016	.009	.047	.107	-.012	.057	.083	.035	.032	-.057	.002	.039	.001	-.002
Q81	.876	.048	.162	.129	.141	.103	.016	.128	.065	.120	.056	.113	-.004	-.026	.027	-.028	.063	.052	.053	.030	-.036	.016	-.055	-.051	.094	.006	-.009
Q82	.832	.149	.058	.067	.075	.070	.135	.084	.118	.070	-.020	-.051	.224	.001	.028	-.081	.053	.110	.005	.040	.017	.083	.039	-.073	.181	.025	.003
Q83	.650	.153	.271	.061	.086	.122	.222	.018	.182	.110	-.018	-.136	.127	.040	.102	-.130	-.007	.157	.034	.058	.113	-.026	.081	.009	.079	.124	.066
Q84	.697	-.071	.063	-.035	.317	.040	.194	.030	.025	.555	.096	.139	.013	-.020	.198	.119	-.093	.108	-.001	.146	.147	.031	.029	.068	-.146	.118	.040
Q85	.666	.091	.080	-.037	.244	.009	.419	.121	.024	.032	.122	-.046	.104	.021	.013	.002	.012	.044	-.116	.101	.111	.034	-.092	.111	.087	.134	.153
Q86	.298	.006	.075	.123	.764	.110	.140	.054	.032	.051	.061	.014	.077	.065	-.073	.032	.067	.040	-.002	.165	.018	.004	.007	.032	.056	-.066	.059
Q87	.331	.068	.084	.224	.677	-.039	.191	-.023	.143	.012	.044	.005	.029	.046	.066	-.012	.143	-.056	.195	.012	.102	-.030	.053	.035	.106	.070	.070
Q88	.199	.106	.056	.103	.831	.048	.149	.065	.098	.081	.108	.125	.012	.071	.022	.020	.080	-.005	.066	.078	.034	-.061	.004	-.017	-.016	-.006	-.030
Q89	.274	.023	.148	.191	.567	.011	.338	.074	-.006	-.129	-.013	.060	.054	-.020	-.033	.180	.195	.090	.130	.089	.042	.109	.071	.060	.020	.166	-.122

CHAPTER 8: ECO-DESIGN INDICATORS COMBINATION

Q90	.203	-.012	-.076	.337	.103	.069	.039	-.033	.065	-.032	-.071	.112	.082	.172	-.086	.125	.118	.170	.132	.008	-.108	-.075	.024	.641	.042	.014	.054
Q91	.484	.071	.197	.231	.173	.153	.359	.129	.088	.069	-.010	.033	.193	-.016	.169	.319	-.004	.102	.062	.043	-.072	.039	-.015	.095	-.062	-.066	-.318
Q92	.241	.089	.151	.200	.262	.050	.897	.115	.141	.099	.159	.057	.080	-.015	.066	.000	.016	.122	.124	.054	-.057	.069	.008	-.128	.021	-.030	-.081
Q93	.379	.084	.089	.049	.274	.049	.686	.094	.058	.108	.100	-.019	-.018	.035	-.025	.143	.005	-.094	.100	.112	-.065	-.042	-.014	-.059	.043	.050	-.002
Q94	.276	.143	.078	.109	.280	.135	.657	.133	.108	.073	.099	.090	.100	.074	.056	.139	.167	-.078	.080	.083	.061	.078	.090	.105	-.017	-.008	.112
Q95	.169	.081	-.040	.576	.275	.077	.307	.036	.189	-.051	.002	-.096	.067	-.032	.164	-.120	.026	.161	-.036	.295	.060	.195	-.116	.134	.048	.138	-.043
Q96	.384	.061	.130	.543	.364	.019	.111	.092	.110	-.091	-.108	.098	.094	.110	-.035	-.061	-.012	-.028	.015	-.050	.146	.035	.127	.264	.115	-.104	-.098
Q97	.192	.044	-.016	.311	.133	-.080	.293	.202	.052	-.077	.023	-.078	.229	-.016	.109	.315	-.052	-.075	.225	.224	-.052	.119	-.018	.232	.054	-.073	-.313
Q98	.207	.087	-.028	.095	.220	.007	.361	.442	.080	-.061	.082	-.035	.213	-.054	.143	.244	.213	.028	.039	.086	.097	.134	-.012	.208	.258	.099	-.147
Q99	.181	.280	-.063	.162	-.003	.267	.400	.450	.008	.105	.171	-.015	.057	.129	.015	-.079	.168	.019	.087	.205	.120	-.020	.201	.144	.146	-.039	-.040
Q100	.082	.889	.031	.027	.126	.405	.165	.049	.038	.019	.044	-.132	.236	.090	.004	-.021	-.052	.086	.011	-.023	.038	-.122	.097	.052	.047	.092	.106
Q101	.200	.761	.118	.026	.019	.222	.000	-.021	-.001	.152	.091	-.017	.112	.167	-.015	.038	-.062	.015	-.037	.210	.018	.039	-.188	-.061	-.019	.149	-.015
Q102	.106	.600	.116	.112	.030	-.009	-.041	.100	.158	.041	-.141	-.053	-.224	.088	.322	.154	.070	-.093	.069	.124	-.110	.056	-.017	-.052	.239	.107	-.098
Q103	.219	.809	.129	-.048	.031	-.009	-.032	.071	.030	.065	.018	.094	-.163	.161	.228	.081	-.008	.003	.049	.058	.057	-.011	-.054	.054	-.002	.019	-.028
Q104	.125	.780	.025	.056	.044	.189	.127	.057	-.026	.119	.049	-.070	.234	.052	-.077	-.100	.019	.082	.048	.077	.066	-.107	.185	-.017	.036	-.004	.117
Q105	.050	.833	.037	.045	.112	.005	.113	.073	-.003	-.013	.009	.116	-.072	.031	.153	-.062	-.040	.050	.052	-.117	.101	-.005	.157	.052	-.074	-.129	.012
Q106	-.032	.885	.054	.002	.040	.078	.066	.017	-.026	.041	.076	.018	.098	-.021	-.010	.130	.079	-.055	.088	.097	.043	.157	-.022	-.074	.101	.017	.008
Q107	.003	.785	.170	.077	.112	.011	-.051	-.185	.093	.059	.075	.068	-.015	-.203	.083	.084	-.095	.063	-.151	-.039	-.084	.099	-.066	.041	-.145	-.035	-.096
Q108	.220	.056	.134	.099	.346	.085	.074	.332	-.012	.180	.124	.480	.140	-.180	-.103	-.051	-.047	.116	-.057	-.118	.128	.041	.097	.174	-.078	.179	.209
Q109	.229	.177	.021	-.018	.261	.105	.072	.323	.076	.216	-.089	.210	.610	-.134	-.054	-.049	.010	.045	.148	-.028	.074	-.138	-.131	.029	-.020	-.009	.117
Q110	.064	.145	.044	.206	.101	.033	-.216	.371	.060	.399	-.127	.098	.153	-.165	.096	.061	-.043	-.047	.298	.076	.046	.251	-.171	.191	-.177	.239	-.093
Q111	.223	.013	.034	.124	.069	.009	.046	.843	.095	.100	.018	.126	.089	.035	.126	.101	.051	.001	.097	.025	.095	.029	.005	-.055	-.028	-.030	-.002
Q112	.237	.023	.034	.120	-.004	-.028	.144	.847	.060	.010	.070	.005	.134	.040	.085	.051	.052	-.026	-.017	.055	.057	.066	.023	.016	.047	.115	.033
Q113	.060	-.018	.138	.175	.069	-.103	.306	.552	.127	-.032	-.035	.188	.019	.006	.146	-.044	-.053	.239	.075	.002	.052	.344	.119	-.089	-.183	.090	-.206
Q114	-.044	.206	.342	-.026	-.153	.094	.325	.245	.161	.071	-.164	.332	.099	-.073	.186	.109	-.008	-.017	-.087	-.077	.051	.136	.348	.143	.063	.228	-.015
Q115	.036	-.006	-.023	.097	.094	.041	.016	.068	.132	.109	.031	.781	.052	.054	.171	-.038	.083	.075	.131	.051	.099	.010	.008	.014	-.050	-.016	.059

Extraction Method: Principal Component Analysis. Rotation Method: Varimax with Kaiser Normalization.
a. Rotation converged in 38 iterations.

Table 8.3 Data Analysis: Elementary Factor Reduction

Component 1	Component 2	Component 3	Component 4	Component 5
Q81. Water Pollution Q82. Earth Pollution Q80. Air Pollution Q77. Ozone Layer Q84. Land Fill Q85. Solid Residues Q79. Energy Consumption Q83. Ecological Deterioration Q76. Green House Effect Q78. More Efficient Use of Water	Q106. Social Inclusion Q105. Self-Determination Q103. Personal Development	Q9. Added Function to Main Function Q10. Renovation & Upgrading Q7. Upgradeability/ Extension Q8. Flexibility in Use Stage Q4. Adaptability To New Changes Q6. Adaptability to the Environment Q5. Adaptability To Surroundings	Q27. Energy & Eco-efficiency Q26. Control of Emission	Q88. Natural Ventilation Q86. Natural Light Q87. Passive Heating Q89. Passive Cooling
Component 6	**Component 7**	**Component 8**	**Component 9**	**Component 10**
Q17. Effect of Function on Human Behaviour Q13. Physical Aspects of Safety & Health	Q92. GEO Thermal Benefits Q93. Sewage & Landfill Gas Benefits Q94. Biomass Benefits	Q112. Pollution Prevention Costs Q111. Pollution Rehabilitation Costs	Q19. Landscape (Blg/Env Interactions) Q35. Landscape Design (Exterior Spaces)	Q2. Functional Zoning Q3. Compatibility
Component 11	**Component 12**	**Component 13**	**Component 14**	**Component 15**
Q32. Distribution of Activities	Q115. Saving Running Costs Or Capital Costs / Running Costs	Q60. Maintainability in Design Service Life	Q59. Longevity in Design Service Life	Q54. Fashion Q53. Style
Component 16	**Component 17**	**Component 18**	**Component 19**	**Component 20**
Q73. Innovation in Use of Technology Q74. Vernacular	Q38. Climate Q37. Building Orientation Q36. Natural Physical Conditions	Q42. Form-built-Ability	Q12. Longevity of the Function Q11. Performance	Q71. Vibration of Equipments Q70. Noise of Equipments
Component 21	**Component 22**	**Component 23**	**Component 24**	**Component 25**
Q24. Government Q23. Society Q25. Organisations	Q50. Disassembling Q51. Reusability & Recycling	Q44. Geometry of Form (Aesthetic & Stability)	Q90. Insulation & Air tightness	Q49. Reliability & Usability
Component 26	**Component 27**			
Q75. Vernacular Technology	Q41. Site Restrictions			

Table 8.3 is the summary of Table 8.2. In Table 8.3 the most important and influential eco-indicators of each component are extracted and shown. The 6 clusters shown in Table 8.4 are formed based on the 27 extracted components and their most important indicators shown in Table 8.3. The new

clusters are considered as ***eco-building design*** indicators clusters for assessing building design eco-efficiency. The percentage of variance of each component (extracted from Table 8.1) are presented and added up in order to calculate the percentage of variance of each cluster in eco-building design indicators.

The percentage of variance of each indicator is taken from Table 8.1, and then the cluster percentage of variance is calculated through summation of each indicator's variance (see Table 8.3). The out come of calculations are presented in Table 8.4. In Table 8.4 each cluster degree of effect in eco-building design is calculated based on percentage of variance of each component derived from Table 8.1. For example, the third column in Table 8.4 which presents site analysis as one of six clusters for eco-building design, is composed by components 9 (%variance of 2.698%), presenting Q19 as the main indicator of its set, component 17 (%variance of 1.605%), presenting Q38 and Q37 as the main indicators of its group, and Component 27 (%variance of 0.924%) presenting Q41 as the main indicator of its set. Therefore the % of variance for cluster 3 (Site Analysis) in Table 8.4 is calculated through summation of its components' %s of variance. Thus the % of variance for cluster 3 is computed as:

$$2.698 + 1.605 + 0.924 = 5.227 \%$$

This value of 5.227 % is out of 83.170 % (4.347% out of 100% of data) which was shown as % of variances for first 27 components extracted through principal component analysis presented in Table 8.1. The summation of %s of variance for the 6 new clusters is also the same as 83.170%, which means these clusters can definitely be appropriate representatives of all eco-design indicators and explains 83.170 % of information in the survey questionnaire. The use of data reduction techniques in SPSS has helped to reduce the number of factors (115 indicators) to 32 indicators. These are grouped into 6 clusters, which are highly manageable without losing a large amount of data and just 100 - 83.170 = 16.83 % of existing information are compromised.

By applying factor analysis and data reduction in this survey, the questionnaire 115 indicators are reduced to 27 components, and then categorised into 6 pivotal clusters which include just 32 original indicators of the questionnaire, represents the major relevant data on eco-building design. For the extraction of the final 32 indicators, results of factor analysis in Table 8.3 and weighted ranking of indicators in chapter 8 were used. The final results of data reduction are presented in Table 8.4.

Table 8.4 Factor Reduction: Six New Categories (Final Data Reduction and Factor Analysis)

Cluster 1 Environmental Impacts	Cluster 2 Design Environmental Strategies	Cluster 3 Site Analysis	Cluster 4 Social Aspects	Cluster 5 Economy	Cluster 6 Design Aspects
Component 1	Component 4 Component 5 Component 7 Component 24	Component 9 Component 17 Component 27	Component 2 Component 21	Component 8 Component 12	**Function** Component 3 Component 6 Component 10 Component 11 Component 19 **Form** Component 15 Component 18 Component 22 Component 23 Component 25 **Space Technology** Component 13 Component 14 Component 16 Component 20 Component 26
Q81. Water Pollution Q82. Earth Pollution Q80. Air Pollution	Q27. Energy & Eco-efficiency Q26. Control of Emission Q88. Natural Ventilation Q86. Natural Light Q87. Passive Heating Q89. Passive Cooling Q90. Insulation & Air tightness	Q19. Landscape Q38. Climate Q37. Building Orientation Q41. Site Restrictions	Q106. Quality of Life Q24. Government Q23. Society Q25. Organisations	Q112. Pollution Prevention & Rehabilitation Costs Q115. Saving Running Costs Or Capital Costs / Running Costs	Q7. Flexibility Q6. Adaptability Q17. Mental Aspects Q13. Physical Aspects Q2. Functional Zoning Q11. Durability Q42. Form-built-Ability Q50. Disassembling Q51. Reusability & Recycling Q49. Reliability & Usability Q60. Maintainability Q73. Innovation
24.649	4.241+ 3.815 2.948 0.995	2.698+ 1.605 0.924	7.476+ 1.245	2.771+ 2.045	4.584+ 3.002 2.529 2.305 1.361 1.750 1.436 1.152 1.058 0.963 1.931 1.779 1.646 1.304 0.956
24.649	11.999	5.227	8.721	4.816	27.756

The six generated clusters will be subjected to further analysis and will also be used for developing a fuzzy model for assessing building design for eco-efficiency in chapter 9.

8.5 Interpretation of the Clusters

Based on the relationship between the chosen indicators, the clusters' names are selected. These clusters are presented and discussed in the following sections.

8.5.1 Cluster 1: *Environmental Impacts*

The extracted indicators for cluster one are all related to environmental impacts or consequences of building design. As it can be seen in Table 8.3, there are 10 indicators in component 1, but by examining them it can be derived that all of them are related to the different types of pollutions caused by building industries. Therefore, all of these ten indicators can be presented by 3 main indicators namely: water pollution, Earth pollution, and air pollution in cluster 1 renamed as *Environmental Impacts* category embodying a share near to 25% of whole percentage of variance in eco-building design indicators (See Table 8.4 and calculation of % variances). This cluster plays a pivotal role in design because of its high score in the eco-building design survey.

8.5.2 Cluster 2: *Environmental Design Passive and Active Strategies*

This cluster has a percentage of variance of 12% and embraces indicators such as: Energy & Eco-efficiency, Control of Emission, Natural Ventilation, Natural Light, Passive Heating, Passive Cooling, Insulation & Air tightness. All of aforementioned indicators are related to the environmental design strategies. This cluster takes advantage of technology and design intelligence, knowledge, and experience over the life cycle (LC) of building. The indicators of environmental design strategies can provide the winning factors for projects. These indicators according to Kano model belong to excitement threshold regarding customers' satisfaction (See Figs 4.3 and 4.4, in chapter 4). Setting these indicators in building design establishes the level of success relatively to eco-design. Thus, utilisation of environmental design strategies in eco-building relates to satisfaction of user in future application of through providing the building applicants with higher quality of life and comfort. The achievements derived from environmental design strategies include both ecological and economical aspects over the whole life cycle (WLC). For example employment of renewable sources of passive energies like solar energy, passive cooling and ventilation not only provides better natural living conditions but also in long terms save a large amount of energy and financial costs (Langston and Ding, 2001; Roaf et al., 2001; Smith, 2001).

8.5.3 Cluster 3: *Site Analysis*

Cluster 3 has a percentage of variance of 5.22% and consists of indicators such as: Landscape, climate, Building orientation and Site restrictions. The cluster is renamed as *Site Analysis* cluster. The indicators presented in this cluster are all concerning project's site analysis and specifications and include the policies and strategies which should be followed in the early design stage of building to fulfil higher quality of design to achieve customer's satisfactions. In other words it embraces the context of the projects. It is obvious that disregarding the context is not acceptable in the field of design, but what is important is that in eco-building design a specific emphasis is placed on this category in early design stage. Higher perception of site characteristics enhances the quality of design and reduces the rate of risk and uncertainties due to limitations which embraces site restrictions and specifications related to context. Prudent site analysis leads to more efficient design services. Design based on climate, landscape and choosing an appropriate orientation for the building will provide the asset with many advantages such as: natural light, natural ventilation and passive energy applications. The eco-efficiency gained through the application of these environmental site related strategies will lead to cost-efficiency and financial savings in long terms as well.

8.5.4 Cluster 4: *Social Aspects*

Cluster 4, renamed *Social Aspects* with percentage of variance of 8.72% and consists of 4 indicators, quality of life, Government, Society, and Organisations all require different level of involvement in design. Here, all customers and their expectations are captured by a cluster named *Social Aspect*. Customers as the main users of the building have the main role in determining the level of success for a building and its design. Eco-building design as a school of philosophy seeks the fulfilment of customer's expectations through application of certain strategies in building design over WLC of buildings. Customer satisfaction and social aspects can be discussed and explained by Keno model (See Fig 4.3, in chapter 4). EBD as a new design concept attempts to fulfil needs based on user orientations.

8.5.5 Cluster 5: *Economy*

Cluster 5, economy in eco-building design involves financial and monetary aspects of building over its WLC. It embraces two main indicators as: pollution costs and running costs. The ratio of capital cost in comparison to running cost should be minimised. Pollution costs are associated with both pollution avoidance and pollution rehabilitation. Running costs should be considered in long term for the maintenance of building over its WLC period. Recovering the impacts and pollutions generated by building process in WLC embraces a large amount of budgets. Hence, building design through application of environmental design strategies is capable to present solutions generating lower rate of emissions and cheaper to maintain over project WLC. Here, the value of passive solar energy and other renewable sources application generating no pollution and impact and having no financial loads on the building occupants is encouraged.

8.5.6 Cluster 6: *Design Aspects and Strategies*

This cluster consists of 12 main indicators embracing 27.75% of variance in eco-building design indicators which are more than a quarter. All of the indicators in this cluster are relating to design strategies. The pivotal difference of this research with others in eco-design field is that in this work, the cardinal emphasis is placed on design aspects of building design, and it is assumed that design stage has a main influence on the result of building process and operation. Design strategies reinforced with environmental strategies, will provide solutions towards higher physical and mental quality of life for users. All impacts are established in design stage through a better quality design strategies. Author believes that the impacts generated by building process are the result of both design and implementation process, therefore the solutions should be sought through identification and addressing these problems in the decision stages. There are many strategies for enhancing the design eco-efficiency. Employment of these influential strategies mitigates the rate of environmental impacts as well as improving building quality and eco-efficiency.

Indicators belonging to design aspects and strategies are: Flexibility, Adaptability, Mental Aspects, Physical Aspects, Functional Zoning, Durability, Form-built-ability, Disassembling, Reusability and Recycle ability, Reliability and Usability, Maintainability, Innovation. Each of these indicators is employed by various schools of philosophy to design sustainable buildings. Eco-indicators in cluster 6 (design aspects and strategies) are considered as functional aspects of design. *Rematerialisation* and *dematerialisation* (See chapter 2) are two philosophies used in DfE.

8.6 Conclusions

Subjectivity regarding eco-building design indicators has generated a vast range of responses. This fact can be illustrated by histograms and data distribution curves (See histograms in chapter 6).

By using Data reduction and factor analysis techniques in SPSS, the 115 indicators in questionnaire were reduced to 32 indicators and grouped into six clusters. The extracted eco-building design clusters based on their orders of importance are presented below:

1. Design Aspects and strategies (Percentage of variance 27.75%)
2. Environmental Impacts (Percentage of Variance 24.64%)
3. Design Environmental Strategies (Percentage of Variance 11.99%)
4. Social Aspects (Percentage of Variance 8.72%)
5. Site analysis (Percentage of Variance 5.22%)
6. Economy (Percentage of Variance 4.81%)

In this research design aspects and strategies are introduced as an influential category in eco-building design. In comparison with other eco-design researches, focusing mainly on environmental impacts and other related aspects, this research places the main emphasis on the design aspects and strategies and believes that the rate of environmental impacts and future impacts of a building are established and controlled in the early design stage. Thus, this work looks for passive and active solutions offered in design stage. The study in this research focuses on the new 6 clusters which present the major eco-building design characteristics.

In the next chapter a model will be developed based on these six clusters to assess the eco-efficiency of design.

CHAPTER 9*

Fuzzy Eco-Building Design Model Development

9.1 Introduction

Brandon and Lombardi (2005) highlighted *'the lack of an agreed structure'* and subjectivity in sustainable decision making processes. As the majority of sustainability assessment methods are based on subjective aspects of design, a tool which is capable to turn these qualitative aspects to a quantitative decision making model is needed. In this chapter, the development of a model to evaluate building eco-efficiency is proposed. To develop the model, this work uses fuzzy theory. Fuzzy logic is described as the language of nature and involves in the rules based on reality. The fuzzy theory approach, introduced in the literature review of this study in chapter 5, is developed by Zadeh (1965). The theory could be useful for the representation of eco-building design indicators which are assessed based on subjectively and qualitatively. Fuzzy techniques are used in order to indicate the significance of each attribute of eco-building design. Fuzzy techniques are an approximation that can be used to model decision processes for which mathematical precision is impossible or impractical (Boussabaine and Elhag, 1998). Due to inclusive ability of fuzzy theory it is expanding and is being applied in different fields. Fuzzy theory is finding wide popularity in various applications that include management, economics, and engineering (Zadeh, 1994). Fuzzy theory deals with uncertainties and ambiguities in decision making process. Although fuzzy theory deals with imprecise information, it is based on sound quantitative mathematical theory (Chen and Hang, 1992).

This study uses a set of extracted variable, consisting of 32 eco-building design indicators, arranged in 6 main clusters for developing an eco-building design assessment model. The degree of membership of each indicator in the total set was extracted and computed. The model was designed based on three linguistic variables. The developed model is able to indicate the low eco-efficient and high eco-efficient bands of a particular design through its main clusters scores based on indicators MBF value (See chapter 5). The process, findings, discussions and conclusions are presented in the next sections of this chapter.

*Note: *The main part of this chapter was published in the journal of Building and Environment by Elsevier (Vakili-Ardebili and Boussabaine, 2007).*

9.2 Background

Many methods have been developed for sustainable building assessment. The majority of them are related to manufacturing. Some of them, like GBC (GB tools), BREEM, LEED, and others are related to buildings (See chapter 3). These methods attempt to establish a set of indicators for sustainable building design through application of rules, codes, and focus on specific variables. The majority of them place the main emphasis on the environmental impacts and a series of scores are given to the selected indicators based on experience and subjective opinion of assessors and then the scores are multiplied by the weights, given to each parameter for deriving a final score for each indicator. Few highlighted differences exist in comparison with this research.

1. In this work the main emphasis is placed on passive and active design aspects and strategies as well as environmental impacts. In this study it is believed that a sound selection of strategies in design stage, besides a standard quality of design can prevent many environmental impacts, risks, and other inappropriate consequences in design decisions.
2. The next difference is concerned with the application of fuzzy theory in the assessment of building design for eco-efficiency.
3. Although fuzzy theory is based on the subjective opinions of individuals, it is taking advantage of application of a set of linguistic variables to develop a model, capable to handle all different conditions (possible existing scenarios for design decisions). Therefore it can be stated that a more precise and accurate method of evaluation is achieved through using fuzzy theory.
4. The mathematical algorithms used to develop the model, can be improved and turned into assessment software using measurable numeric values.

9.3 Applied Methodology

Fuzzy logic is based on the theory of sets and subsets. If set of S and its subset F are assumed, then the degree of membership of each element of S belonging to F is defined as a "membership function" (MBF). As shown in Figs 9.4 to 9.9 a membership function for each selected eco-indicator (See Table 8.4 in chapter 8) is generated which gives the degree of membership of each indicators in each cluster (a subset) belonging to eco- indicators (the set). In this research MBF is constructed based upon indicators' statistical characteristics such as the average weighted mean and standard deviation.

A model is developed that addresses different scenarios and possibilities for each indicator. These scenarios are formed on MBF of each indicator based on different level of significance in linguistic variables. Then the combination of different scenarios of each indicator with other indicators scenarios is considered. The low and high eco-efficient bands of each cluster can be calculated through summation of scenarios. The scenarios are assumed as components consisting of linguistic variables and degree of membership of each indicator. Boussabaine and Elhag, (1998) believe that linguistic variables as described by Zadeh (1993) provide a mean of modelling human tolerance for imprecision by encoding decision relevant information into labels of fuzzy sets. In this research fuzzy average technique with linguistic variables is employed to represent eco-building design indicators. The result from this computation is presented as the scores of clusters on a spider net which indicates both building lower and upper eco-efficiency bands of a particular design.

The method which is employed in this research is based on application of fuzzy techniques with linguistic variables to represent eco-building design indicators. Dubios and Prade (1984) developed an approach for taking into account the weight of each indicator using the following formula:

$$F(y) = \sum W_i F_i(x) \quad \text{for} \quad \sum W_i = 1 \quad (9.1)$$

Later on, Dong and Wong (1987) solved the problem by developing an approximation technique that applies alpha cuts (a) (A horizontal line which creates cross-section at the level of membership) and interval analysis as well (See the following section for detailed explanation). MBF of each eco-indicator is calculated based on estimated alpha cuts (a), and then each cluster receives a weighted average membership based on MBF of its indicators by using the following equation:

$$F_i(y) = \sum W_j F_{ij}(x) \Big/ \sum W_j \quad (9.2)$$

Where $F_{ij}(x)$ is the membership function at a certain alpha cut (a)

and W_j is the weighting coefficient for criterion (a)

This equation is used to compute the final score of each category of eco-building design. The process of calculating alpha cuts for each indicator and weighted average membership of each indicator are discussed in detail in section 9.9 of this chapter. Fig 9.1 shows the process of development of a Fuzzy eco-building design Model (FEBDM).

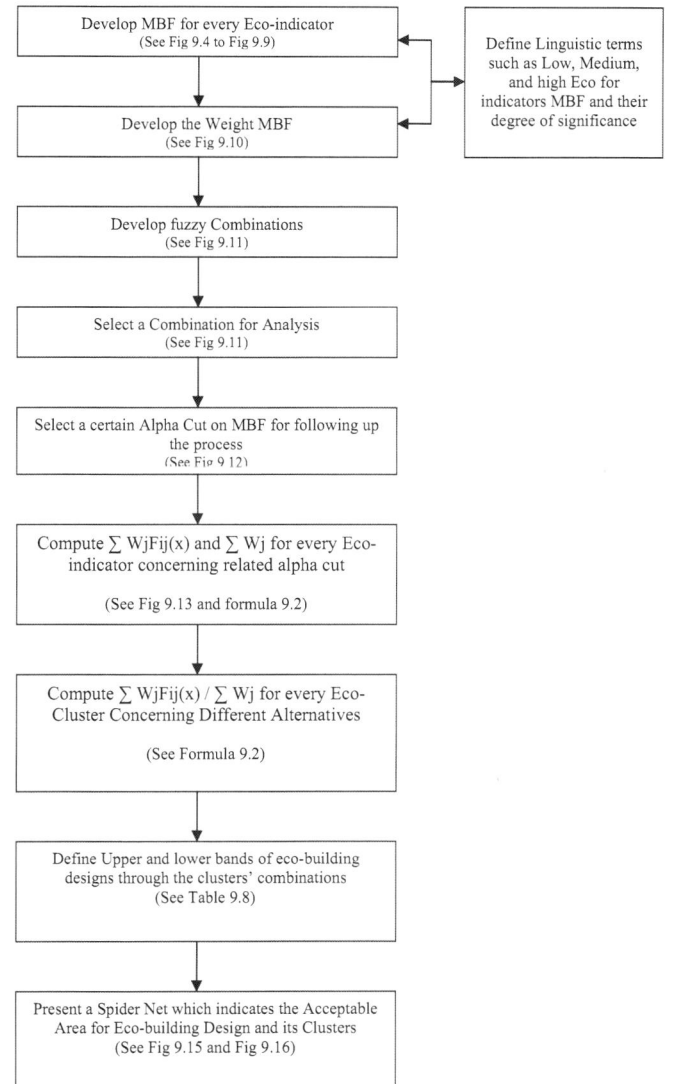

Fig 9.1 The Process of Calculation and Developing the *Fuzzy Eco-Building Design Model* (FEBDM)

9.4 Fuzziness of Eco-Building Design Indicators

Fuzzy theory is finding wide popularity in various applications that include management, economics, and engineering (Zadeh, 1994). Architecture and Eco-building design as a multidisciplinary profession, consisting of many characteristics, combining art and engineering might benefit from using fuzzy theory. Initially the theory was presented by Zadeh (1965) more than forty years ago, but its level of significance has only recently been found out.

Each variable in fuzzy theory carries a certain value, formed on linguistic expressions. For better perception one of the best examples of fuzzy logic is presented as following:

If two values of 0 and 1 are assumed for two colours of pure black and pure white, due to mathematical logic, there is no more colour and value presenting the existing relationship, But in fuzzy logic all tints of grey, locating in the range between pure black and pure white will have a certain value which increases when it moves from black toward white. This means that for each certain shade of grey, there is a value of x that exists in $0<x<1$. In the next sections of this chapter the variable linguistics will be presented in more details (See Fig 9.11 and Table 9.7 in this chapter).

Application of fuzzy logic can help to establish a method for evaluating and measuring the value of eco-indicators through their membership function (truth value or degree of their membership to eco-building design as the main set). Each fuzzy set carries a distinct membership function belonging to the interval 0 to 1, Degree of membership varies from 0 (non-membership) to 1 (full membership). This is in contrast to crisp or conventional sets, where an element can either be or not be part of the set (Boussabaine and Elhag, 1998). Based on this paradigm, the MBF for each indicator is calculated and presented (See Figs 9.4 to 9.9).

9.5 Construction of the Membership Functions

Extraction of the membership function (MBF) of the sets is the most important stage in a fuzzy decision support systems development. There are many guidelines on developing the membership functions for fuzzy sets (Dubios and Prade, 1980). Despite most of the methods used in past, were based on heuristics, but recent studies prefer to develop MBF based on statistics which are more compatible to the most naturally fuzzy sets. It is quoted by Boussabaine and Elhag (1998) that:

"The advantage of statistically based membership function is that they are naturally quantitative, that is, there is reason to believe that the membership function has a relationship to some physical property of the set". Hence this study uses criteria which result in a perceivable and accurate (but approximated) method to define membership functions for eco-building design of fuzzy sets which are formed on a statistical base. In this research, all indicators memberships of functions are based upon the mean and standards deviation of a defining feature of its members in the universe of discourse. The crucial problem is related to how to create MBF of each eco-indicator according to its statistical measures. There are conditions that should be considered to make the set work with the subjective judgement of a decision maker and underlying statistics of defined indicators. Based on other researches findings the most likely elements like average weighted mean should be considered as the high membership value. Choosing the average weighted mean as the highest value of membership is based on its statistical characteristics which represents the major priorities of the set. These sets of conditions might be represented in a quantitative way (Civanlar and Trussell, 1986) in the following section.

Note: The contents of this part are adopted and modified from (Boussabaine and Elhag, 1998):

1. $E\{F_{(x)}\} \mid X$ is distributed according to the underlying mean and standard deviation.
2. $0 \leq X \leq 1$, this is a classical interval that the membership function is defined in it. [0, 1]
3. $\int F_{(x)}2$ should be minimised: this is because, the number of parameters in the functional representation should be as small as possible.

The fuzzy membership of x defined as, $F_{(X)}$ which belongs to [0, 1], are estimated by using the following formulae.

(a) For low level of significance of a defined indicator

$$F_{(X)} = \mid (a-x) \div b \mid \quad \text{for } a-b < x < a \quad (9.3)$$

(b) For medium Level of significance of a defined indicator

$$F_{(X)} = \mid (x-a+b) \div b \mid \quad \text{for } x < a \quad (9.4)$$

$$F_{(X)} = \mid (x-a-b) \div b \mid \quad \text{for } x > a \text{ or } x = a$$

(c) For high level of significance of a defined indicator

$$F_{(X)} = \mid (x-a) \div b \mid \quad \text{for } a < x < a+b \quad (9.5)$$

Here a is the average weighted mean and b is the standard deviation. As it can be seen in the formula, there is a focal central member (a) for which $F_{(X)}$ is greater than other members of set. Also (b) is working as a controlling parameter in the formulae above. Fig 9.2 shows how these two parameters cause modifications in the shape and distribution of the $F_{(X)}$ based on the results obtained through equations in the formulae (9.1). In Fig 9.2, scale values indicated on the horizontal axis represent level of significance of a defined eco-indicator using statistical data, such as: average weighted mean, standard deviation, and variances. The fuzziness and MBF depend on parameters a and b. The parameter b determines the fuzziness of peripheral members.

In this research, since mean is a moderated representative, it can be an ideal choice for a. Fig 9.2. shows the medium range of level of significance of the eco-indicator from values from $(a-2b)$ to $(a+2b)$, with the highest degree of membership at the value of $(a-2b)$ for eco-indicator level of significance, (a) for medium level of significance and at $(a+2b)$ for high level of significance. Assuming that the distribution is normal in each indicator case, 95% of responses are within the range of membership functions and lie in interval of $[a-2b, a+2b]$.

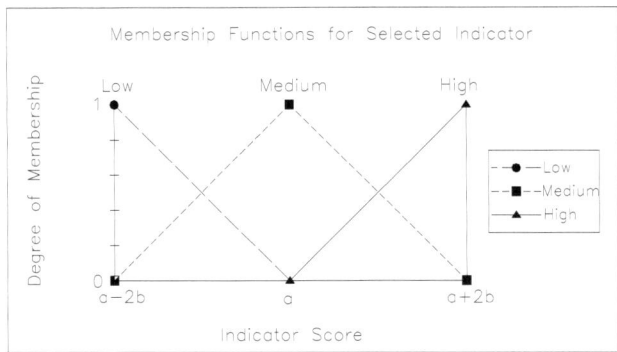

Fig 9.2 Membership Function of Eco-Building Indicators

9.6 Statistical Data Used to Develop Membership of Functions (MBFs)

Thirty two eco-indicators were extracted (See Table 8.4 in chapter 8) and renamed into six clusters. By utilisation of related statistical information of these data (See chapter 6 statistical data, also see histograms of each factor) the membership function of each eco-indicator is developed. Tables 8.1 to 8.6 show the data, used in this research, to develop the membership function of each eco- indicator. The order of tables is based on the level of influence of each cluster on eco-building design (See Table 8.4 and calculations). The level of influence of each cluster was discussed in chapter 8. The level of influence of each cluster is shown by percentage of variance in Table 8.4.

The reason that interval of [a-2b, a+2b] is selected is based on the distribution of data. In a normal distribution it is proven in probabilities that the %68 of data locate in interval of [a-b, a+b], while %95 are shown in the interval of [a-2b, a+2b], and %99.7 are presented in the interval of [a-3b, a+3b] as shown in Fig.10.3.

Where **a** presents **average weighted mean** and **b** indicates **standard deviation**.

Fig 9.3, presents the distribution of data in a normal curve. In this study interval of [a-2b, a+2b] is selected which embraces %95 of data and is shown as the hatched triangle in Fig 9.3. The hatched area in the triangle is the base for calculation of membership function of eco-indicators.

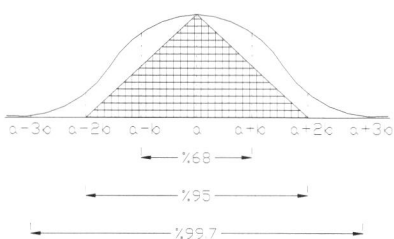

Fig 9.3 Probabilities Associated with a Normal Distribution, adopted from Montgomery and Runger (1999).

Table 9.1 *Design Aspects and Strategies* Cluster Data

Cluster	Indicator	Weighted Average Mean (a)	Standard Deviation (b)	a – 2b	a – b	a + b	a – 2b
Design Aspects and Strategies	Flexibility	6.10	1.48	3.14	4.62	7.58	9.06
	Adaptability	6.97	1.40	4.17	5.57	8.37	9.77
	Mental Aspects	5.88	1.97	1.94	3.91	7.85	9.82
	Physical Aspects	5.82	1.92	1.98	3.90	7.74	9.66
	Functional Zoning	5.06	1.92	1.22	3.14	6.98	8.90
	Durability	6.70	1.29	4.12	5.41	7.99	9.28
	Form-built ability	5.36	1.62	2.12	3.74	6.98	8.60
	Disassembling	4.77	1.95	0.87	2.82	6.72	8.67
	Reusability & Recycling	6.16	1.83	2.50	4.33	7.99	9.82
	Reliability & Usability	6.32	1.43	3.46	4.89	7.75	9.18
	Maintainability	6.72	1.25	4.22	5.47	7.97	9.22
	Innovation	5.67	1.88	1.91	3.79	7.55	9.43

Table 9.2 *Environmental Impacts* Cluster Data

Cluster	Indicator	Weighted Average Mean (a)	Standard Deviation (b)	a − 2b	a − b	a + b	a +2b
Environmental Impacts	Water Pollution	7.09	1.34	4.41	5.75	8.43	9.77
	Earth Pollution	6.96	1.38	4.20	5.58	8.34	9.72
	Air Pollution	7.18	1.32	4.54	5.86	8.50	9.82

Table 9.3 *Design Environmental Strategies* Cluster Data

Cluster	Indicator	Weighted Average Mean (a)	Standard Deviation (b)	a − 2b	a − b	a + b	a +2b
Design Environmental Strategies	Energy & Eco-efficiency	7.22	1.18	4.86	6.04	8.40	9.58
	Control of Emission	6.86	1.52	3.82	5.34	8.38	9.90
	Natural Ventilation	7.18	0.97	5.24	6.21	8.15	9.12
	Natural Light	7.14	1.09	4.96	6.05	8.23	9.32
	Passive Heating	7.04	0.98	5.08	6.06	8.02	9.00
	Passive Cooling	6.94	1.19	4.56	5.75	8.13	9.32
	Insulation & Air Tightness	7.13	1.20	4.73	5.93	8.33	9.53

Table 9.4 *Social Aspects* Cluster Data

Cluster	Indicator	Weighted Average Mean (a)	Standard Deviation (b)	a − 2b	a − b	a + b	a +2b
Social Aspects	Quality of Life	4.27	2.17	−0.07	2.10	6.44	8.61
	Government	5.75	1.82	2.11	3.93	7.57	9.39
	Society	5.73	1.77	2.19	3.96	7.50	9.27
	Organizations	4.91	1.78	1.35	3.13	6.69	8.47

Table 9.5 *Site Analysis* Cluster Data

Cluster	Indicator	Weighted Average Mean (a)	Standard Deviation (b)	a − 2b	a − b	a + b	a +2b
Site Analysis	Landscape	6.13	1.45	3.23	4.68	7.58	9.03
	Climate	6.81	1.48	3.85	5.33	8.29	9.77
	Building Orientation	7.10	1.23	4.64	5.87	8.33	9.56
	Site Restrictions	5.65	1.73	2.19	3.92	7.38	9.11

Table 9.6 *Economy* Cluster Data

Cluster	Indicator	Weighted Average Mean (a)	Standard Deviation (b)	a – 2b	a – b	a – b	a +2b
Economy	Pollution Costs	6.07	1.51	3.05	4.56	7.58	9.09
	Saving Running Costs (Capital Costs / Running Costs)	6.69	1.49	3.71	5.20	8.18	9.67

9.6.1 Membership of Functions (MBF) of Eco-Indicators

Information in Tables 9.1 to 9.6 is used to construct membership functions of eco-indicators for each cluster. Figs 9.4 to 9.9 illustrate the MBF of eco-indicators of each cluster.

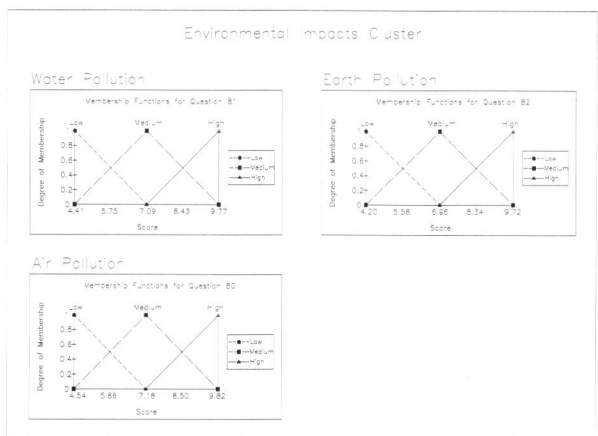

Fig 9.4 Membership of Functions of *Environmental Impacts* Cluster

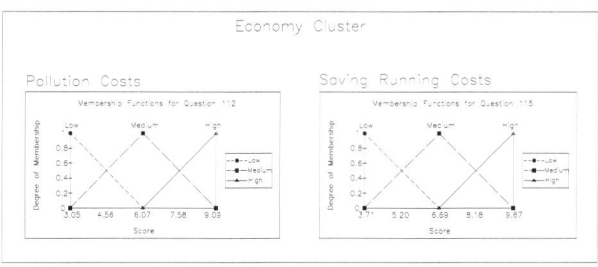

Fig 9.5 Membership of Functions of *Economy* Cluster

CHAPTER 9: FUZZY ECO-BUILDING DESIGN MODEL DEVELOPMENT

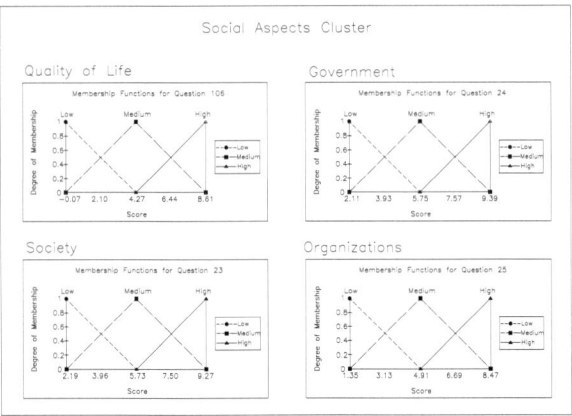

Fig 9.6 Membership of Functions of *Social Aspects* Cluster

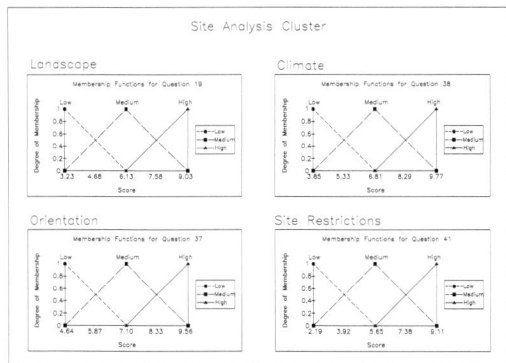

Fig 9.7 Membership of Functions of *Site Analysis* Cluster

Fig 9.8 Membership of Functions of *Design Environmental Strategies* Cluster

Fig 9.9 Membership of Functions of *Design Aspects and Strategies* Cluster

9.7 Defuzzification

"The defzzification process (output inference) translates the linguistic outputs of the inference step into numerical values so it can be used for ranking or comparisons" (Wanous, 2000). This stage of process is merged by integration of MBFs and linguistic variables and the outcome is presented as a scoring system which enables the researcher to interpret the data and comparisons them with each other. Fuzzy techniques use weights and scores for developing a numeric and quantitative scoring system. The formula, presented in methodology section is used in the assessment of six extracted clusters (See Table 8.4 in chapter 8).

$$F_i(y) = \sum W_j F_{ij}(x) \div \sum W_j \qquad (9.2)$$

Where $F_{ij}(x)$ is the score membership function at a certain alpha cut (*a*)
and W_j is the weighting coefficient for criterion (*a*)

Formula 9.2 provides the final score of each cluster. For the purpose of this research three linguistic variables that show the level of significance in respondents' answers are chosen the score MBF. The scores from **0 to 2** are considered as *(Low Eco)*, from **3 to 5** as *acceptable eco (Medium Eco),* and from **6 to 8** as *efficient eco (High Eco).* Linguistic variables provide a mean of modelling human tolerance for imprecision by encoding decision-relevant information into labels of fuzzy sets (Zadeh, 1995). By evaluating eco-indicators in terms of linguistic approximation a multi-answer to a crisp (singleton) problem can be provided, allowing decision makers to test all different alternatives for eco-indicators. The terms of linguistic variables are unlimited. Consideration of more linguistic variables will provide more scenarios and accuracy. The linguistic variables used for the evaluation of weight in the formula (9.2), are presented at the beginning of this section.

9.8 Linguistic Variables and Linguistic Terms (Possible Scenarios)

The next stage; after the development of eco-indicators membership functions is related to the definition of their linguistic variables. In this stage, the real value of each eco-indicator is translated into a linguistic value through application of linguistic variables. The possible values in linguistic variables do not include the numeric quantities, but the linguistic terms. For example here, three terms of *Low-eco*, *Medium-eco*, and *high- eco* are used as linguistic variables. The variables can be described in more detailed terms for example in the groups consisting of 5, 7, 9 or even more. There is no limitation for the number of variables terms, but since their calculation is time consuming, therefore in this research a linguistic term of three is selected to carry out the study.

Fig 9.10 illustrates membership function of significance of an eco-indicator.

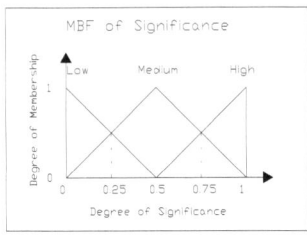

Fig 9.10 Membership Function of Eco-indicator Significance

Through Fig 9.10, the weight of each indicator can be estimated and used in formula 9.2 to compute the final score. Boussabaine and Elhag (1998) mentioned that" weight can expressed in either numeric (crisp) or linguistic (fuzzy) terms. All the weights must be defined in the same manner." In this study a fuzzy weighted average is extracted via using linguistic weights. Hence, in this study, linguistic weights are being expressed in terms of degree of significance of eco-indicator, including, *Low Eco*, *Medium Eco*, and *High Eco* (See fig 9.10). The developed model is created based on a combination of MBF of eco-indicator (Fig 9.2) and MBF of significance for each indicator (Fig 9.10). As the possibility of occurrence for each eco-indicator based on each figure is 3, therefore the whole possibilities for alternatives can be 3×3=9 for reach eco-indicator. MBF of eco-indicator always can occur in 3 possibilities, but the number of linguistic terms could be unlimited depending on the required accuracy of research being carried out. Thus the total possibility of alternatives for each eco-indicators can be 3×N, in which 3 is different alternatives of an eco-indicator MBF and N is different alternatives (terms) that represent weights in the MBF of significance for each eco indicator.

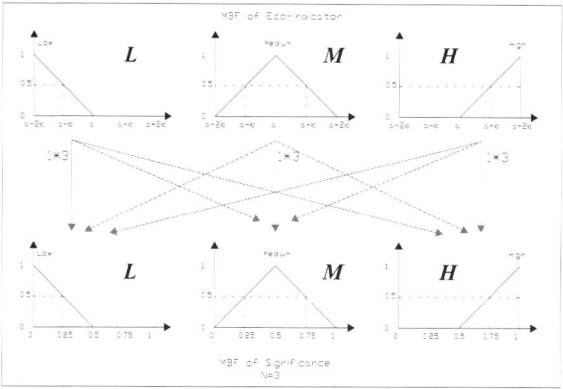

Fig 9.11 Number of Alternatives (Possible Scenarios) for each Eco-indicator

In Fig 9.11 different alternatives are collaborated. As it can be seen, these combinations can provide the study with all $W_jF_{ij}(x)$s which are needed for the computation of each cluster's MBF using equation (9.2).

9.9 Combination of Scenarios and Fuzzy Computation

For better understanding of calculation a general example for clarification is presented below. It attempts to illustrate the process of alpha cut through MBF and significance of MBF. In Fig 9.11 the alpha cuts at points 0, 0.5, and 1 are illustrated, but generally it can be regularised as shown in Fig 9.12. The combination always happen between two triangles as it can be extracted from Fig 9.11. One triangle describes the MBF of eco-indicator (*MBF* or *Indicator Score*), and the latter one, presents the MBF of significance of eco-indicator (*Linguistic terms* or *Weights*). From one triangle the score is derived and from the next one the weight is extracted, then combination of them which is presented as the multiplication of score by weight creates the fuzzy computation of $W_jF_{ij}(x)$ which is applied to extract the average weighted MBF through formula (9.2).

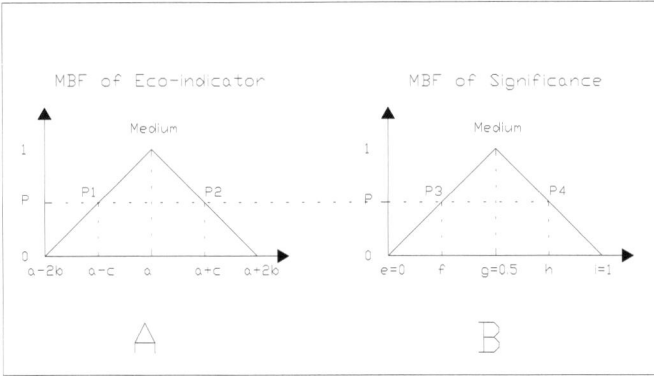

Fig 9.12 The Process of Combination of Alternatives

Clarification of combination of alternatives is carried out via assumption of two triangles shown in Fig 9.12 as triangle A and B. Supposed that from point P on the vertical axis (degree of membership) a horizontal line is drawn and point P shows the alpha cut point, (this horizontal cross-sections at various levels of membership) will create two intersection with the other two sides of triangle which are not parallel to it. These intersections in triangle A are shown as P1 and P2, and in triangle B are illustrates as P3 and P4. Then the projection of P1 and p2 on horizontal axis will have the values or scores equal to a-c, and a+c, shown on the horizontal axis (score axis in triangle A). The same would be for triangle B, the projection of P3, and P4 on the horizontal axis will show the extracted weight of the alpha cut relating to score in triangle A. Thus it can be stated that for point P (alpha cut) the MBF of eco-indicator with score of (a-c) will have the weight equal to (f) and MBF of eco-indicator with the score of (a+c) will be equal to (h). Therefore the process of combination can be summarised as follows:

Alpha cut at P=0: $W_1F_{11} = (a-2b) \times e$; and $W_1F_{12} = (a+2b) \times i$

Alpha cut at P=P: $W_1F_{11} = (a-c) \times f$; and $W_1F_{12} = (a+c) \times h$

Alpha cut at P=1: $W_1F_{11} = a \times g$

Therefore:

$$\sum W_j F_{ij}(x) = [(a-2b) \times e] + [(a+2b) \times i] + [(a-c) \times f] + [(a+c) \times h] + [a \times g]$$

The combination of two triangles $A \times B$ are shown as one triangle, presented in Fig 9.13.

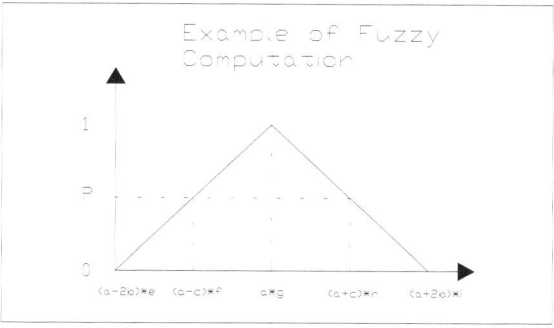

Fig 9.13 Example of Fuzzy Computation A × B

The above fuzzy computation can be replaced by the multiplication of the following matrices:

$$\sum W_j F_{ij}(x) = \begin{vmatrix} a-2b \\ a-c \\ a \\ a+c \\ a+2b \end{vmatrix} \times [e\ f\ g\ h\ i] = \{(a-2b) \times e\} + \{(a+2b) \times i\} + [\{(a-c) \times f\} + \{(a+c) \times h\} + \{a \times g\}$$

The first matrix shows the scores and the second represents the weights. Multiplication of the two matrices like fuzzy computation, presents as a numeric value, presenting average weighted membership of each cluster concerning its eco-indicators.

9.9.1 Notes in Computation

Calculation is based on triangles that have a 90 degree angles (height and one side of triangle are overlaid on each other). These triangles, also obey the same rule that is descried in former section in Fig 9.12, but the following points should be noted. In Fig 9.14, the conditions are shown in details. Imagine that triangle Y is turning into triangle Z in Fig 9.14.
What will happen?
As drawn and shown in the Fig 9.14, the triangle's side is going to overlay on its height, then it can be seen that point Q1 and Q4 are transferring on the height of the triangle. This assumption will lead to overlay of points R and S on the point T which means in triangle Z, not only T is considered as

the projection of Q3 on the horizontal side of triangle, but also, it presents the projections of points Q1 and Q4, (R and S).

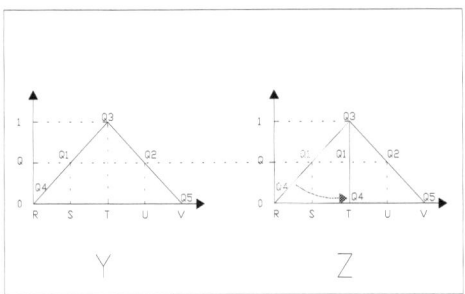

Fig 9.14 Calculation in Triangle with an Angle of 90 Degree

Thus in calculating the value for points Q1, Q4, and Q3, is assumed as the value for point Q3, but it should be calculated for three time in the process of calculation. Therefore the matrix that present the values for triangle Z is presented as follows:

Matrix for Triangle Z: [T T T U V] that indicates the values (scores or weights on the triangle's base as the horizontal axis)

The value of height of triangle should be repeated three times in the matrix. Once is done for the value of mean (peak) and twice for the transferred values of R and S which are now overlaid on T.

The extractions of matrices for all alternatives are carried out in the same process, as illustrated in Fig 9.12 and Fig 9.14. Through use of this method and its technique, the $\sum W_j F_{ij}(x)$ for different alternative represented in numeric data (See section 9.9) and matrices used for computation in Fig 9.13 in this chapter) which is easier to understand, and handle.

Then

$F_i(y) = \sum W_j F_{ij}(x) \div \sum W_j$ is calculated for each cluster.

In Fig 9.11 the scenarios of the MBF of an eco-indicator are described as **Low**, **Medium**, and **High-Eco** and presented by **L**, **M**, and **H**, and the possible MBFs of significance of eco-indicator are illustrated as **Low**, **Medium**, and **high**, and are presented by **L,M, H** as well, then the 9 possible combinations are available in Table 9.7 as follows:

Table 9.7 Possible combinations (Alternatives) of eco-indicator

$W \downarrow$ $N=3$ $F_{(x)}$	Low Eco (L)	Medium Eco(M)	High Eco(H)
Low Significance (L)	LL	ML	HL
Medium Significance(M)	LM	MM	HM
High Significance(H)	LH	MH	HH

Table 9.7 presents the created possible scenarios for each indicator. Thus for each eco-indicator 9 alternatives should be calculated. Table 9.8 presents the fuzzy computation of each eco-indicator based on possible alternatives in each cluster.

Then the MBF of each cluster will be computed based on these indicators and their existing alternatives which depend on the way they are combined with each other. In practice, decision makers, designers and stakeholders for their evaluations and assessment, combine a set of variables for arriving at particular design decisions. Therefore the range and rate of significance of eco-indicators differs in each case. This research attempts to establish a certain approximation for making the assessment easier to understand and handle. To achieve this objective, based on findings in Table 9.8, both lower and upper bands for each cluster are calculated and then the result is presented in a spider net diagram (Figs 9.15 and 9.16). The lower band for clusters consists of all minimum alternatives, here presented as **LL** alternative for each eco-indicator in its cluster.

Table 9.8 Possible Alternatives Fuzzy Computation of Eco-indicators

Cluster	Indicator	LL $W_\sim$	LL $W*F(x)$	LM $W_\sim$	LM $W*F(x)$	LH $W_\sim$	LH $W*F(x)$	ML $W_\sim$	ML $W*F(x)$	MM $W_\sim$	MM $W*F(x)$	MH $W_\sim$	MH $W*F(x)$	HL $W_\sim$	HL $W*F(x)$	HM $W_\sim$	HM $W*F(x)$	HH $W_\sim$	HH $W*F(x)$
Design Aspects and Strategies	Flexibility	0.75	4.205	2.5	11.92	4.25	17.785	0.75	6.425	2.5	18.95	4.25	27.775	0.75	6.795	2.5	22.28	4.25	35.915
	Adaptability	0.75	4.8775	2.5	14.275	4.25	21.9225	0.75	6.9775	2.5	20.925	4.25	31.3725	0.75	7.3275	2.5	24.075	4.25	39.0725
	Mental Aspects	0.75	3.9175	2.5	10.2675	4.25	14.155	0.75	6.8725	2.5	19.625	4.25	27.4525	0.75	7.365	2.5	24.0575	4.25	38.2875
	Physical Aspects	0.75	3.885	2.5	10.23	4.25	14.175	0.75	6.765	2.5	19.35	4.25	27.135	0.75	7.245	2.5	23.67	4.25	37.695
	Functional Zoning	0.75	3.315	2.5	8.33	4.25	10.945	0.75	6.195	2.5	17.45	4.25	23.905	0.75	6.675	2.5	21.77	4.25	34.465
	Durability	0.75	4.7025	2.5	13.8475	4.25	21.38	0.75	6.6375	2.5	19.975	4.25	30.0875	0.75	6.96	2.5	22.8775	4.25	37.1825
	Form-built ability	0.75	3.615	2.5	9.755	4.25	13.87	0.75	6.045	2.5	17.45	4.25	24.805	0.75	6.45	2.5	21.095	4.25	33.715
	Disassembling	0.75	3.09	2.5	7.5375	4.25	9.5475	0.75	6.015	2.5	16.8	4.25	22.71	0.75	6.5025	2.5	21.1875	4.25	33.435
	Reusability & Recycling	0.75	4.1625	2.5	11.2825	4.25	16.115	0.75	6.9075	2.5	19.975	4.25	28.4675	0.75	7.365	2.5	24.0925	4.25	38.5325
	Reliability & Usability	0.75	4.3825	2.5	12.5825	4.25	18.995	0.75	6.5275	2.5	19.375	4.25	28.6475	0.75	6.885	2.5	22.5925	4.25	36.5125
	Maintainability	0.75	4.7275	2.5	13.9875	4.25	21.685	0.75	6.6025	2.5	19.925	4.25	30.1225	0.75	6.915	2.5	22.7375	4.25	36.9975
	Innovation	0.75	3.7825	2.5	9.945	4.25	13.7575	0.75	6.6025	2.5	18.875	4.25	26.4475	0.75	7.0725	2.5	23.105	4.25	36.7875
Env. Impacts	Water Pollution	0.75	4.9825	2.5	14.71	4.25	22.7625	0.75	6.9925	2.5	21.075	4.25	31.8075	0.75	7.3275	2.5	24.09	4.25	39.1775
	Earth Pollution	0.75	4.875	2.5	14.295	4.25	21.99	0.75	6.945	2.5	20.85	4.25	31.305	0.75	7.29	2.5	23.955	4.25	38.895
	Air Pollution	0.75	5.055	2.5	14.98	4.25	23.255	0.75	7.035	2.5	21.25	4.25	32.165	0.75	7.365	2.5	24.22	4.25	39.425
	Energy & Eco-efficiency	0.75	5.12	2.5	15.395	4.25	24.195	0.75	6.89	2.5	21	4.25	32.16	0.75	7.185	2.5	23.655	4.25	38.65
	Control of Emission	0.75	4.765	2.5	13.73	4.25	20.795	0.75	7.045	2.5	20.95	4.25	31.055	0.75	7.425	2.5	24.37	4.25	39.415
Design Environmental Strategies	Natural Ventilation	0.75	5.1425	2.5	15.7675	4.25	25.18	0.75	6.5975	2.5	20.375	4.25	31.7275	0.75	6.84	2.5	22.5575	4.25	37.0625
	Natural Light	0.75	5.0825	2.5	15.3975	4.25	24.35	0.75	6.7175	2.5	20.575	4.25	31.7075	0.75	6.99	2.5	23.0275	4.25	37.7025
	Passive Heating	0.75	5.035	2.5	15.395	4.25	24.53	0.75	6.505	2.5	20.05	4.25	31.145	0.75	6.75	2.5	22.255	4.25	36.535
	Passive Cooling	0.75	4.9075	2.5	14.6725	4.25	22.95	0.75	6.6925	2.5	20.325	4.25	30.9825	0.75	6.99	2.5	23.0025	4.25	37.5275
	Insulation & Air Tightness	0.75	5.0475	2.5	15.125	4.25	23.7025	0.75	6.8475	2.5	20.825	4.25	31.8025	0.75	7.1475	2.5	23.525	4.25	38.4025

CHAPTER 9: FUZZY ECO-BUILDING DESIGN MODEL DEVELOPMENT

Table 9.8: Possible Alternatives Fuzzy Computation of Eco-indicators

Cluster	Indicator	LL		LM		LH		ML		MM		MH		HL		HM		HH	
		$W_\sim$	$W*F(x)$	$W_\sim$	$W*F(x)$	$W_\sim$	$W*F(x)$	$W_\sim$	$W*F(x)$	$W_\sim$	$W*F(x)$	$W_\sim$	$W*F(x)$	$W_\sim$	$W*F(x)$	$W_\sim$	$W*F(x)$	$W_\sim$	$W*F(x)$
Social	Quality of Life	0.75	2.66	2.5	5.7925	4.25	6.2125	0.75	5.915	2.5	16.1	4.25	20.86	0.75	6.4575	2.5	20.9825	4.25	32.795
	Government	0.75	3.8575	2.5	10.28	4.25	14.4275	0.75	6.5875	2.5	18.925	4.25	26.7125	0.75	7.0425	2.5	23.02	4.25	36.7225
	Society	0.75	3.855	2.5	10.3425	4.25	14.6175	0.75	6.51	2.5	18.75	4.25	26.565	0.75	6.9525	2.5	22.7325	4.25	36.3
	Organisations	0.75	3.2375	2.5	8.27	4.25	11.0775	0.75	5.9075	2.5	16.725	4.25	23.0925	0.75	6.3525	2.5	20.73	4.25	32.8825
Site Analysis	Landscape	0.75	4.235	2.5	12.0625	4.25	18.0775	0.75	6.41	2.5	18.95	4.25	27.865	0.75	6.7725	2.5	22.2125	4.25	35.84
	Climate	0.75	4.7375	2.5	13.695	4.25	20.8025	0.75	6.9575	2.5	20.725	4.25	30.7975	0.75	7.3275	2.5	24.065	4.25	38.9325
	Building Orientation	0.75	5.0175	2.5	14.9825	4.25	23.41	0.75	6.8625	2.5	20.825	4.25	31.7125	0.75	7.17	2.5	23.5925	4.25	38.4775
	Site Restrictions	0.75	3.805	2.5	10.2325	4.25	14.4975	0.75	6.4	2.5	18.45	4.25	26.175	0.75	6.8325	2.5	22.3425	4.25	35.69
Economy	Pollution Costs	0.75	4.15	2.5	11.7025	4.25	17.3925	0.75	6.44	2.5	18.95	4.25	27.685	0.75	6.8175	2.5	22.3475	4.25	35.99
	Saving Running Costs	0.75	4.645	2.5	13.3725	4.25	20.2375	0.75	6.88	2.5	20.45	4.25	30.295	0.75	7.2525	2.5	23.8025	4.25	38.49

To calculate the lower band of cluster formula (9.2) is used:

$$F_i(y) = \sum W_j F_{ij}(x) \div \sum W_j \qquad (2)$$

Just all $W^*F_{(x)}$ (**LL**) alternatives are used instead of $\sum W_j F_{ij}(x)$ and then the result of summation is divided to the summation of weights (All calculations, done in table 8). For example lower and upper bands for cluster 1 (***Environmental Impacts***) is calculated as follows:

$$C\ min = W_1 F_{1(X)} + W_2 F_{2(X)} + W_3 F_{3(X)} \Big/ W_1 + W_2 + W_3$$

$C_1\ min = (4.98+4.87+5.05) \div (0.75 + 0.75 + 0.75)$

$C_1\ min = 6.62$

The same process is used for calculation of upper bands, but instead of the **LL** alternatives, the **HH** ones are used in formula (10.2). Similar trends are employed for calculation of medium band. In medium band all **MM** alternatives are used in the equation. The result of calculation and approximations of each cluster is presented in Table 9.9.

Table 9.9 Calculation of Lower, Middle, and upper bands of Eco-building Design Clusters

Cluster	Minimum (MIN)	Medium (MED)	Maximum (MAX)
Environmental Impacts	6.62	8.42	9.21
Design Environmental Strategies	6.68	8.23	8.91
Site Analysis	5.92	7.89	8.76
Social Aspects	4.53	7.04	8.15
Economy	5.86	7.88	8.76
Design Aspects and Strategies	5.40	7.62	8.59

9.10 Fuzzy Eco-Building Design Model (FEBDM)

After the extraction and calculation of lower, middle and upper bands of each eco-building design cluster, a spider net diagram seems to be an appropriate tool to illustrate the result. The Fig 9.15 is used to determine building design eco-efficiency. In the diagram, the *Min*, *Med*, and *Max* of each cluster are shown on an axis (radius of co-centred circles as the scale of the measurements) which indicates each cluster by its name, and then all *Min* points of clusters are connected to each other. These connected points (lines) shape a looped polygon that presents the lower band of eco-building design. The same process is used to plot *Med*, and *Max* points to determine the medium and high eco-efficient bands of eco-building design.

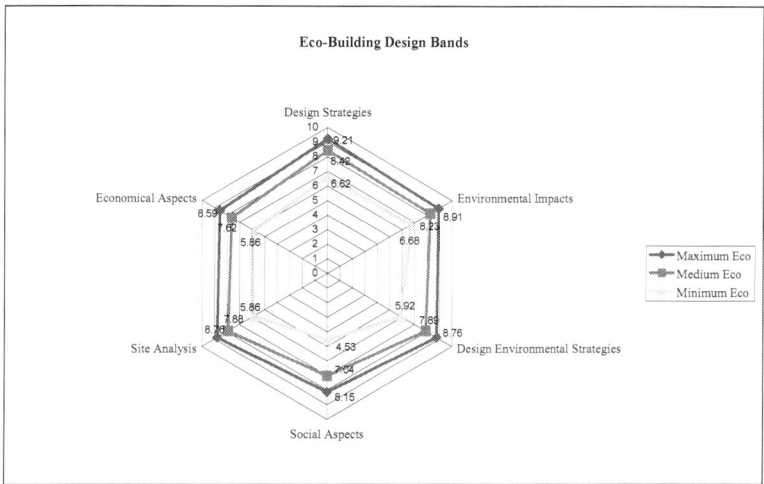

Fig 9.15 Illustration of Lower, Middle, and Upper Bands for Eco-building Design

In Fig 9.15 the highest score in diagram is 9.21 on the axis of C1. For easier assessment, if this score is assumed as 10, then all scores should be divided by 9.21 and the results is presented in Fig 9.16 which is the evolutional version of Fig 9.15 to obtain better range of scores.

Kano model (See Fig 4.3 and Fig 4.4, section 4.4 and 4.5 in chapter 4) and its relations to design process were presented in chapter 4. Based on Kano model *Min eco*, *Med eco* and *Max eco* in achieving eco-efficiency in building design are interpreted.

Min Eco embraces all rational requirements needed for a building design as found in contemporary building design whereas Med Eco includes all factors needed for a Min eco as well as added values to the design process to enhance building efficiency and quality. Max Eco embraces all emotional and rational requirements as well as passive and active design strategies to add value to eco-efficiency of building assets. The implications of max eco might be economical and environmental benefits in addition to end users satisfaction.

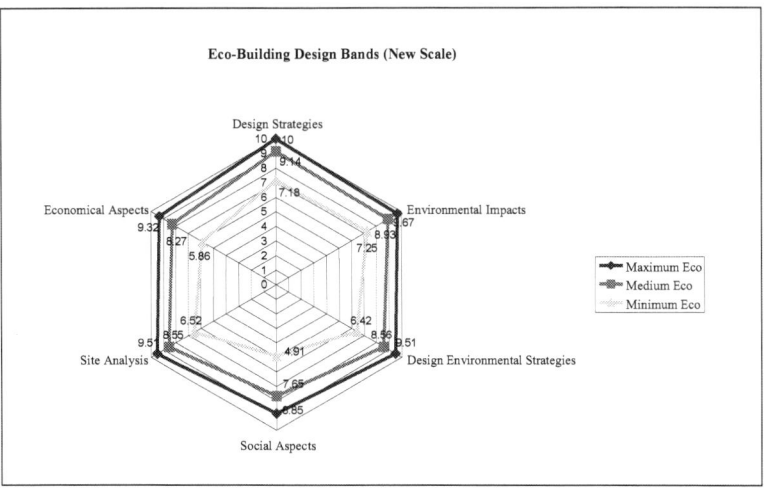

Fig 9.16 Illustration of Lower, Middle, and Upper Bands for Eco-building Design, with New Scale

9.11 Conclusions

In this chapter it was attempted to prove that fuzzy theory is an appropriate tool to deal with the subjectivity exists in the assessment of building design eco-efficiency. In fuzzy techniques the language of subjectivity is translated to mathematical approximations that seem to be easier to understand and apply for evaluations and comparisons. Through use of fuzzy logic and data analysis, a model is developed based on approximation, which is capable to indicate the minimum and maximum boundaries of eco-building design via calculation of various alternatives, which may assist in practical design decision making processes. The development of this model might partially solve the current problem in the assessment of design for eco-efficiency. The model can be expanded over time. In comparison with available assessment models in literature, this model has the advantages of taking into account design strategies alongside other indicators in existing models. Hopefully, this model provides advancement from existing methods and contributes towards achieving SBD and ultimately SD.

CHAPTER 10

Overview of Ecological Design Indicators Application

10.1 Introduction

The main objectives of this study were to uncover the most influential indicators that affect the eco-efficiency of building design. The current chapter is devoted to discuss the most important findings of the research presented in this thesis and to compare it with the other available methods in the building industry. The discussion focuses on type of indicators, selected for consideration in EBD, the techniques applied to extract the eco-indicators and finally the proposed model contributions to SBD.

10.2 Indicators Affecting Eco-Building Design (EBD)/Eco-Indicators

A number of surveys have been carried out in different countries with the aim of identifying the indicators, affecting SBD. There are some common parts among these surveys but based on the priorities considered in each study, the results might differ (see Table 3.1). BREEAM (1993, UK), LEED (1998, USA), BEPAC (1993, Canada), LCAid (Australia) and GBA (1998-2005) are all examples of efforts done in SBD and eco assessment methods. Each method is based on a certain set of assumptions resulted from those studies differ considerably. Therefore, identifying indicators characterising EBD (as a subset of SBD), seems to be essential. Based on previous researches on different methods of SBD, semi-structured interviews, brainstorming with the supervisor of the research and author's personal experience in architectural design, potential indicators were identified. Then the list of indicators was transformed into a questionnaire and the opinions of a number of architects were asked in the research pilot study. In this survey 65% of indicators (75 indicators out of 115) belong to building design category which indicates that the study is a design focused one. For clarification of the survey, the four most important and applicable methods of assessments in SBD are chosen. According to research carried out by (Crawley and Aho, 1999) and shown in Table 10.1 in this chapter the areas covered by each method are divided into six main groups, namely: Environmental management, Product marketing, building performance targeting, design guidelines, performance based codes and environmental auditing in existing buildings. The comparison of four assessment methods is presented in Table 10.1 below.

Table 10.1 Application of Environmental Assessment Methods

Assessment method	Application					
	Environmental management	Product marketing	Building performance targeting	Design guidelines	Performance-based codes	Environmental auditing in existing buildings
BREEAM		X	X	X		X
BEPAC	X	X	X	X		
LEED		X		X		X
GBA	X	X	X	X	X	X

Adopted from (Crawley and Aho, 1999).

As it is shown in the Table 10.1, each method carries certain weaknesses and strengths in the assessment of SBD. As shown in the Table 10.1, the GBA method covers more aspects than other assessment methods. "It is interesting to note that all four methods effectively deal with resources consumption issues. Beyond consumption, they vary in focus and hence, in scope and potential applicability". (Crawley and Aho, 1999, p.306)

From these four methods in the table GBA is the only one that has addressed a few design characteristics such as Indoor environment, Longevity, Process and contextual factors. These factors provide a set of design guidelines in building design which are clearly needed in the process and are considered as the design success establishing factors. Thus, this research is founded on compensation of existing weaknesses in methods available in the design assessment process. As the majority of assessments ignore or poorly focus on indoor environment, functionality of design and specific design characteristics in solving the environmental issues, hence, in this study the pivotal concern is placed on design issues and their influences in preventing environmental impacts in early stages of design process. Based on the assumption of this study the questionnaire designed for this survey consists of four main sections of *building design category* (Author's focus and Partially GBA), *environmental profile* (available methods in the market such as BREEAM, LEED, BEPAC, LCA, GBA and etc.), *energy and resources consumption profile category* (available methods in the market) and *socio-economics category* (Author's point of view and few studies). Therefore the influential indicators in EBD are classified in this survey as follows:

10.2.1. Design Strategy Indicators

Design strategies are those focusing on characteristics of building design which enhance design performance, quality and functionality. Different researchers advocated dissimilar concepts to improve design quality. Flexibility of design (Slaughter, 2001), Building performance concept

(Alexander, 1982; Gibson, 1982; Chatagnon *et al.*, 1998; winch *et al.*, 1998; CIB, 2003), building indoor quality, longevity, process, contextual factors considered by GBA (Crawley and Aho, 1999), Design for adaptability, durability, form built-ability, disassembling, decommissioning and disposal (NASA, 2001), reusability (Kibert,1994), innovation, personal safety and security and maintainability (Chew *et al.*, 2004), mental aspects, physical aspects, functional zoning, worker productivity (NASA, 2001) and design for life cycle cost (Kibert, 1994) in a building are factors that can affect the quality of design and performance of a building regarding its effectiveness in EBD.

10.2.2 Environmental Design Strategy Indicators

The indicators of this group are those found in design strategies category but because of the importance of this group the author has preferred to categorise them as an independent cluster in EBD. Design characteristics such as performance, longevity, durability (NASA, 2001), flexibility (NASA, 2001; Slaughter, 2001), maintainability (NASA 2001), energy efficiency (Fisher, 1992), embodied energy (NASA, 2001) and eco-efficiency and healthier and safer materials consumption (Fisher, 1992; Kibert, 1994) are those mentioned in design strategies. The examples of this group could be Natural ventilation and light, passive cooling and heating, insulation and air tightness and over ally, policies providing better conditions of indoor quality. (Langston and ding, 2001; Nicholls, 2001; Roaf *et al.*, 2001 and Smith, 2001).

The application of these indicators in a building design indicates the level of innovation, design knowledge and technology to control emissions and existing environmental impacts.

10.2.3 Site Analysis Indicators

The majority of designers and specifically architects are aware that eco-efficiency achievement is impossible unless prudent considerations of landscape, climate, site restriction and particularly building orientation are made in early stages of design. Based on the importance and influence of this group in the result of design process this cluster is particularly focused in EBD and relevant assessment method. The researches handled by (Kibert, 1994; NASA, 2001; Nicholls, 2001; Roaf *et al.*, 2001; Smith, 2001) approve the decisions made in this study. It should be known that application of different types of renewable energy and enhancing eco-efficiency of a building is achievable just through consideration of site and surrounding characteristics and specifications. In macro scale point of view site selection can definitely minimise the rate of both environmental and transportation impact (NASA, 2001).

10.2.4 Environmental Impact Indicators

This group of indicators are those that are emphasised by all assessment methods available in the market. The reason is that they are considered as the main indicators in DFE and SBD. Boussabaine and kirkham (2004) classified the impacts into three main groups namely: air impacts, water impacts and earth impacts. The impacts are caused by material consumption and the design applied technology during the building process. There are many different precise findings about environmental impacts embracing both qualitative and quantitative assessment methods. These methods are discussed and surveyed in product industry more efficiently than in building design (see Table 3.3). There are many common attributes between product and building designs. Hence, methods used in manufacturing might be applied in building design assessment.

10.2.5 Social Indicators

Many researchers like (Du Plessis, 2001) believe that ignorance of this category leads to failure of research in SBD. They also stated that SD and SBD should embrace social aspects as fundamental aspect of SD. Thus in this research indicators like quality of life, influence of government, society and different types of organisations in EBD are addressed and focused on.

10.2.6 Economical Indicators

Economical profits are good motivators for human activities. Therefore the orientation of development in human activities should be harmonised with the rate of profits and economical issues. In this research two main indicators are introduced as the most important factors which should be taken into account in SBD. Those two are *pollution costs* and *saving running costs* in building design.

Pollution costs include the costs of prevention and rehabilitation of impacts. Saving running costs embodies all efforts done to reduce the assets running costs (e.g. application of more efficient appliances and equipments in properties, application of renewable energy types) (Nicholls, 2001; Roaf *et al.*, 2001)

10.3 Modelling Technique

The model developed in this study, entitled fuzzy eco-building design model (FEBDM), has been created based on former assessment methods, attempting to improve the weaknesses of them partially to some extents. As explained in the former sections the current methods do not include factors embracing potential design, design environmental strategies and functionality attributes. They mainly focus on environmental impacts. In the next section of this chapter the differences between (FEBDM) model and other available models are addressed and explained.

10.3.1 Differences

The differences between this model and current models can be summarised and categorised in following main groups: concept, analysis method, assessment categories and model development.

10.3.1.1 Conceptual differences in indicators selection

EBD in this research embraces all design characteristics as well as consideration of environmental strategies (See eco-indicators in the questionnaire). Hence, the selection of indicators was based on the definition of EBD presented by this study in chapter 4. Since this research focuses highly on early stages of design to prevent probable environmental impacts, therefore, application of strategies and concepts that enhance the performance, energy and eco-efficiency in the building should be the essential priorities at this stage of design.

10.3.1.2 Methods of Analysis of Data

In this research the data obtained from questionnaire survey, was processed based on scientific methods. Descriptive analysis and statistical data obtained through statistics and computer precision (See chapter 6). Factor ranking and data reduction were carried out by computer processing through employment of SPSS and Excel softwares (See chapters 7 and 8).

10.3.1.3 Assessment Categories

Based on distinct objectives followed in this survey, specific categories were selected to carry out the research. As the research is seeking to develop an EBD assessment method, thus all dimensions of SD should be recognisable in the study and its relevant terms. The final result of the study is the development of a fuzzy model. The research categorised the eco-indicators into six distinctive classes. These six groups based on their degree of significance in EBD assessment are: Design Strategies, Environmental Impacts, Design Environmental Strategies, Social concerns, Site Analysis and Economic Concerns. The strength of this classification is related to significance in addressing SD issues. (Campbell,1996 and Ryding,1998)

10.3.1.4 Model Development

The model is based on fuzzy theory to reduce the influence of subjectivity and qualitative data in EBD assessment. Application of fuzzy theory in this model makes it more reliable and applicable in comparison with other methods. Other methods rely completely on qualitative assessment that is based on scoring or weighting but fuzzy theory application enables the fuzzy eco-building design model (FEBDM) to have a higher accuracy in its assessment. (See chapter 9).

Also the model was developed based on the extracted eco-indicators in data processing stage. As the questionnaire contents were formed based on SD dimensions, thus the extracted eco-indicators in this research are the representative of all eco-indicators carrying characteristics of SBD. Hence it is possible to state that fuzzy eco-building design model presented in this research is formed in accordance with sustainability principles. This fact confirms why author believes that EBD is a subset of SBD. The aspects being included in this study embrace design and design environmental strategies, precise site analysis, environmental impacts, social and economical concerns related to building process over WLC whereas current assessment methods exclude design strategies and focus mainly on the impact of material and energy consumption. Only GBA has addressed design longevity, process and contextual factors, environmental loading and indoor environment.

10.3.2 Model Testing

Testing is essential for approving the validity of the model. To test the fuzzy eco-building design model (FEBDM), three architectural practices were contacted and they were asked to fill a form, related to one of the projects designed by their practice. The form contains 32 eco-indicators, clustered into six categories which were developed through factor analysis and data reduction in chapter 8. In the form, the designers were asked to score their projects for each eco-indicator's level of consideration and implementation in design of the project. Tables 10.2 to 10.4 present the scores and the result of calculations belonging to each project. Based on the given scores the computations were carried out and the final scores of each project were extracted through the use of the FEBDM. The illustration of final scores results extracted through FEBDM are presented in Fig 10.2 to Fig 10.4. The light grey coloured area indicates the proposed area of eco-building design whereas the dark grey surface portrays the obtained score by the project. The uncovered area which is remained and is shown by light grey shows the eco-inefficiencies of project design based on eco-efficiency in FEBDM assessment.

As shown in Fig 10.2 and Fig 10.3 both projects weaknesses are related to environmental impacts which are derived from lack of design environmental strategies. This fact and the results imply the author's point of view about application of environmental strategies in early design stages.

The model enables architects and stakeholders to find out where the weaknesses are laying and provide them with a graphic illustration of their designs based on scores given to 32 extracted eco-indicators. Figs 10.2, 10.3 and 10.4 are the results of three real design projects provided and assessed by practices.

CHAPTER 10: OVERVIEW OF ECOLOGICAL DESIGN INDICATORS APPLICATION

1. **Project Name: New Primary School**
2. **Architect: A**
3. **Location: Liverpool**

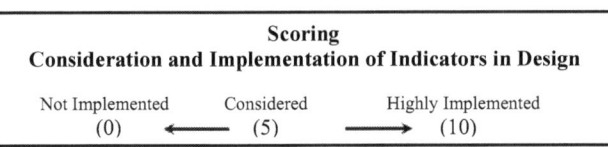

Scoring
Consideration and Implementation of Indicators in Design

Not Implemented   Considered   Highly Implemented
(0)   ←   (5)   →   (10)

Table 10.2 Project 1

	Project One (New Primary School -Liverpool)				
	To what extents the following eco-indicators are implemented and considered in this design?	Score	W_i	$F_{ij(x)}$	$\Sigma W_i F_{ij(x)} / \Sigma W_i$	Score in the Model
Design Aspects	1. Flexibility of Building (e.g. in use, extension, capacity)	5	4	0.65	7.80	8.47
	2. Adaptability of Building	5	4	0		
	3. Mental Aspects (Spiritual Effects)	7	5.6	0.96		
	4. Physical Aspects	7	5.6	0.97		
	5. Functional Zoning regarding Eco-Efficiency	5	4	0.86		
	6. Durability of Building	8	6.4	0.94		
	7. Building Form-Built-Ability	8	6.4	0.84		
	8. Building Dismantling, Disassembling and Deconstruction Regarding WLC	3	2.4	0.70		
	9. Reusability and Recycling of Building Components	3	2.4	0		
	10. Reliability and Usability of Building	8	6.4	0.89		
	11. Building Maintainability	8	6.4	0.93		
	12. Level of Innovation applied in Building	3	2.4	0.57		
Environmental	1. Water pollution	5	4	0	0	0
	2. Air Pollution	5	4	0		
	3. Earth Pollution (Solid Wastes and landfills)	2	1.6	0		
Design Environmental Aspects	1. Energy and Eco-Efficiency	5	4	0	5	5.40
	2. Control of Emission	5	4	0.53		
	3. Natural Ventilation	7	5.6	0.59		
	4. Natural Light	7	5.6	0.65		
	5. Passive Heating	2	1.6	0		
	6. Passive Cooling	2	1.6	0		
	7. Insulation and Air tightness	6	4.8	0.85		
Social Aspects	1. Quality of Life (User expectations Fulfilment)	8	6.4	0.74	7.80	8.47
	2. Government (Policies)	9	7.2	0.80		
	3. Society (Culture and Level of Acceptance)	9	7.2	0.79		
	4. Organisations (Benefits)	8	6.4	0.79		
Site Analysis	1. Landscape	7	5.6	0.82	7.80	8.47
	2. Climate	6	4.8	0.66		
	3. Building Orientation	8	6.4	0.85		
	4. Site restrictions	9	7.2	0.77		
Economy	1. Pollution Prevention and Rehabilitation Costs	3	2.4	0	6.90	7.49
	2. Saving Running Costs (Capital Costs / Running Costs)	8	6.4	0.95		

209

CHAPTER 10: OVERVIEW OF ECOLOGICAL DESIGN INDICATORS APPLICATION

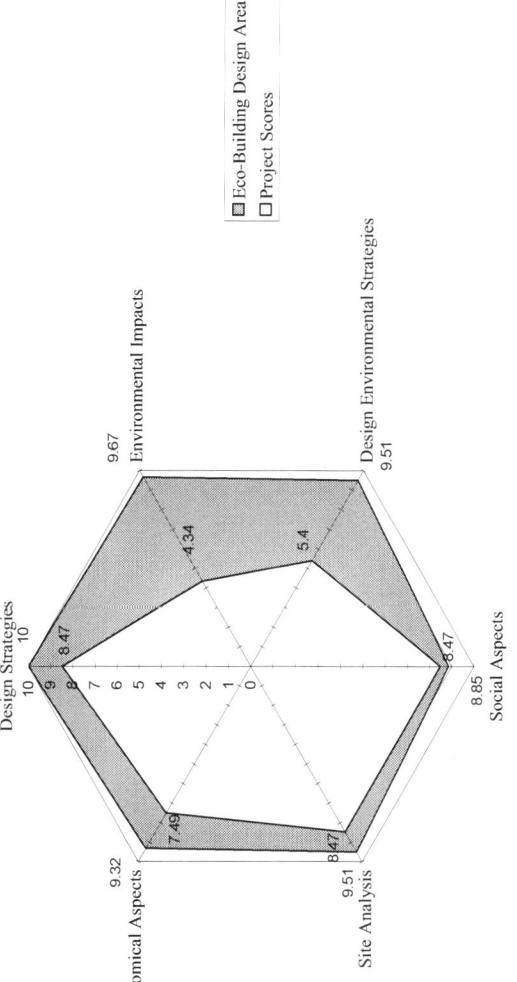

Fig 10.1 Project 1 Assessment

1. Project Name: Royal Mill Apartments
2. Architect: B
3. Location: Manchester

Scoring
Consideration and Implementation of Indicators in Design

Not Implemented   Considered   Highly Implemented
(0)   ⟵⟶   (5)   ⟶   (10)

Table 10.3 Project 2

	Project Two (Royal Mill Apartments - Manchester)					
	To what extents the following eco-indicators are implemented and considered in this design?	Score	W_i	$F_{ij(x)}$	$\Sigma W_i F_{ij(x)} / \Sigma W_i$	Score in the Model
Design Aspects	1. Flexibility of Building (e.g. in use, extension, capacity)	9	7.2	0.81	8.51	9.24
	2. Adaptability of Building	9	7.2	0.95		
	3. Mental Aspects (Spiritual Effects)	4	3.2	0.84		
	4. Physical Aspects	7	5.6	0.97		
	5. Functional Zoning regarding Eco-Efficiency	8	6.4	0.82		
	6. Durability of Building	10	8	0.74		
	7. Building Form-Built-Ability	8	6.4	0.84		
	8. Building Dismantling, Disassembling and Deconstruction Regarding WLC	3	2.4	0.70		
	9. Reusability and Recycling of Building Components	1	0.8	0		
	10. Reliability and Usability of Building	8	6.4	0.89		
	11. Building Maintainability	8	6.4	0.93		
	12. Level of Innovation applied in Building	6	4.8	0.95		
Environmental	1. Water pollution	5	4	0.50	5.00	5.40
	2. Air Pollution	5	4	0.50		
	3. Earth Pollution (Solid Wastes and landfills)	5	4	0.50		
Design Environmental Aspects	1. Energy and Eco-Efficiency	5	4	0	1.54	1.67
	2. Control of Emission	5	4	0.53		
	3. Natural Ventilation	4	3.2	0		
	4. Natural Light	4	3.2	0		
	5. Passive Heating	3	2.4	0		
	6. Passive Cooling	3	2.4	0		
	7. Insulation and Air tightness	3	2.4	0.51		
Social Aspects	1. Quality of Life (User expectations Fulfilment)	7	5.6	0.70	7.00	7.60
	2. Government (Policies)	7	5.6	0.96		
	3. Society (Culture and Level of Acceptance)	8	6.4	0.80		
	4. Organisations (Benefits)	5	4	0.24		
Site Analysis	1. Landscape	5	4	0.63	6.61	7.18
	2. Climate	5	4	0.53		
	3. Building Orientation	5	4	0.63		
	4. Site restrictions	9	7.2	0.77		
Economy	1. Pollution Prevention and Rehabilitation Costs	5	4	0.65	7.75	8.41
	2. Saving Running Costs (Capital Costs / Running Costs)	6	4.8	0.88		

CHAPTER 10: OVERVIEW OF ECOLOGICAL DESIGN INDICATORS APPLICATION

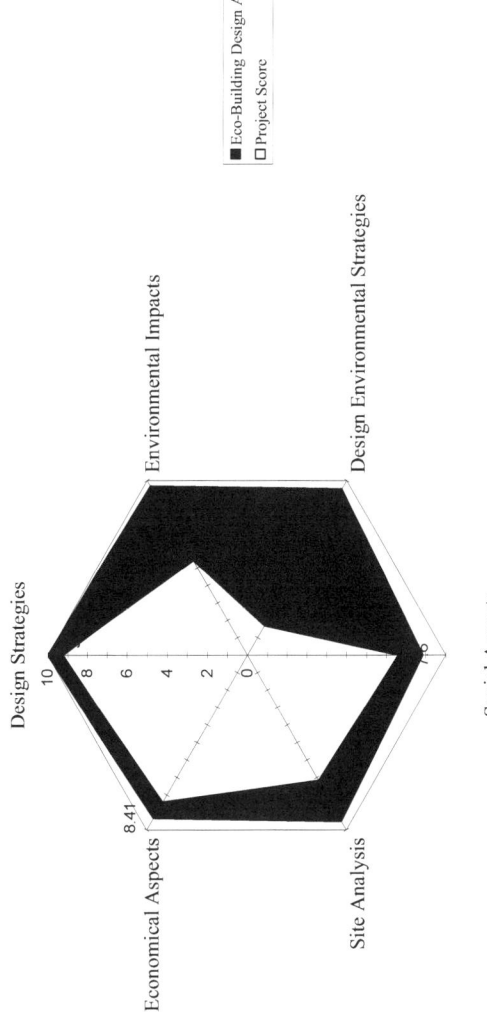

Fig 10.2 Project 2 Assessment

1. **Project Name: Kaskenmaw School for Disabled**
2. **Architect: C**
3. **Location: Oldham**

```
                    Scoring
    Consideration and Implementation of Indicators in Design

        Not Implemented    Considered    Highly Implemented
             (0)      ←——      (5)      ——→      (10)
```

Table 10.4 Project 3

	Project Three (Kaskenmaw School for Disabled, Oldham)					
	To what extents the following eco-indicators are implemented and considered in this design?	Score	W_i	$F_{ij(x)}$	$\Sigma W_i F_{ij(x)} / \Sigma W_i$	Score in the Model
Design Aspects	1. Flexibility of Building (e.g. in use, extension, capacity)	5	4	0.65	7.30	7.93
	2. Adaptability of Building	5	4	0		
	3. Mental Aspects (Spiritual Effects)	10	8	0.73		
	4. Physical Aspects	10	8	0.71		
	5. Functional Zoning regarding Eco-Efficiency	8	6.4	0.82		
	6. Durability of Building	8	6.4	0.94		
	7. Building Form-Built-Ability	10	8	0.59		
	8. Building Dismantling, Disassembling and Deconstruction Regarding WLC	5	4	0.90		
	9. Reusability and Recycling of Building Components	5	4	0.70		
	10. Reliability and Usability of Building	8	6.4	0.89		
	11. Building Maintainability	8	6.4	0.93		
	12. Level of Innovation applied in Building	8	6.4	0.69		
Environmental	1. Water pollution	7	5.6	0.50	5.00	5.40
	2. Air Pollution	7	5.6	0.50		
	3. Earth Pollution (Solid Wastes and landfills)	7	5.6	0.50		
Design Environmental Aspects	1. Energy and Eco-Efficiency	7	5.6	0.65	6.76	7.34
	2. Control of Emission	8	6.4	0.92		
	3. Natural Ventilation	7	5.6	0.59		
	4. Natural Light	10	8	0.80		
	5. Passive Heating	6	4.8	0		
	6. Passive Cooling	6	4.8	0.55		
	7. Insulation and Air tightness	9	7.2	0.81		
Social Aspects	1. Quality of Life (User expectations Fulfilment)	10	8	0.57	6.22	6.75
	2. Government (Policies)	10	8	0.69		
	3. Society (Culture and Level of Acceptance)	10	8	0.67		
	4. Organisations (Benefits)	10	8	0.56		
Site Analysis	1. Landscape	10	8	0.67	7.63	8.28
	2. Climate	9	7.2	0.93		
	3. Building Orientation	10	8	0.81		
	4. Site restrictions	10	8	0.66		
Economy	1. Pollution Prevention and Rehabilitation Costs	8	5.6	0.92	8.24	8.94
	2. Saving Running Costs (Capital Costs / Running Costs)	8	5.6	0.81		

CHAPTER 10: OVERVIEW OF ECOLOGICAL DESIGN INDICATORS APPLICATION

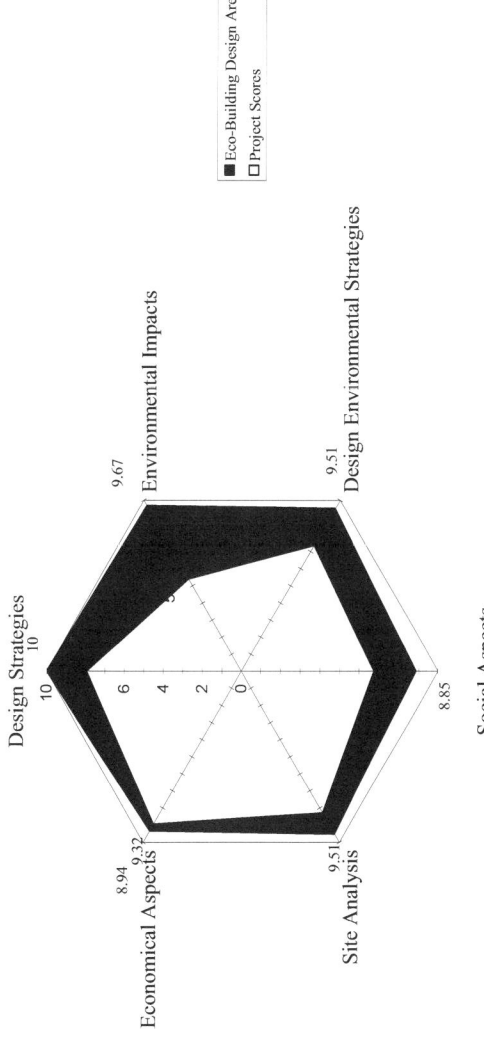

Fig 10.3 Project 3 Assessment

10.3.3 Advantages

Advantages of FEBDM are presented as follows:

1. Weighting is based on mathematical rules and created based on scientific methods.
2. The model is developed based on a context-sensitive approach.
3. The model is developed based on design strategies, environmental design strategies, and environmental performance indicators as indicated by SD in Fig 2.2 in chapter 2.
4. The model was simplified in order to be used easily.
5. The model attempts to minimise the level of subjectivity in the assessment of eco-indicators through application of *fuzzy theory*.

10.3.4 Comparison with Other Methods

Table 10.5 illustrates the aspects covered by EBD and makes a comparison between EBD and the four available methods (BREEAM, BEPAC, LEED and GBA) in SBD. As shown in the Table 11.5 many factors are addressed by current available methods as these methods concentrate on environmental issues.

It can be concluded from the Table 10.5 that BREEAM and BEPAC mainly cover aspects such as environmental impacts and physical design attributes whereas LEED in addition to the aforementioned attributes deals with maintainability as well. GBA includes more characteristics of functionality in design such as: adaptability, durability and maintainability as well as a number of aspects in social and site analysis concerns.

There is a lack of consideration of design attributes among the majority of environmental assessment methods. In addition to this, transport factors should also be added to the assessment factors. This factor was considered as an eco-indicator in this research and embraces energy, resources consumption and embodied energy related issues. As it is seen in the table there are many areas in design strategies which are not covered by current environmental assessments methods. The author believes that; since environmental impacts are implications of our designs and their related terms, therefore solutions to problems should be sought in design stage specifically in the early stages of design through concepts and applied passive design strategies.

Illustration in Table 10.5 shows that other methods still have some weaknesses in aspects such as social, economical and environmental design strategies. Building design is the art of architect to advocate all aspects of SD simultaneously in the form of building (Williamson *et al.*, 2003). The comparison made through Table 10.5 clarifies the strength and weak aspects of current methods.

Table 10.5 Scopes of Assessment Methods

Cluster	Indicator	Assessment Method				
		BREEAM	BEPAC	LEED	GBA	FEBDM
Design Aspects and Strategies	Flexibility	-	-	-	-	+
	Adaptability	-	-	-	+	+
	Mental Aspects	-	-	-	-	+
	Physical Aspects	+	+	+	+	+
	Functional Zoning for Eco-Efficiency	-	-	-	-	+
	Durability	-	-	-	+	+
	Form-built ability	-	-	-	-	+
	Disassembling and Decommissioning	-	-	-	-	+
	Reusability & Recycling	-	-	-	-	+
	Reliability & Usability	-	-	-	-	+
	Maintainability	-	-	+	+	+
	Innovation	-	-	-	-	+
Environmental Impacts	Water Pollution	+	+	+	+	+
	Earth Pollution	+	+	+	+	+
	Air Pollution	+	+	+	+	+
Design Environmental Strategies	Energy & Eco-efficiency	+	+	-	+	+
	Control of Emission	-	-	-	+	+
	Natural Ventilation	-	-	-	-	+
	Natural Light	-	-	-	-	+
	Passive Heating	-	-	-	-	+
	Passive Cooling	-	-	-	-	+
	Insulation & Air Tightness	-	-	-	+	+
Social Aspects	Quality of Life	-	-	-	+	+
	Government	-	-	-	-	+
	Society	-	-	-	+	+
	Organizations	-	-	-	-	+
Site Analysis	Landscape	-	-	-	+	+
	Climate	-	-	-	+	+
	Building Orientation	-	-	-	-	+
	Site Restrictions	-	-	+	+	+
Economy	Pollution Costs	-	-	-	-	+
	Saving Running Costs Or Capital Costs / Running Costs	-	-	-	-	+

Poorly Concerned (-)
Strongly Concerned (+)

10.4 Scope

The majority of previous assessment methods and models are concerned with environmental impacts and poor considerations of design characteristics. This research looks at passive design strategies as the main influential factors in coping with environmental impacts. Functionality and performance of design can improve EBD through application of both design technical and environmental strategies in early stages of design. EBD aims to uses mainly passive design strategies to solve environmental impact problems.

10.5 Impacts

EBD contributions in the field of building design embrace many aspects. The impacts of EBD indicators and application of FEBDM will provide the following design impacts:
1. Design quality and decision making enhancement through application of design guidelines provided by EBD indicators.
2. Moving towards SBD based on the use of SD components as eco-indicators in EBD.
3. Obtaining more eco-efficient and environmental compatible buildings.
4. Moving towards self- sufficient building systems (an environmental equilibrium).
5. The use of EBD will lead to providing buildings with efficiency, safety and health, quality, performance and socio-economical issues.
6. Retrospective consideration of flexibility in various concepts of design will enhance the evolutional process of EBD.

10.6 Conclusions

This study aims to provide a systematic, scientific and qualitative approach in assessing eco-building design. The developed model based on EBD indicators helps architects and stakeholders in early stages of building design in their decision making to overcome the weaknesses leading to environmental impacts occurrences.

Achieving Eco-efficiency and high performance in buildings are the main objectives of EBD. As the absence of an agreement among researchers on a suitable assessment method was strongly tangible, thus EBD was developed based on SBD principles embracing all SD dimensions and their relevant issues. The developed model is a very flexible model in the sense that its attributes can be modified and improved. This means new rules and eco-indicators can be added and the former ones could be omitted. It provides the model with *flexibility in sustainability* (Guy and Moore, 2005).

The major conclusion of this work is that; since FEBDM is based on SBD principles, it can successfully be employed to assess building design. It is an enhancement on many of previous methods because it not only has formed on their achievements but also attempted to add values to the previous methods through new design strategies and its specific focused terms. Moreover FEBDM is a promising development tool in SBD which might be applied to model the decision making of both building design and building management. This chapter discussed the objectives followed by EBD indicators leading to FEBDM development.

References

Alexander, M. (1997), *The Rebound Effect in Energy Conservation*, Ph.D. Dissertation (www.leprechaun.com/econ.html) [Accessed on 18/8/2005]

Allenby, B. R. and Fullerton, A. (1991-92), Design for Environment: A New Strategy for Environmental Management. *Pollution Preventation Review*, winter, pp.51-61.

American Heritage on line dictionary at http://education.yahoo.com/reference/dictionary/entry?id=p0580800 [accessed on 24/8/2005]

ARBE 121, Sustainability, Sustainable Development Definitions [online source] http://www.liv.ac.uk/~jabr05/ARBE121Sustainabledevelopment.ppt#12 [Accessed on 24/8/2005)

ASHRAE (American Society of Heating, Refrigerating and Air-Conditioning Engineers), (2000) Seminar on Maintainability of HVAC Systems, Annual meeting in Minneapolis, http://edesign.state.fl.us/fdi/edesign/news/0008/ash.htm [Accessed on 10/6/2004]

Ashworth, A. (2004), *Cost Studies of Buildings* (4th edition), Harlow, Prentice Hall, ISBN: 013145322X

Bakker, C. (1995), *Environmental Information for Industrial Designers*, Delft University, Delft

Baldwin, R. et al., (1991), *BREEAM 2/91: An Environmental Assessment for New Superstores and Supermarkets*, Building Research Establishment, Gaston., UK

Barnes, M. (1988), Construction project management, *International Journal of Project Management*, No. 6, pp 69–79.

Barrett, P. and Sexton, M. G. (1998) *Integrating to Innovate, Report for the Construction Industry Council*, DETR/CIC, London.

Barringer, H. P. (1997), *Life Cycle Costs and Reliability for Process Equipment, Energy week 1997*, Sponsored by ASME & API and organised by Penn Well Conference, Houston, TX.

Bartholomew, D.J., and Knott, M. (1999), *Latent variables models and factor analysis*, Oxford University Press, London.

BATE (1998) Cleaner production reduces costs for Chinese manufacturer. *Business and the Environment ISO 14000 Update*, No.4, pp. 3-4.

BBCPersian.com by Payam Yazdian in Farsi [online source accessed on 5/5/2005] available at: Http://www.bbc.co.uk/persian/iran/story/2005/05/05/05/05_mj-yazdian-zadeh-berlin

Berger, Gene and Herzl Marouni, H. (1993), *ASQC Section 1405 Certified Reliability Refresher Course*, Published by Gene Berger, Houston, TX.

Berggren, B. (1999), Industry's contribution to sustainable development, *Building Research and Information*, Vol. 27, No. 6, pp.432-436.

Bhamra, T., Evans, S., van der Zwan, F. & Cook, M. (2001) "Moving from Eco-Products to Eco-Service", *Journal of Design Research v2:* http://jdr.tudelft.nl/articles/issue2001.02/article3.html [Accessed on 7/9/2005]

Bisset A.F. (1994), Designing a Questionnaire: Send a Personal Covering Letter, *BMJ*, Vol. 308, pp.202-203.

Blanchard, B. S. and Lowery, E.E. (1969). *Maintainability: Principles and practices*, McGraw-Hill, New York.

Blanchard, B. S.; Verma, D. and Peterson, E. L., (1995), *Maintainability: A key to Effective Serviceability and maintenance Management*, Prentice-Hall, Englewood Cliffs, NJ.

Bloom M. and Fischer J. (1982), *Evaluating Practice: Guild lines for the accountable professional*, Prentice Hall, New Jersey.

Bourdeau, L. (1999), Sustainable Development and the Future of Construction: A comparison of vision from Various Countries, *Building Research and Information*, Vol. 27, No. 6, pp. 354-366

Boussabaine, A. H. and Elhag, T. (1999), Applying fuzzy techniques to cash flow analysis, *Construction Management and Economics*, Vol.17, No. 6, pp.745-755

Boussabaine, H. and Kirkham, R. (2004), *Whole Life-Cycle Costing: Risk and Risk Responses*, Blackwell publishing, Oxford, The UK, ISBN: 1405107863

Brand, S. (1994), *How Buildings Learn: What Happens after They're Built*, Vikings Press, New York, NY.

Brandon, P. S. (1999), Sustainability in management and organization: the key issues? *Building Research and Information*, Vol. 27, No. 6, pp. 391-397.

Brandon, P.S. and Lombardi, P. (2005), *Evaluating sustainable Development: In the Built Environment*, Blackwell Science, Oxford, The UK, ISBN: 0632064862

BREEM, http://www.breeam.org/, [Accessed on 1/9/2005]

Brennan, J. (1997), Green Architecture: style over content. *Architectural Design*, Vol. 67, No. 1-2, pp. 23-25.

Brezet, J.C., Hemel, C. (1997), *Ecodesign-A promising approach to sustainable production and consumption*, Delft University of Technology, Delft.

Brochner, J.; Ang, G.K.I. and Fredriksson, G. (1999), Sustainability and the performance concept: encouraging innovative environmental technology in construction. *Building Research and Information*, Vol. 27, No.6, pp. 368-373.

Bruntland, G.H., et al. (1987), *Our Common Future:* Report of the World Commission on Environment and Development. Oxford, Oxford University Press, P. 8.

Bunker, S.G. (1996), Raw material and the Global Economy: Oversights and Distortions in industrial ecology, *Society & Natural Resources*, Vol.9, pp 419-429

Burati, J. L., Farrington, J. J., and Ledbetter, W. B. (1992), Causes of quality deviations in design and construction, *Construction Engineering and Management, Vol.* 118, No. 1, pp. 34-49.

Burns R. (2000), *Introduction to Research Methods*, 4th Edition, Sage Publication, London, pp. 556-594

Cambridge Dictionary [Accessed on 14/10/2005] available at: http://dictionary.cambridge.org/results.asp?searchword=modelling

Campbell, S. (1996), Green cities, growing cities, just cities? Urban planning and the contradictions of sustainable development, *APA Journal (Journal of the American Planning Association)*, Summer, Vol.62, No. 3, pp. 296-312.

Carson, R. (1962), *Silent Spring*, Penguin Books, UK, ISBN 0-14-013891-9

Chaharbagi, K. and Willis, R. (1999), Stusy and Practice of Sustainable Development, *Engineering Management Journal*, Vol.9, No.1, Feb.1999, pp.41-48.

Charter M., Chick A., (1997) *Welcome to the first issue of the Journal of Sustainable Product Design*, April 1997

Charter, M. and Chick, A. (1997), Editorial; *The journal of Sustainable product Design*, Issue. 1, pp. 5-6.

Chatagnon, N., Nibel, S. and Achard, G. (1998), ESCALE: a method of assessing a building's environmental performance at the design stage, *Proceedings: Green Building Challenge '98*, Vancouver, BC, 26-28 October.

Chen, S.J. and Hang, C.L. (1992), *Fuzzy Multiple Attribute Decision-Making: Methods And Applications*, Springer-Verlag, Berlin

Chew, M.Y.L., Tan, S.S. and Kang, K.H., (2004), Building Maintainability—Review of State of the Art , *ASCE, Journal of Architectural Engineering*, Vol. 10, No. 3, pp. 80-87.

Chisnall, P.M. (1992), *Marketing Research*, 4th Edition, McGraw-Hill.

CIB (International Council for Research and Innovation in Building and Construction) (2003), *Performance Based Building, 1st International State-of-the-Art Report*, Annex: *PeBBu Domain Synthesis Reports*. Report No. 291, CIB, Rotterdam

Civanlar, M.R. and Trussell, H.J. (1986), Constructing membership functions using statistical data, *Fuzzy Sets and Systems*, 18, pp. 1-13

Clift, M., and Butler, R. (1995), The performance and cost in use of buildings: A new approach. *BRE Report*, Building Research Establishment, Garston, U.K.

Cnuddle, M. (1991). Lack of quality in construction—Economic loss, *Proceeding, 1991 European Symposium. on Management, Quality and Economics in Housing and other Building Sectors*, Lisbon, Portugal, pp. 508–515.

Cole, R. J. (1999), Building environmental assessment methods: clarifying intensions, *Building research and information*, Vol. 27, No. 4/5, pp. 230-246.

Cole, R.J. (2005), Building environmental assessment methods: redefining intentions and roles, *Building Research and Information*, Vol. 33, No. 5, pp. 455-467.

Cole, R.J. and Larsson, N.K. (1998), Preliminary assessment of the GBC assessment process, in: *Proceedings of Green Building Challenge' 98*, Vancouver BC, 26-28 October, Vol.2, pp.251-67.

Crawley, D. and Aho, I. (1999), Building environmental assessment methods: application and development trends, *Building Research and Information*, Vol. 27, No. 4/5, pp. 300-308.

Curwell, S., Tates, A., Howard, N., Bordass, B. and Doggart, J. (1999), The Green Building Challenge in the UK., *Building Research and Information*, Vol. 27, No. 4/5, pp. 286-293.

Dasmann, F.R. and Milton, J.P. and Freeman, P.H. (1973), *Ecological Principles for Economic Development* London, John Wiley and Sons LTD, ISBN 0 471 19606 1

Deakin, M. (2005), Evaluating sustainability: is a philosophical framework enough? , *Building Research and Information*, Vol. 33, No. 5, PP. 476-480.

Design Council, (1997), More for Less: Design for Environmental Sustainability, The Design Council, London.

DETR (1998), (Department of the Environment, Transport and the Regions) Opportunities for Change: consultation paper on a revised UK Strategy for Sustainable Development, London, HMSO.

DETR (2000), Http://www.arch.hk/research/BEER/sustain.htm

Dewberry, E. (1996), *Ecodesign: Present Attitudes and future Directions. Studies of UK Company and Design Consultancy Practice*, Ph.D. Thesis, The design Discipline, Technology Faculty, The Open University, Milton Keynes.

Dincer, I. (2000), Renewable energy and sustainable development: A crucial review, *Renewable and Sustainable Energy Reviews*, Vol. 4, No. 2, 2000, pp. 157 – 175.

Dincer, I and Rosen M. A., (1999), Energy, environment and sustainable development, *Applied Energy*, Vol. 64, No.1, 1999, pp. 427 – 440.

Dong, W. and Wong, F. (1985) Fuzzy computation and risk in decision analysis, *Civil Engineering systems*, 2, pp.201-8

Dresner, S. (2002), *The Principles of Sustainability*, Earthscan Publication Ltd, The UK, ISBN: 185383842X

Dubois, D. and Prade, H. (1980), *Fuzzy Sets and Systems: Theory and Application*, Academic Press, New York.

Dubois, D. and Prade, H. (1984) A Review of fuzzy set aggregation connectives. *Information Science*, No.36, pp.85-121.

Ducey, M. J. and Larson, B. C. (1999), A fuzzy set approach to the problem of sustainability. *Forest Ecology and Management*, Vol. 115, No: 1, pp. 29-40.

Du Plessis, C. (1999), Sustainable development demands dialogue between developed and developing worlds, *Building Research and Information*, Vol. 27, No. 6, pp. 379-390

Du Plessis, C. (2001), Sustainability and Sustainable Construction: the African Context, *Building Research and Information*, Vol. 29, No. 5, pp. 374-380.

Dutta, S. (1993), Fuzzy Logic Application: Technological and Strategic Issues, *IEEE Transactions on Engineering Management*, Vol. 40, No. 3, August 1993, pp.237-253.

Edmunds, K. (1999), HK-BEAM: Improving the life cycle performance of new residential buildings, *Proceedings, Better homes in the next Millennium,* Nov.24-25, 1999, Hong Kong

Edwards, B. (Guest Editor) (2001), Green Architecture, *Architectural Design.*

Ernzer, M.; Oberender, C. and Birkhofer, H. (No time) METHODS TO SUPPORT ECODESIGN IN THE PRODUCT DEVELOPMENT PROCESS, Darmstadt University of Technology, Institute for Product Development and Machine Elements, Germany [Online source Accessed on 22/2/2005] http://aix.meng.auth.gr/helcare/CAREO2/ordnerstruktur/paper%20presentation/04.4.pdf

Ethernfeld, J. and Lenox, M. (1997), The Development and implementation of DfE Programmes, *Journal of sustainable Product Design*, Issue 1.

Fiksel, J. (1994) *Design for Environment: Creating Eco-Efficient Products and Processes*, New York, McGraw-Hill.

Fisher, T.A. (1992), *Principles of Environmental Architecture*, AIA, Nov. 1992.

Gann, D.M. and Barlow, J. (1996), Flexibility in building use: the technical feasibility of converting redundant offices into flats. *Construction Management and Economics*, Vol. 14, No. 1, pp. 55-66.

Gibson, E.J. (1982), *Working with the Performance Approach in Building, Report 64,* CIB, Rotterdam.

Giedion, S. (1980), *Space, time and architecture: the growth of a new tradition,* Harvard University Express

Glaumann, M. (2000), Eco Effect-A holistic tool to measure environmental impact of building properties, *Proceedings, Sustainable Building 2000*, Maastricht, The Netherlands.

Glen, W. (1994), Use value of historical space structures in relation to adaptability for housing, *International Journal for Housing Science and Its Applications*, Vol.18, No. 1. , pp. 63-68.

Goedkoop, M.J., Halen van J.G., Riele, te H.R.M, Rommens, P.J.M., 1999. Product Service Systems: Ecological and Economic Basics, The Hague, NL.

Gottwald, S. (1993), *Fuzzy Sets and Fuzzy Logic*, Vieweg, Braunschweig Wiesbaden.

Green Building Pages: Sustainable **Design Checklist** [online source] http://www.greenbuildingpages.com/checklist/checklist.html [accessed on 3/9/2005]

Guy, G. B. and Kibert, C.J. (1998), Developing indicators of sustainability: US experience, *Building Research and Information*, Vol. 26, No. 1, pp. 39-45.

Guy, S. (2005), Forum: Cultures of architecture and sustainability, *Building Research and Information*, Vol. 33, No. 5, pp. 468-471.

Guy, S. and Farmer, G. (2001), Re-interpreting sustainable architecture: the place of technology. *Journal of Architectural Education*, Vol. 54, No. 3, pp. 140-148.

Guy, S. and Moore, S. (eds) (2005), *Sustainable Architecture: Cultures and Natures in Europe and North America*, E&FN Spon, London.

Guy, S. and Shove, E. (2000), A sociology of Energy, *Building and Environment*, Routledge, London.

Hammarlund, Y., and Josephson, P. E. (1991). ''Sources of quality failures in building.'' *Proc., European Symp. On Management, Quality and Economics in Housing and other Building Sectors*, Lisbon, Portugal, pp. 671–679.

Hart, S. L. (1997), Beyond greening: strategies for a sustainable world, *Harvard Business Review*, Vol. 75, No. 1, pp. 67-76.

Hattis, D. (1996) Role and significance of human requirements and architecture in application of the performance concept in building, in Proceedings of the 3rd CIB–ASTM–ISO– RILEM International Symposium, National Building Research Institute, Haifa, Israel.

Heine, K. (2001), Potential application of fuzzy methods in geodetic fields, Brandenburg University of Technology at Cottbus, Universitätsplatz 3-4, D-03044 Cottbus, Germany [Accessed on 22/9/2005] available at: http://www.tucottbus.de/BTU/Fak2/Vermwes/publikationen/heine_zuerich_2001.pdf#search='fuzzy%20logicbbczadeh'

Henerson M., Morris L., and Fitz-Gibbon C. (1987), *How to Measure Attitudes*, Sage Publications, London

Herring, H. (1998), Does energy efficiency save Energy: the implication of accepting the Khazzoom-Brookes postlate, EERU, the Open University (http://technology.open.ac.uk/eeru/staff/horace/kbpotl.htm)

Hill, R.C. and Bowen, P.A. (1997), Sustainable construction: principles and a framework for attainment, *Construction Management and Economics*, Vol.15, No.3, pp.233- 239.

http://www.bauinf.tu-cottbus.de/mitarbeiter/dilip/fuzzy.html [Accessed on 10/10/2005]

Holton E.H. and Burnett M.B. (1997), Qualitative Research Methods, In Swanson, R.A. and Holton, E.F. (Eds.), *Human resource development research handbook: Linking research and practice*, San Francisco: Berrett-Koehler Publications.

Hurson, A. R., Pakzad, S. and Jin, B. (1994), Automated knowledge acquisition in a neural network-based decision support system for incomplete database systems, *Microcomputers in civil engineering*, Vol.9, pp. 129-143.

Hyper online Dictionary at http://www.hyperdictionary.com/search.aspx?define=product [accessed on 24/8/2005]

Iselin, D.G. and Lemer, A.C. (1993), *The Fourth Dimension in Building: Strategies for Minimizing Obsolescence (Studies in Management of Building Technology)*, National Academy Press, Washington, DC. ISBN: 0309048427

ISO 14000, [online Source] (http://www.iso14000.com/) [Accessed on 3/9/2005]

IUCN /UNEP/ WWF. (1991). *Caring for the Earth. A Strategy for Sustainable Living*. Gland, New Zealand

Jamison, A. (2001), *The Making of Green Knowledge: Environmental Politics and Cultural Transformation*, Cambridge, Cambridge Press.

Jeganathan, C. (2003) *Development of Fuzzy Logic Architecture to assess the sustainability of the Forest Management*, International Institute for Geo-Information Science and Earth Observation, ENSCHEDE, The Netherlands, Master degree Thesis
Available at: http://www.itc.nl/library/Papers_2003/msc/gfm/jeganathan.pdf [Accessed on 20/9/2005]

Johnson, R.C. (1989), NEW LIFE for Fuzzy Logic, *Electronic Engineering Times*, pp.39-42, sep.18, 1989.

Keoleian, G. and Menerey, D. (1994), Sustainable Design by Design, *Air &Waste*, (May), No.44, pp. 645-668

Kerlinger, F. (1986), *Foundations of Behavioural Research*, 3rd edition, Holt, Rinehart and Winston, Inc.

Keymer, M.A.(2000), *Design strategies for new and renovation construction that increase the capacity of building to accommodate change*, Master of Science, MIT, Cambridge, MA.

Khalfan, (2001), *Sustainable Architecture and Building Design*,
http://www.c-sand.org.uk/Documents/WP2001-01-SustainLitRev.pdf [Accessed on 17/8/2005]

Kibert, C.J. (1994) Establishing principles and a model for sustainable construction. *Final Session of First International Conference of CIB TG 16 on Sustainable Construction*, Tampa, Florida, 6- 9 November, pp.3- 12.

Kibert, C.J., Sendzimir, J. and Guy. G.B. (1999), Natural Systems as a Model for the Built Environment, *Alternatives Journal*, Fall 1999

Kibert, C J. ,Sendzimir, J. and Guy, B. (2000), Construction Ecology: Natural Systems Models for the Built Environment. *Proceedings of the 2nd South African Conference on a Sustainable Built Environment*, 23-25 August 2000, Johannesburg, South Africa.

Kibert, C. J., Sendzimir, J. and Guy, B. (2000), Construction ecology and metabolism: natural system analogues for a sustainable built environment, *Construction Management and Economics*, Vol.18, No. 8, pp. 903-916.

Kuswari, R. (2004), Assessment of Different Methods for Measuring the Sustainability of Forest Mangement, International Institute for Geo-Information Science and Earth Observation, ENSCHEDE, The Netherlands, Master degree Thesis.
[Accessed on 22/9/2005] Available at: http://www.itc.nl/library/Papers_2004/msc/nrm/kuswandari.pdf

Lagerstedt, J. (2003), *Functional and Environmental Factors in Early Phases of Product Development-Eco Functional Matrix*, Ph.D. Thesis, (http://www.lib.kth.se/fulltext/lagerstedt030124.pdf) [Accessed on 21/1/2005]

Lagerstedt J., Grüner C., (2000), *Company Internal Communication in DFE –survey in German and Swedish Industry*, CIRP 7th International Seminar on Life Cycle Engineering, Tokyo, Japan

Langston, C.A. and Ding, K.C.G. (Eds) (2001), *Sustainable Practices in the Built Environment (2nd edition)*, Butterworth-Heinemann, Oxford. ISBN: 0 7506 5153 9

Larsson, N. (1998) Green Building Challenge '98: international strategic intentions, *Building Research and Information*, Vol. 26, No. 2, pp 118–121.

Lippiatt, B.C., 1999. Selecting cost-effective green building products: BEES approach. *Journal of Construction Engineering and Management*, Vol. 125, No.6, pp. 448-455.

Love, P. E. D. and Li, H. (2000), Quantifying the causes and costs of rework in construction, *Construction Management and Economics*, Vol. 18, No.4, pp. 479–490.

Lupton, S. (2001), *Architect's Handbook of Practice Management* (7th Edition), RIBA Publication, London, ISBN: 1 85946 1190

Luttropp, C. and Lagerstedt, J. (1999), *Customer Benefits in the context of life Cycle Design, EcoDesign (99)*: 1st International Symposium on Environmentally conscious design and Inverse Manufacturing, Tokyo, Japan.

McAloone, T. C. (1998), *Industrial Experiences of Environmentally Conscious Design Integration: An Exploratory Study*, Ph.D. Thesis, The CIM Institute, Cranfield University, Cranfield, UK.

McAloone T. C., Evans S., (1996), Integrating Environmental Decisions into the Design, *Proceedings of CIRP 3rd International Seminar on Life Cycle Engineering*, Zurich, Switzerland

Macnaghton, P. and Urry, J. (1998), *Contested Natures*, Sage, London.

Macozoma, D.S. (2002), UNDERSTANDING THE CONCEPT OF FLEXIBILITY IN DESIGN FOR DECONSTRUCTION, Design for Deconstruction and Materials Reuse CIB Publication 272, *Proceedings of the CIB Task Group 39 – Deconstruction Meeting, 9 April 2002*, Edited by Chini, A. R. and Schultmann, F., pp.118-127.

Markeset, T. and Kumar, U. (2003) Integration of RAMS and risk analysis in product design and development work processes: a case study, *Journal of Quality in Maintenance Engineering*, Vol. 9, No. 4, pp. 393-410

Mintzer, (1992), http://www.gdrc.org/sustdev/definitions.html [Accessed on 2/8/2005)

Miyatake, M. (1996), Technology Development and sustainable construction, *Journal of management in Engineering*, Vol. 12, No. 4, pp.23-27

Montgomery, D. C. Douglas. and Runger, C. G. (1999), Applied Statistics and Probability for Engineers, 2nd edition, p.159, John Wiley and Sons, USA, ISBN:0-471-17027-5 (acid free paper)

Munn P. and Drever E. (1999), *Using Questionnaires in Small-scale Research*, SCRE Publication104.

Muster, A.P.A. (1995), The Rebound Effect: An Introduction, Netherlands Energy Research Foundation (www.ecn.nl) [Accessed on 18/8/2005]

NASA, (2001), *Report on Sustainable Design, Design for Maintainability and Total Building Commissioning, for National Aeronautics and Space Administration Facilities Engineering Division (NASA) (March 7, 2001)* [Accessed on 22/8/2005]
(http://www.wbdg.org/pdfs/nasacommissioning.pdf#search='building%20maintainability)

Newell R. (1993), Questionnaires, In N Gilbert (ed.), *Researching Social Life*, Sage, London, pp. 94-116.

Nicholls, R. (2001), *Heating, Ventilation and Air Conditioning (3rd edition)*, Interface Publishing, Oldham, England, ISBN: 0-9539409-1-8

Norusis, M. J. (2000), *SPSS 10.0 Guide to data analysis*, Prentice Hall, Englewood Cliffs, N.J.

Oakland, J. S. and Aldridge, A. J. (1996), Quality management in civil and structural engineering consulting, *International Journal of Quality and Reliability Management*, Vol. 12, No. 3, pp. 32–48.

Online Source: http://nhi.or/online/issues/103/sustain.html [Accessed on 2/8/2005].

Papanek, V. (1995), *The Green Imperative*, Thames and Hudson, London

Parasumraman, A. (1991), *Marketing Research*, Addison-Wesley, Reading (Mass).

Parkin, S. (2000), Sustainable development : the concept and the practical challenge, Proceedings of ICE, Vol. 138, Nov. 2000, pp. 3 – 8.

Patermann, C. (1999), The fifth EU framework programme and its consequences for construction industry, *Bulding Research and Information,* Vol. 27, No, 6, pp.413-419.

Paul, G. and Beitz, W. (1996) in Wallace, K. (Ed.), *Engineering Design: A systematic Approach, (2nd edition)*, Springer, Berlin

Pettersen, T.D., Strand, S., Haagenrud, S. and Krigsvoll, G. (2000), Eco Profile-A simplistic environmental assessment method experiences and new challenges, *Proceedings, Sustainable Building 2000*, 22-5 October, Maastricht, The Netherlands.

Pearce, D. (1996), Sustainable Development: the political and institutional challenge, in J. Kirby, P. O'keefe and L.Timberlake (eds): *The Earthscan Reader in sustainable Development*, Earthscan Publication Ltd, London.

Pearce, D.W. (2001), *Measuring resource productivity*, Paper to DTI/Green Alliance Conference, February 2001.

Phillis Y. A. and Andriantiatsaholiniaina, Luc. A. (2001), *Ecological Economics*, vol. 37, issue 3, pp. 435-456

Pilvang, C. and Sutherland, I. (1998), Research Information, Environmental management in project Design, *Building research and information*, Vol. 26, No. 2, pp. 113-117.

Prior, J. (ed.) (1993), *Building Research Establishment Environmental Assessment Method (BREEAM)*, Version1/93. New Offices, Building research establishment, Garston, UK.

Raj, D. (1972), *The Design of Sample Survey*, McGraw Hill.

Redclift, M. and Sage, C. (1994), *Strategies for Sustainable Development, Local Agendas for Southern Hemisphere*, John Wiley and Sons, Chichester.

RIBA (Royal Institute of British Architects), April 2005 (http:/www.ribafind.org/)

Roaf, S. and Fuentes, M. and Thomas, S. (2001), *Eco House: A Design Guide*, Oxford, Architectural Press, pp. 52-3, ISBN 0 7506 4904 6

Roaf, S. and Fuentes, M. and Thomas, S. (2001), *Eco House: A Design Guide*, Oxford, Architectural Press, ISBN 0-7506-4904-6

Robinson, J. (2004), Squaring the circle? Some thoughts on the idea of sustainable development, *Ecological Economics*, Vol. 48, pp. 369–384.

Ryan, C. (1996), From Eco Redesign to Eco design, *Eco design*, Vol. 4, Issue 1, pp. 5-7.

Ryding, S-O. (1998), Miljöanpassad produktudveckling, Förlags AB Industrilitteratur, Stockholm, Sweden, (in Swedish) adopted from: Lagerstedt, J. (2003) *Functional and Environmental Factors in Early Phases of Product Development-Eco Functional Matrix*, Ph.D. Thesis, (http://www.lib.kth.se/fulltext/lagerstedt030124.pdf) [Accessed on 18/8/2005]

Saunders, H. (1992), The Khazzoom-Brookes Postulate and Neoclassical Growth, *Energy Journal*, Vol. 13, No. 4, pp. 131-148.

Sexton, M.G., Barrett, P., Miozzo,M., Wharton, A.&Leho, E., (2001), Innovation in Small Construction Firms: Is it Just a Frame of Mind?, *Proceedings of the Seventeenth Annual Conference of the Association of Researchers in Construction Management*, Salford, 5th– 7thSeptember.

Shen, Q. and Liu, G. (2003), Critical Success Factors For Value Management Studies in Construction, *Journal of Construction Engineering and Management*, September/October, pp.485-491

Sherwin, C. and Bhamra, T. (2001), Early Eco design Integration: Experiences from a Single Case, *The Journal of Design Research*, Issue 2001.02, http://jdr.tudelft.nl/articles/issue2001.02/article4.html [Accessed on 6/10/2004]

Sherwin C. and Evans, S. (2000), Eco design Innovation: Is Early Always Best? In 2000 IEEE *International Symposium on Electronics and the Environment Conference Proceedings*, May 8-10-

2000, The Institute of Electrical and Electrical Engineers Inc. Computer Society, Technical Committee on Electronic and the Environment, San Francisco, California, pp. 112-117.

Shipworth, D. (2002), Environmental impact mitigation is not sustainable development, *Building research and information*, Vol. 30, No. 2, pp. 139-142.

Shrivastava, P. (1995) Environmental technologies and Competitive Advantages, *Strategic Management Journal*, Vol. 16, pp. 183-200.

Siegel, S. and Castellan, J. (1987), *Non Parametric Statistics for Behavioral Science*, McGraw-Hill

Slaughter, E.S. (2001), Design Strategies to Increase Building Flexibility, *Building Research and Information*, Vol. 29, No. 3, pp. 208-217.

Smith, P.F. (2001), *Architecture in a Climate of Change: A Guide to Sustainable Design,* Oxford, Architectural Press. ISBN: 0-7506-5346-9

SPSS Inc. (July 2004). *SPSS 12.0.1 for Windows*, Apache Software foundation (The University of Liverpool, Computer Service Department)

Stacey M. (1969), *Method in Social Research*, Pergamon Press, Oxford.

Stahel, W. (1994), The Utilization-Focused Service Economy: Resource Efficiency and Product Life- Extension, *The Greening of Industrial Ecosystems*, pp.178-190, Washington DC, National Academy Press.

Stahel, W. (1998), *From Products to Services: Selling Performance Instead of Goods*, IPTS Report, Vol. 27.

Stevens, S. (1951), *Handbook of Experimental Psychology,* New York.

Stigson, B. (1999), Sustainable development for industry and society, *Building Research and Information*, Vol. 27, No. 6, pp. 425-431.

Todd, J. A. and Geissler, S. (1999), Regional and cultural issues in environmental performance assessment for building, *Building Research and Information*, Vol. 27, No. 4/5, pp. 247-256.

Todd, J.A.; Crawley, D.; Geissler, S. and Lindsey, G. (2001), Comparative assessment of environmental performance tools and the role of the Green Building Challenge, *Building Research & Information*, Vol. 29, No. 5, pp.324-335.

USBDC (US Green Building Council) (2000), Leadership in Energy and Environmental Design (LEED) Rating System, Version 2.0, March, San Francisco, CA.

Vakili Ardebili, A. (2005), *Development of an Assessment Framework for Eco-Building Design Indicators*, PhD Thesis, The University of Liverpool, Liverpool, The UK.

Vakili-Ardebili, A. (2007), Complexity of Value Creation in Sustainable Building Design (SBD), the Journal of *Green Building*, Volume 2, Number 4, pp.171-181.

Vakili-Ardebili, A. and Boussabaine, A.H. (2007), Design Eco-Drivers, *the journal of Architecture*, Voume12, Number 3, pp. 315-332.

Vakili-Ardebili, A. and Boussabaine, A.H. (2007), Application of fuzzy techniques to develop an assessment framework for building design eco-drivers, the journal of *Building and Environment*, Volume 42, Issue 11, pp. 3785-3800.

Vakili-Ardebili, A. and Boussabaine, A.H. (2010), Ecological Building Design Determinants, the journal of *Architectural Engineering and Design Management*, Volume 6, Number 2, pp. 111-131.

Van Bueren, E. M. (2000), Essay competition, A sustainable built environment: the institutional challenges, *Building Research and Information*, Vol. 28, No. 1, pp. 79-81.

Van Hemel, C. G. (1998), *Eco design Empirically Explored. Design for Environment in Dutch Small and Medium Sized Enterprises*, Design for Sustainability Research Programme, Delft University of Technology, Delft, The Netherlands.

Van Nes, N. and Cramer, J. (1997), Eco-Efficiency Assessment for Strategic Product Planning. In: *Towards Sustainable Product Design 2 Conference Proceedings*, The royal College of Pathologists, London, The Centre for Sustainable Design, Farnham, Unpaginated.

Walker, S. (1998), Experiments in Sustainable Product Design, *The journal of Sustainable Product Design*, Issue 7, pp. 41-50.

Walonick D.S. (1997-2003), *experts from: Survival Statistics, Stat Pac,* Published by: Stat Pac Inc., Available URL: http// www.statpac.com 20/7/2005

Wanous, M. (2000), *A Neuro Fuzzy Expert System for Competitive Tendering in Civil Engineering*, PhD thesis, The University of Liverpool, P. 42.

(WBCSD) World Business Council for Sustainable Development, (1997), *Exploring Sustainable Development Global Scenarios 2000-2050*, Summary Brochure

WCED (1987), *Our common Future*, (The Brundtland Report) Oxford University Press, Oxford, P.43.

White, A., Stoughton, M. and Feng, L. (1999), *Servicizing: The Quiet Transition to Extended Product Responsibility Submitted to: U.S. Environmental Protection Agency*, Office of Solid Waste.

Wikipedia, [online encyclopaedia] (http://en.wikipedia.org/wiki/Repair_and_maintenance) [Accessed on 23/8/2005]

Williams, B. (1993), What a performance! *Property Management, Vol.* 11, No. 3, pp. 190–191.

Williamson, T., Radford, A. and Bennetts, H. (2003), *Understanding Sustainable Architecture*, E&FN
Spon, London.

Wilson, A., Uncappher, J., McManigal, L., Lovins, A., Cureton, M., and Browing, W. (1998), *Green Development: Integriting Ecology and Real Estates,* New York, John Wiley and Sons, Inc

Winch, G., Usmani, A., and Edkins and A. (1998), Towards total project quality: A gap analysis approach, *Construction Management and Economics*, Vol.16, No.2, pp.193–207.

Wines, J. (2000), The art of architecture in the age of ecology, in D.E. Brown, M. Fox and M.R. Pelletier (EDS): *Sustainable Architecture: White Papers*, Earth Pledge Foundation, New York, PP. 12-18.

Yeang, K. (1995) *Designing with Nature*, McGraw-Hill, New York.

Zadeh, L.A. (1965), fuzzy sets. *Information and Control*, No. 8, pp.338-353

Zadeh, L.A. (1979), A theory of approximate reasoning. In: Hayes, J., Michie, D. and Mikulich, L., Editors, 1979. *Machine Intelligence* Vol. 9, Halstead, New York, pp. 149–194.

Zadeh, L.A. (1994), Fuzzy Logic, neural Networks, and soft computing. *Communications of the ACM*, Vol. 37, No. 3, pp. 77-84.

Zimmermann, H.J. (1991). In: *Fuzzy Set Theory and Its Applications*, Kluwer, Boston, p. 399

Zimmermann H. J. (1996), *Fuzzy Set Theory and its Applications*. Boston.

VDM publishing house ltd.

Scientific Publishing House
offers
free of charge publication

of current academic research papers, Bachelor´s Theses, Master's Theses, Dissertations or Scientific Monographs

If you have written a thesis which satisfies high content as well as formal demands, and you are interested in a remunerated publication of your work, please send an e-mail with some initial information about yourself and your work to *info@vdm-publishing-house.com.*

Our editorial office will get in touch with you shortly.

VDM Publishing House Ltd.
Meldrum Court 17.
Beau Bassin
Mauritius
www.vdm-publishing-house.com

Made in the USA
Lexington, KY
21 May 2011